Art's Work in the Age of Biotechnology

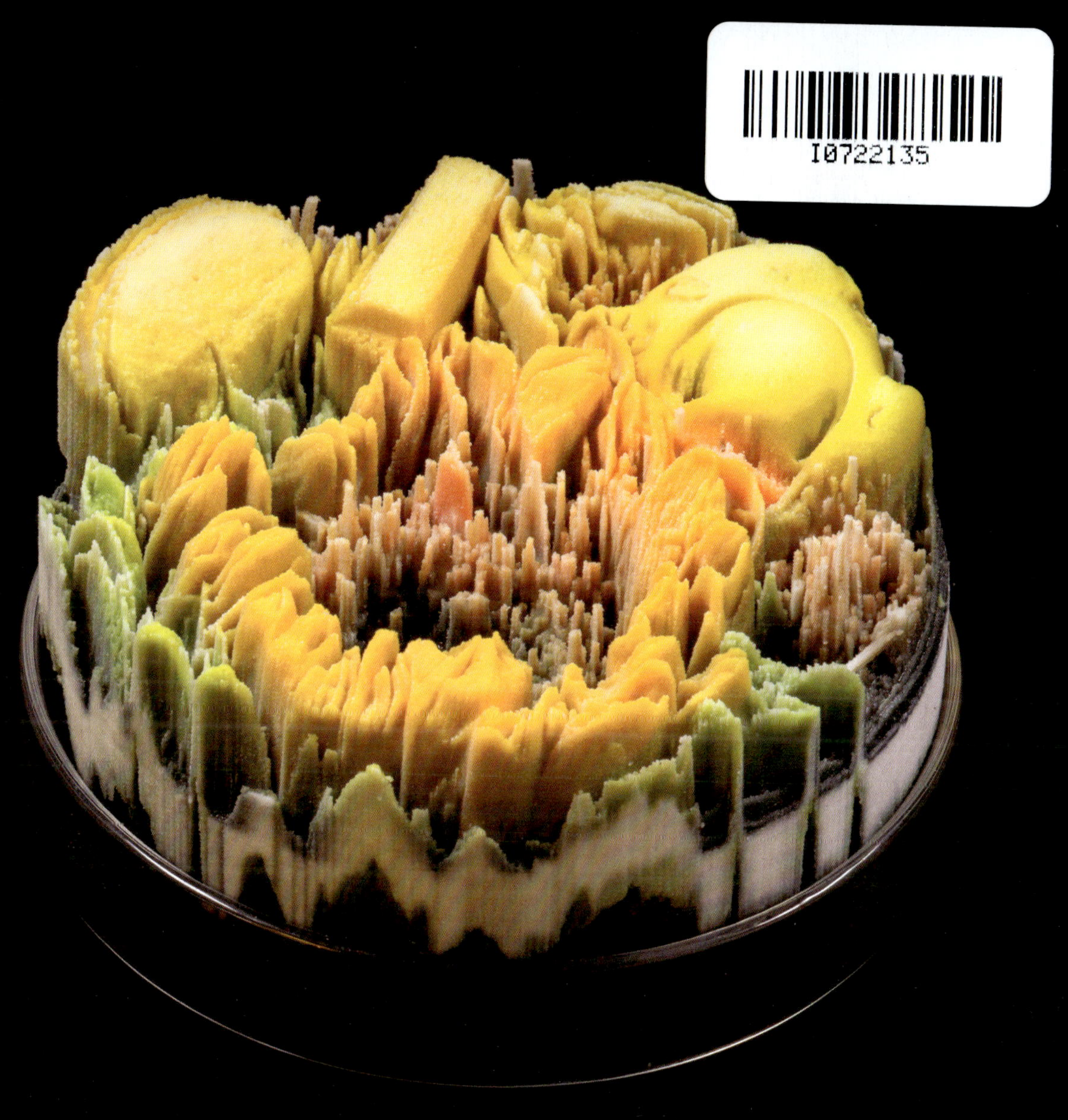

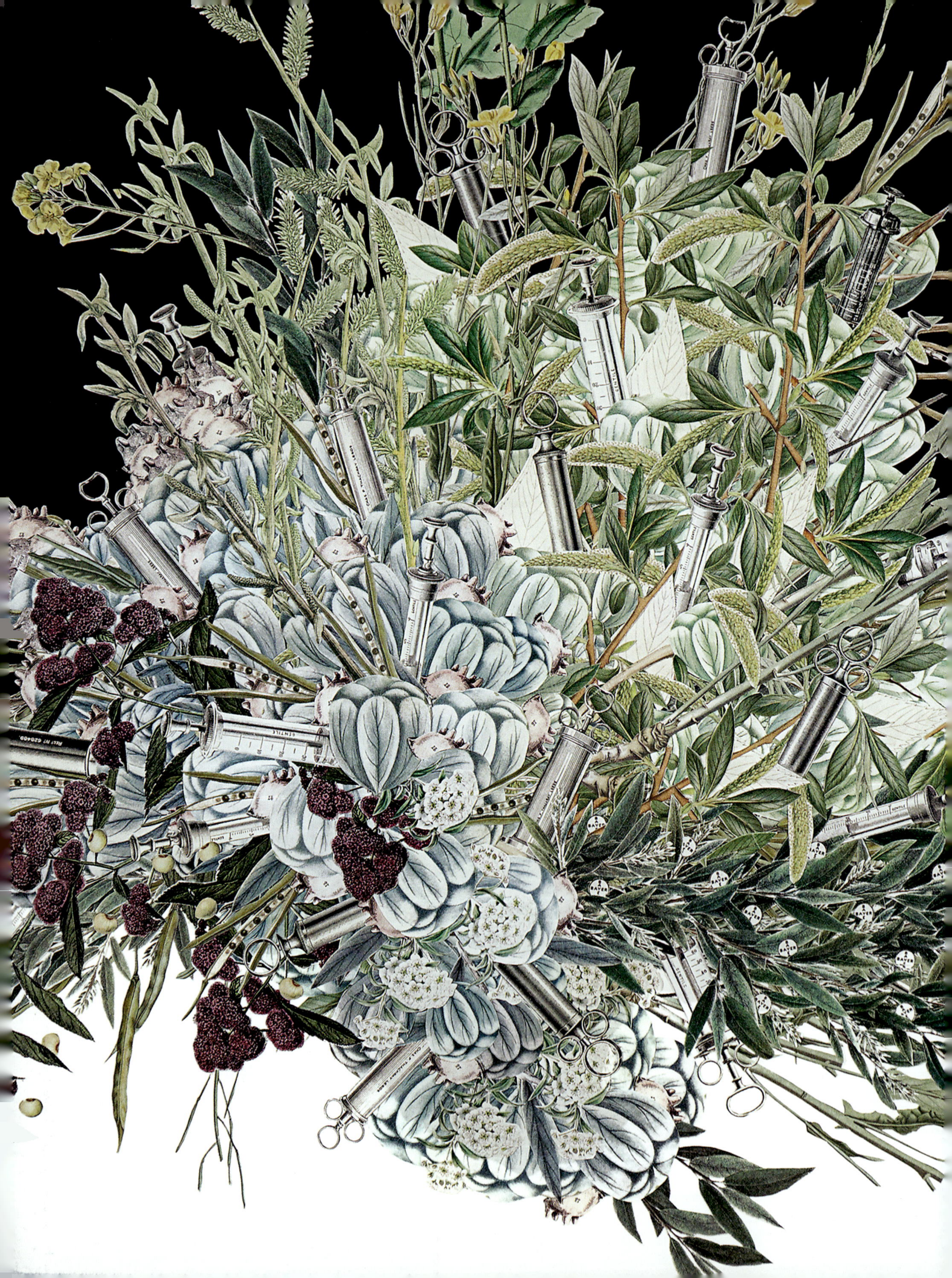

CURATED BY

Hannah Star Rogers

WITH AN ESSAY BY

William Myers

AND CONTRIBUTIONS BY

Roger Manley

Fred Gould
  and Molly Renda

Megan Serr
  and John Godwin

Todd Kuiken

ART'S WORK IN THE AGE OF BIOTECHNOLOGY: SHAPING OUR GENETIC FUTURES

Suzanne Anker

Joe Davis

Jonathan Davis

Heather Dewey-Hagborg

Aaron Ellison and
  David Buckley Borden

Emeka Ikebude

Charlotte Jarvis

KERASYNTH
  Diana Eusebio
  Erin Kirchner
  Grace Kwon
  Rachel Rusk
  Sydney Sieh-Takata

Maria McKinney

Joel Ong

Richard Pell

Ciara Redmond

Kirsten Stolle

Emilia Tikka

Paul Vanouse

Jennifer Willet

Adam Zaretsky

NC STATE University Libraries

2019

Heather Dewey-Hagborg, *New York: Sample 7,* from the series *Stranger Visions,* 2012–13, found genetic materials, custom software, 3D prints, documentation. Courtesy of the artist and Fridman Gallery, New York.

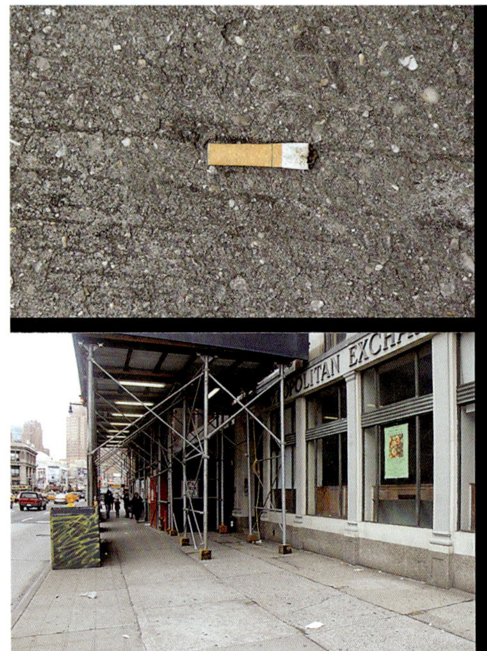

Art's Work in the Age of Biotechnology: Shaping Our Genetic Futures is published on the occasion of the exhibition of the same title presented at the Gregg Museum of Art & Design and the NC State University Libraries.

October 17, 2019–March 15, 2020

Art's Work/Genetic Futures has been developed through a partnership between the Genetic Engineering and Society Center, the NC State University Libraries, and the Gregg Museum of Art & Design.

ISBN 978-1-4696-5926-8

Published by
NC State University Libraries
Campus Box 7111
Raleigh, NC 27695-7111

Funding for this publication is generously supported by the NC State University Libraries' Goodnight Educational Foundation Endowment for Special Collections.

Distributed by
UNC Press
116 South Boundary Street
Chapel Hill, NC 27514-3808

Copy edited by Chris Vitiello and Julie Johnson. Typeset and designed by Molly Renda in Darwin Pro and Meta Serif Pro. Printed and bound in Canada by Friesens Corporation.

ART'S WORK/GENETIC FUTURES TEAM

Molly Renda, *NC State University Libraries*
Fred Gould, *Genetic Engineering and Society Center*
Hannah Star Rogers, *Guest Curator*
Todd Kuiken, *Genetic Engineering and Society Center*
Elizabeth Pitts, *University of Pittsburgh*
Roger Manley, *Gregg Museum of Art & Design*

Page 1: Suzanne Anker, *Remote Sensing, #36,* 2013–18, rapid prototype sculptures; plaster, pigment, resin, glass petri dish. Photograph by Raul Valverde.

Page 2: Kirsten Stolle, *Chemical Bouquet II* (detail), 2016, collage on paper. Courtesy of the artist and Tracey Morgan Gallery, Asheville.

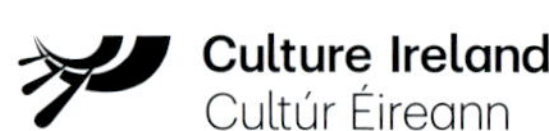

Maria McKinney's work is supported by Culture Ireland / Cultúr Éireann.

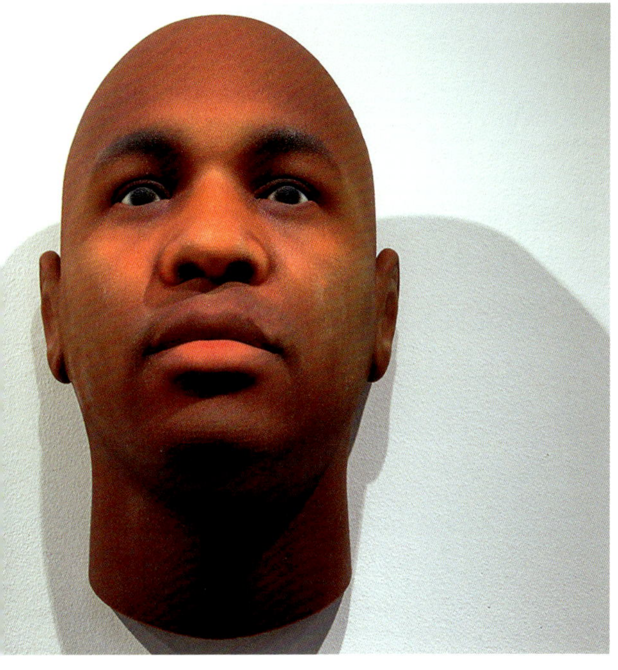

CONTENTS

[Science] enables us to "experience" atoms and galaxies, heredity and evolution, entropy and energy. It does not tell us what we have learned about human experience nor discover what is possible for human experience. Such discoveries, such predictions, such communications, constitute the domain of the arts. . . . Both endeavors are deeply rooted in culture and heritage; both expand our awareness and sensitivity to what is happening in nature, and in ourselves.[1]

—Frank Oppenheimer, physicist and founder of San Francisco's Exploratorium art and science museum; brother of Robert Oppenheimer

In Dreams Begin Responsibilities[2]

ROGER MANLEY

Art is the Queen of all sciences, communicating knowledge to all the generations of the world.
—*Leonardo da Vinci, Italian Renaissance polymath*

It is through science that we prove, but through intuition we discover.
—*Henri Poincare, French mathematician, theorist, and philosopher*

1. Oppenheimer, Frank F. 1977. "The Arts: A Decent Respect for Taste." *The National Elementary Principal* 57 (1).

2. The title of this foreword, *In Dreams Begin Responsibilities*, is borrowed from a 1935 short story by Delmore Schwartz, who borrowed it from the epigraph of William Butler Yeats' 1914 book of poems *Responsibilities*, who in turn attributed it to a line from "an old play." Much like the genome, it apparently has a trans-generational history with murky beginnings.

3. Not till the sixteenth century would they also become repositories of artifacts or artworks, and even today not all museums maintain collections of objects. Their function as a nexus for experience and discussion is far older and far more central to their purpose.

When Fred Gould of NC State University's Genetic Engineering and Society Center and Molly Renda of the NC State University Libraries first approached the Gregg Museum of Art & Design about the possibility of mounting an exhibition that would forefront artists who are tapping into the concepts and techniques of genetic engineering, we immediately set about finding space on the calendar and room in the galleries to present this work. We realized it would offer the museum a fine occasion to reach new audiences among the science, technology, engineering, and math (STEM) students and professors who account for the majority of the academic population of this university. But more important, it would present a great opportunity to advance the Gregg's key mission of inspiring creativity, innovation, and the expression of ideas.

Any chance to showcase the experiments and discoveries of living artists, and especially any who are taking a cross-disciplinary approach to addressing real-world issues, is an opportunity to continue fulfilling the original intent of *all* museums. In the beginning, museums—a Latin term derived from the Greek μουσεῖον (*mouseion*)—were shrines to the Muses, the nine deities of creative invention. Museums were places where poets, astronomers, musicians, and philosophers could meet to discuss and explore art, science, and the natural world.[3] The cross-fertilization that took place in such settings was one of the major drivers behind the great advances in cultural development that marked classical antiquity.

As the outward expression of the human imagination, art has been the conjoined twin of technology for as long as humans have existed. Consider cave paintings. Given their settings (typically deep underground), it seems highly unlikely that the sweeping images of horses, aurochs, and ibexes depicted in prehistoric caves were intended as simple reportage or record keeping, or even as decorative features for the delight of passersby. Instead, the paintings must have helped their makers to better comprehend the animal realm, ritually promote its increase, and envision success in hunting and acquiring food

4. Even practical levitation and convincing invisibility may not elude us for much longer. As futurist writer Arthur C. Clarke once pointed out, "Any sufficiently advanced technology is indistinguishable from magic." Considering imaginative writing also as a form of art, Clarke made his own contributions to the art and science partnership by envisioning things like geostationary satellites and other technological advances well before they became a reality.

as well. Often these stirring images of animals were accompanied by representations of spear-wielding humans, suggesting that they served as previsualizations for achieving goals with the most advanced technologies of the day. Solving any problem or realizing any technical achievement always involves first envisioning the possibilities (including the possibility of pitfalls or failures), and then taking a leap to see what actually happens.

The sheer mastery of nearly all prehistoric artworks (and the fact that they were rendered well out of sight of their animal models) is convincing evidence that early humans were keen at observing, imaging, modeling, analogizing, experimenting, transforming, thinking dimensionally, and communicating—i.e., that they had already thoroughly developed most of the skills essential for both art and technology (and, beginning with Aristotle, what we now call science).

Throughout history, nearly every accomplishment that could be visualized in the imagination and communicated through art eventually came into being through the advances of science and technology. Long before Philo Farnsworth exhibited the first working television, ancient Greek, Indian, and Mexican mythmakers had already described the transmission of images over long distances by way of magical bronze or obsidian mirrors. Flight had been envisioned and depicted by artists long before the Wright brothers or even Daedalus. Ages ahead of space stations or satellites, we pictured pagan gods and medieval angels gazing down on the earth from the heavens above, and illustrated the concept on the pediments

of temples and ceilings of churches. One by one, all but a handful of the primal dreams first evoked through art were eventually pursued and attained through technology and science.[4]

With genetic engineering in its present, fast-developing state, we now find ourselves at a point when another of humankind's age-old imaginings—the manipulation and transformation of living substance—is finally coming within reach. Ovid's *Metamorphoses*, written by the Roman poet during the lifetime of Jesus, describes scores of partial or complete transformations from humans into animals, from one animal species into another, or from humans into flowers or trees. These themes were also common subjects in the frescos, mosaics, sculptures, and painted ceramics of his day. Centuries earlier, Egyptian monuments and tomb paintings had featured deities with both animal and human characteristics, their heads borrowed from the creatures that best expressed their personalities, while petroglyphs dating to still further back in time show shamans and shapeshifters transitioning from one animate state to another.

Now, it seems, we are finally getting closer to achieving such changes for real without, we may hope, some of the pitfalls or failures already envisioned in works like H. G. Wells' 1896 novel, *The Island of Doctor Moreau*, horror films from the 1940s and 50s, or modern classics like *Jurassic Park*. Proceeding with simultaneous caution and imaginative experimentation, the artists that curator Hannah Star Rogers has rounded up for *Art's Work in the Age of Biotechnology: Shaping Our Genetic Futures* promise their own challenging and refreshing takes on biotechnology that explore possibilities in directions other than the minotaurs and chimeras that so fascinated the ancients.

These run the gamut from ethics-driven research like the *Kerasynth* team's explorations of the possibilities of using tissue engineering to generate vegan wool, or Charlotte Jarvis' proposal to address age-old gender imbalances caused by patriarchal conventions by creating female sperm, to more art-focused projects like Joel Ong's *Terra Et Venti* piece, which encodes a poem in the *Pseudomonas syringae* bacteria genome, or Emeka Ikebude's *Fragments*, which consists of a traditional portrait created from discarded toothpicks that were embedded with tissues and DNA by thousands of unwitting users.

Other artists in the exhibition present seemingly more playful ventures, like Richard Pell's *The Mermaid De-Extinction Project* or Ciara Redmond's use of selective breeding (the kind of bioengineering that humans have practiced for millennia) to create clover that is much more likely to have the "lucky" four-leaf trait. Even these, however, stimulate serious (i.e., useful) questions for biotechnology. Redmond's clover asks whether four-leaf clovers would still be considered lucky if science made them common—a question that quickly leads to considerations of other innovations that have later been taken for granted, like antibiotics, and with potentially far more grave implications.

Pell's mermaid, meanwhile, never existed except in art and folklore, so is "de-extincting" it one of those age-old dreams that would best be left alone?

The ancients well understood the concept of unintended consequences, and knew that in-between states of being could be dangerous. Transformed into a stag, Actaeon was devoured by Diana's hounds, while "ass-eared" Midas quickly regretted wishing for the golden touch when even his food and drink turned into shiny yellow metal.

As we find ourselves becoming more and more like the ancient gods—destroyers of worlds and creators of new expressions of life—perhaps it is time to choose some different ancient dreams to bring into being. Most of those we have achieved so far have been about ourselves, i.e., about attaining special powers that have increased our domination over nature and each other. It's no wonder, either, since our most distant ancestors must have been keenly aware of their naked helplessness and vulnerabilities above all else. Nearly everything around them seemed to pose a potential threat. If only, they thought, they could speed across the earth like gazelles or cheetahs, fly like birds, or cross rivers like crocodiles, perhaps they might be safer.

Now, however, *we* are the threat and the earth itself seems increasingly helpless and vulnerable, so perhaps it is high time to remember that Eden, too, was also a primal dream. Can biotechnology help bring it into being? Will it help us undo some of our worst mistakes? Can we dream now of trying to restore that ancient vision of the garden sanctuary and do whatever we can to make it happen?

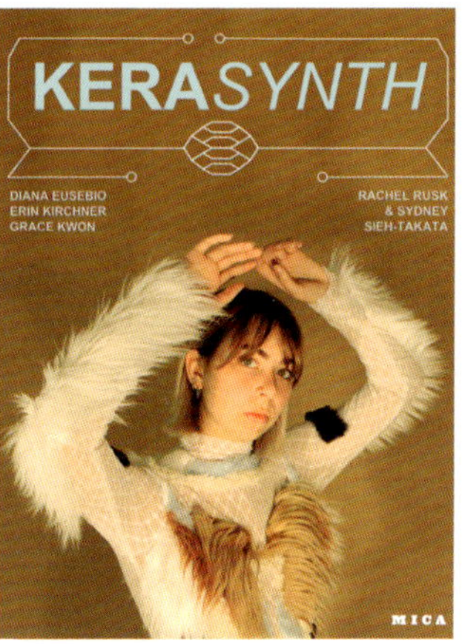

Diana Eusebio, Erin Kirchner, Grace Kwon, Rachel Rusk, Sydney Sieh-Takata, *Kerasynth*, 2018 BioDesign Challenge finalist. Courtesy of the Kerasynth, Baltimore.

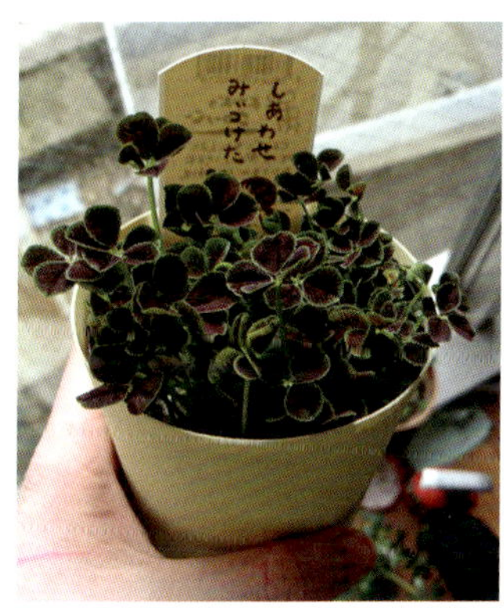

Ciara Redmond, *We Make Our Own Luck Here*, 2018–ongoing. Courtesy of the artist, with support from Waseda University.

From Risk Panic to Innovation Thrill: Art's Role in Navigating Genetic Intervention

FRED GOULD AND MOLLY RENDA

1. Whittingham, N., A. Boecker and A. Grygorczyk. 2019. "Personality traits, basic individual values and GMO risk perception of twitter users." *Journal of Risk Research.* https://doi-org.prox.lib.ncsu.edu/10.1080/13669877.2019.1591491.

2. Geall, S., and A. Ely. 2019. "Agri-food transitions and the 'green public sphere' in China." *Environmental Innovation and Societal Transitions* 30 (SI): 33–42.

3. Pew Research Center. 2016. *The New Food Fights: U.S. Public Divides Over Food Science.* http://www.pewinternet.org/2016/12/01/thenewfoodfights/.

4. National Academies of Sciences, Engineering, and Medicine. 2016. *Genetically Engineered Crops: Experiences and Prospects.* Washington, DC: The National Academies Press. doi:10.17226/23395.

5. National Academies of Sciences, Engineering, and Medicine. 2019. *Science Breakthroughs to Advance Food and Agricultural Research by 2030.* Washington, DC: The National Academies Press. https://doi.org/10.17226/25059.

6. Kaebnick, Gregory E., Elizabeth Heitman, James P. Collins, Jason A. Delborne, Wayne G. Landis, Keegan Sawyer, Lisa A. Taneyhill, and

It's not hard to find a person with a strong attitude about genetically modified organisms (GMOs) or genetically engineered (GE) foods. Indeed, it seems harder to find someone without an opinion about them. Many surveys of US populations and those in other countries have generated plenty of hypotheses but no unambiguous explanation for the wide range of personal and national perspectives on GMOs, or why GE foods elicit so much more response than GE medicines such as insulin.[1,2] While it's tempting to think that the divide in responses could be explained at least in part by whether a person is politically conservative or liberal, as is the case with climate change, no such correlation is found in attitudes toward GMOs.[3]

For those who have been closely watching the breakthroughs in genetic engineering over the past two decades, it feels like the pace of change has been lightning-fast. While we don't know what the future will bring, it's certainly reasonable to expect the pace of change to increase as it did with computing in the recent past. Among those doing research in genetic engineering, there is a general opinion that the currently marketed GE foods are safe[2,4] and that future breakthroughs in the field will be ever more exciting both in terms of basic understanding of biology and in terms of new products.[5] Some members of the general public tend to agree and to see genetic engineering as crucial for feeding the future world population. Others think we can't risk the potential consequences of this technology. In the past, there has been a tendency among those who are developing new technologies to consider themselves rational and their opposition as irrational or as Luddites. An opinion piece in *Science*[6] points out that those developing the technologies may be just as emotionally involved as those opposed to rapid adoption of innovations. The authors use the terms "risk panic" and "innovation thrill" as two ends of this emotional response spectrum. They harken back to Robert Oppenheimer, the nuclear physicist, who is quoted as saying, "When you see something that is technically sweet, you go ahead and do it and you argue about what to do about it only after you have had your technical success."[7]

In the period after WWII, the sense of "innovation thrill" was not restricted to the researchers. At least in the US, much of the public felt that technological advances were needed and would enable the country to survive and flourish. Seventy-five years later, this premise is not so strongly embraced. While most people today would not desire to move back to 1940s technology, the record of technologies bringing "better living" is mixed. Most people would not want to return to an era without cancer therapies and cell phones, but what about rewinding to before hydraulic fracking and the Great Pacific Garbage Patch?

The issue relevant to this exhibition is whether, seventy-five years from now, most people will feel that they have benefited or not from having lived through decades of the continued development of genetic engineering technology. The question raised by this exhibition is whether society—including researchers, policy makers, spiritual leaders, artists, and others—could guide genetic engineering in a way that would be more likely to have a positive impact not only on society, but on the natural world and the intricate systems that support all life.

In 2013, the Genetic Engineering and Society Center was established at NC State University with the vision of "integrating scientific knowledge and public values in shaping the futures of biotechnology." Operating on the premise that we are already immersed in the age of genetic engineering, the GES Center combines expertise in biological sciences, social sciences, and the humanities to help citizens and policymakers make more informed decisions about biotechnology through detailed evidence and culturally informed deliberation. The Center has involved NC State students and faculty in discussions with well-known GMO proponents and detractors, and it has supported dialogues between these individuals. The Center has sponsored events enabling people beyond the NC State community to interact with ethics scholars, molecular biologists, economists, and many others to examine for themselves how genetic engineering may affect society in the future. Although the Center has used a number of approaches in the past to elevate the public conversation about GMOs, this is a continuing struggle. One path that had not been explored is that of reaching students, faculty, and the broader public through art. *Art's Work in the Age of Biotechnology: Shaping Our Genetic Futures* is focused on just that.

The NC State University Libraries is uniquely situated as a gateway to knowledge and knowledge creation for the entire university community. As a nexus of information, as well as the technologies that give those data meaning, the Libraries is a natural partner for the GES Center to realize a project that aspires to examine one of the critical topics of our time through the language of art. To kickstart that effort, resources were made available to create a quarter-acre corn maze in the Ann and Jim Goodnight Museum Park at the North Carolina Museum of Art. The maze, *From Teosinte to Tomorrow*, functions as a metaphorical prelude to the questions posed by the greater exhibition.

Although some view art as an elite enterprise, isolated from the mainstream of society, history proves that wrong. Heroic sculptures evoke great nationalistic pride, but no one can look at Picasso's *Guernica* without feeling the horror of war. During the Industrial Revolution—an epoch of innovation thrill that continues to express both positive and largely unanticipated negative residual effects—artists from the late eighteenth century

David E. Winickoff. 2016. "Precaution and Governance of Emerging Technologies." *Science* 354 (6313): 710–711. doi:10.1126/science.aah5125.

7. Atomic Energy Commission. 1954. *In the matter of J. Robert Oppenheimer: Transcripts of hearing before Personnel Security Board.* Washington, DC: Government Printing Office.

into the early twentieth century were concerned with the battle between the beauty of nature, the promise of technology, and the often brutal effects of industry. Painters such as Jean-François Millet disrupted the Beaux-Arts canon in terms of technique and content by portraying the reality of poverty in agrarian France. Lewis Hine's photographs of conditions in North Carolina cotton mills had a direct impact on child labor laws in the US, while his contemporary, American painter Charles Sheeler, celebrated the powerful forms, products, and architecture of the machine age. Artists continue to comment on our ever-evolving technologies and to push viewers to confront the impact of these changes on their world. Rapid and unpredictable breakthroughs in genetic engineering have been challenging the capacity of society to absorb the ways in which this technology could change individual lives, larger cultures, and the natural world. Artists and designers can both deepen and influence our responses to this new force.

Art's Work in the Age of Biotechnology: Shaping Our Genetic Futures brings together a diverse set of artists who challenge viewers in different ways. Two of our exhibits particularly remind us to be careful of what we wish for through our biotech aspirations. Over the millennia, societies and their artists have envisioned and given heroic status to hybrid beings such as the centaur and the sphinx. A common imaginary has been the mermaid—half fish, half woman— and dreamy stories of mermaid sightings abound. In the late nineteenth century, impresarios and charlatans claimed to have preserved the remains of these sea creatures. Enter biotechnology. The public imagination has recently fixated on the possibility of the de-extinction of species such as the woolly mammoth through the usage of preserved DNA. Richard Pell invites us to think more boldly by introducing *The Mermaid De-Extinction Project*. We've been wishing for these creatures forever. What happens if we can really make one? What would we do with it? Would we really want this wish fulfilled? What other animals, plants, and people have we envisioned that we now could have the power to make? What is the difference between dreaming of it and having it?

Similarly, Ciara Redmond challenges us with *We Make Our Own Luck Here*. At least in the US, it's common for children at play to search the grass for a four-leaf clover. Why? Because the four-leaf clover was considered to have the power to bring luck. Redmond is breeding a variety of clover with plenty of leaves having four leaflets. How wonderful! Or, how terrible. Is she making luck or is she destroying luck by making a rarity common? Maybe kids will start dreaming of five-leaf clovers? Of course, as with Pell's exhibit, Redmond may be trying to get us to think beyond this specific result. Are you still wishing that your child would have the brains of Einstein and the feet of Ginger Rogers? Maybe not. Could we be ushering in a new era of eugenics?

A very different perspective comes from works by artists like Maria McKinney, who help us to look more deeply into the eyes of creatures that we have already created. McKinney's series *Sire*, large-format photographs of pedigree bulls tethered and held calmly by their keepers, confronts the viewer with the addition of a colorful sculptural object harnessed to their backs. Some of these

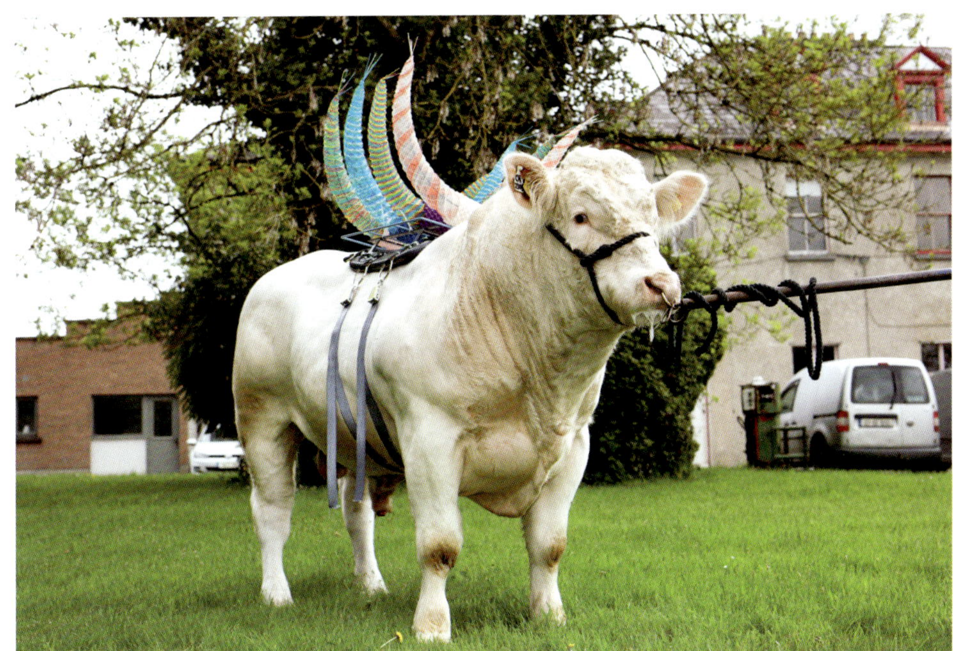

Maria McKinney, *Management /Polled, Doon just the job (CH2305)*, from the series, *Sire*, 2016, archival pigment print. Courtesy of the artist. *Sire* was made possible with support from Culture Ireland / Cultúr Éireann.

objects make obvious references to genetics, such as the chromosome, while other, more ornamental objects echo folk rituals in which animals were adorned with garlands of flowers—such as in the Almabtrieb cattle drives in the Alps. A closer examination of the photograph reveals that the structure is made of bovine semen straws used for artificial insemination. This sire is showing how it came into being through a juxtaposition of itself as both a product and the result of a breeding process. Differing in diameter and color, the straws are not merely an artistic flourish. There is a long history to semen straws that have changed in size and materials over time through scientific advances in artificial insemination. Contemporary practice uses a standardized system of bright colors to indicate breed. The artist applies traditional craft techniques to these tools of modern technology. Does being confronted with the process by which this sire was created change our relationship to it? Or is it only the physical appearance and taste of the meat that matters? The same questions can be asked of the corn we buy at the store. This issue is central to the debate on whether we should label foods developed through genetic engineering. It is also the focus of a central debate in conservation biology over the saving of endangered species through genetically engineered fitness. Would a beautiful rainforest feel as beautiful if you knew it was genetically engineered? Or would beauty be veiled by the concern over the lack of naturalness and potential risks?

Each of the artists in the exhibition aims to use the visual, aural, and conceptual tools of their discipline to engage us with the biotechnology already around us as well as the biotechnology to come. If these artworks succeed in that engagement, we will come away with some new rational and emotional understandings of this technology that include a bit of both "innovation thrill" and "risk panic." We hope that your experiences in this multi-site exhibition will provoke deeper conversations about these technologies, and that those conversations will also help in shaping our genetic futures.

Curating Art and Science: *Art's Work in the Age of Biotechnology* at CAM Raleigh

HANNAH STAR ROGERS

The field trial of the show detailed in this catalog was held at the contemporary art museum, CAM Raleigh, in April 2017 as a one-night, pop-up precursor to the full exhibition at the Gregg Museum of Art & Design and the NC State University Libraries in 2019–20. Six artists presented work that engaged with the ideas and materiality of biotechnology.

Under three glass cloches were versions of the scent of an extinct plant made possible by synthetic biology and art. Synthetic biologist and designer at Ginkgo Bioworks Christina Agapakis displayed her imaginative *Extinct Perfume*: three speculative aromas based on fragments of DNA from an extinct flowering plant, *Hesperelaea palmeri*. The pressed plant was stored in a herbarium for nearly 150 years before Agapakis obtained samples for genotyping. She worked with paleogeneticists and perfumers to produce an experience of the scent of the plant from the samples, based on its genome as well as those of living botanical relatives. The work functioned as a provocation and critique of attempts to recreate extinct organisms from DNA fragments.

Agapakis' work implicitly asks "What is not present?" and "What are the limitations of the interpretation of a new organism based on preserved specimens?" Through this aesthetic and accessible encounter, Agapakis raises questions about what we lose once a species is extinct and only its DNA remains. At CAM, she offered us a memory of the plant through our senses, which triggers a bodily experience in visitors of the loss of a species. Agapakis also showed what is possible in art-science collaborations between different types of experts.

Exhibits on the history of technology always posit arguments for the future of technologies. Along with the turn toward material practice in a variety of humanities fields and the urgency of science and technology policy for academic fields, exhibits in the area of biotechnology are social and political interventions. Curators must necessarily take a stance toward the marking of their controlled public space as a site of intervention. As a scholar of Science and Technology Studies (STS), my curatorial practice is guided by this sensibility, which increasingly informs projects that aim at public transparency. My own efforts have been in the area of art, science, and technology—an area fraught with power differentials but also with the potential to address complex problems.

The 2017 *Art's Work in the Age of Biotechnology: Shaping Our Genetic Futures* pop-up at CAM Raleigh—attended by more than a thousand visitors during a gallery walk night in the city—elicited discussions about genetics in society through provocative contemporary art and offered viewers new ways to think about their role in the genetic revolution. Curatorially, I had been interested in exploring the potential of an exhibit on a technology that was sure to be framed by all concerned as political, while also considering the ways that artworks and technical materials are understood by visitors. STS scholarship has offered pathways to consider how knowledge products might be understood in symmetrical ways,[1] but what is in the mind of a curator or scholar needs to be materially and textually translated for visitors. This engaging pop-up was a successful experiment and provided a blueprint for this larger exhibition at the Gregg Museum of Art & Design and the NC State University Libraries.

The evening's artworks also underscored the importance of the public in relation to the politics of contemporary science. Paul Vanouse, director of Coalesce: Center for Biological Art at the University at Buffalo, has examined this relationship through a series of artworks that use genetic techniques to create social critiques. Through Vanouse's piece in the show, viewers encountered the output of a reverse-engineered gel electrophoresis process In inverting the process by cutting known lengths of DNA, the artist also inverted the political aims of "DNA fingerprinting" and drew out new interpretations of this scientific image-making technology. In *Truth Machine*,[2] scholars of Science and Technology Studies explored how the concept of the "DNA fingerprint" is often misunderstood by the public and by the judicial system as a comprehensive and irrefutable individual identifying marker. Vanouse's work complicates this oversimplification. He draws attention to the hundreds of different enzymes, primers, and molecular probes that can be used to segment DNA and produce banding patterns, and the openness of the image making system to manipulation and artistic possibility. Visitors to CAM Raleigh encountered the lightbox

documentation as a way to experience the artist's classic work of bioart performance and sculptural work, *Latent Figure Protocol* (2007–09). At CAM, the static images provided a history for the bioartworks that have unfolded in the last decade and offered a starting point as visitors entered the space.

On the glass wall across from Vanouse's artwork were the images by Rich Pell. Like many of the pieces in the exhibition, these images were the fruits of art-science collaborations. Richard Pell, Curator for Postnatural Organisms at the Center for PostNatural History (CPNH) in Pittsburgh, presented *Spectres of the PostNatural*—stereoscopic images of 3D-scanned specimens from the center's vault. The CPNH documents species that have been genetically affected by human activities, such as genetically modified mosquitoes or dogs that have been bred for aesthetic or utilitarian traits. The center's work offers viewers opportunities to consider the postnatural in their everyday lives and the ways that definitions impact an understanding of the consequences of human action.

Adam Zaretsky's DIY biolab *DNA Food Art* was a highly interactive, hands-on experience that attendees flocked to. Decked out in a hazmat suit and with a mad scientist's air, Zaretsky showed attendees how to isolate DNA from a mixture of sources using common household items like contact lens cleaner, salt, and Woolite. By using everyday materials to isolate DNA from a monstrous collective blender mash-up, the public had a chance to touch the subject of so much social and scientific foment and gain a bodily experience of the goopy strands in all

1. Barnes, Barry, David Bloor, and John Henry. 1996. *Scientific Knowledge: A Sociological Approach.* Chicago: University of Chicago Press.

2. Lynch, Michael, Simon A. Cole, Ruth McNally, and Kathleen Jordan. 2008. *Truth Machine: The Contentious History of DNA Fingerprinting.* Chicago: University of Chicago Press.

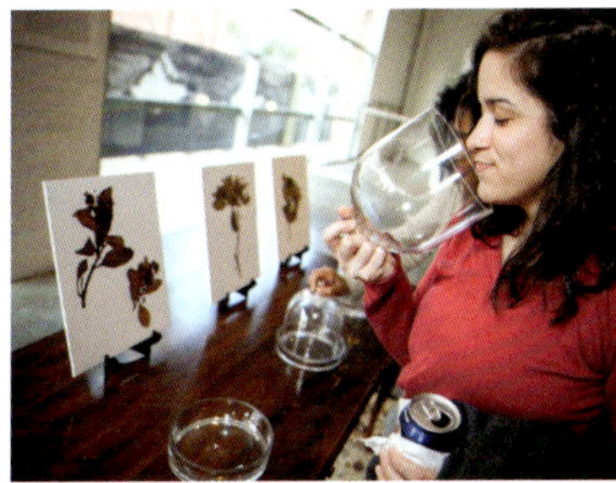

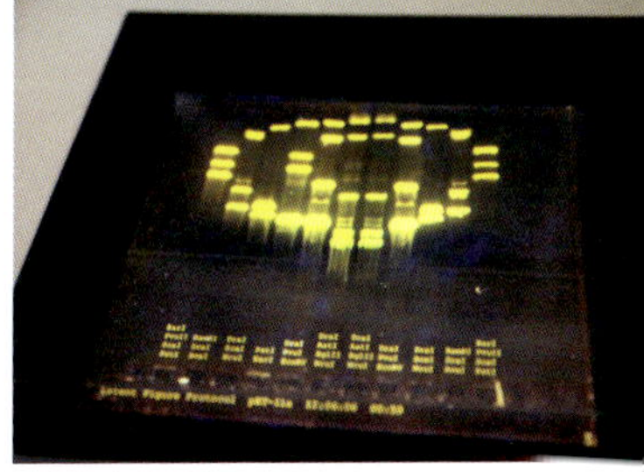

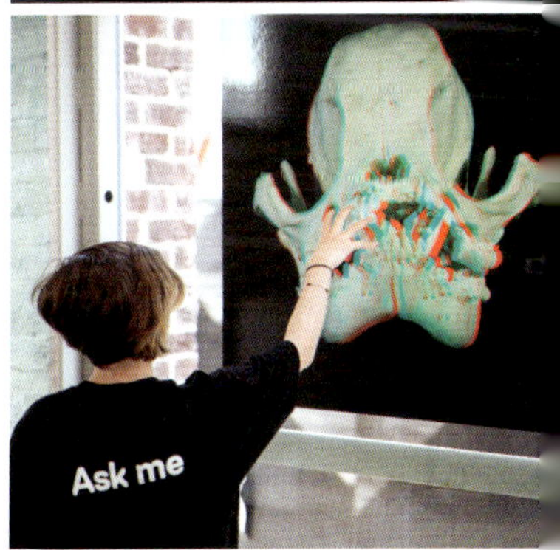

TOP TO BOTTOM: Visitors sample scents of Christina Agapakis' *Extinct Perfumes*; Paul Vanouse's *Latent Figure Protocol*; Richard Pell's *Specters of the PostNatural.* Photographs by York Wilson.

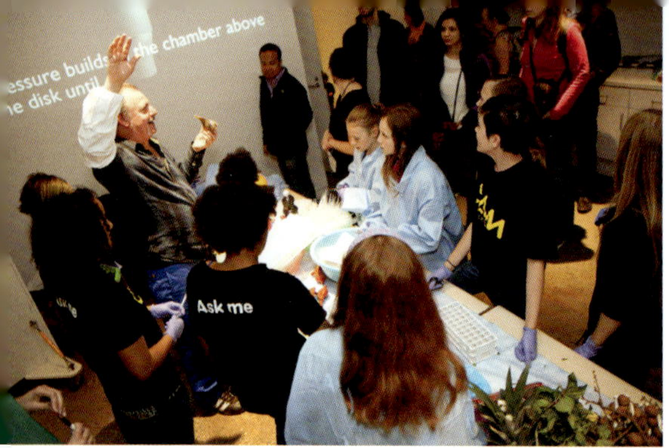

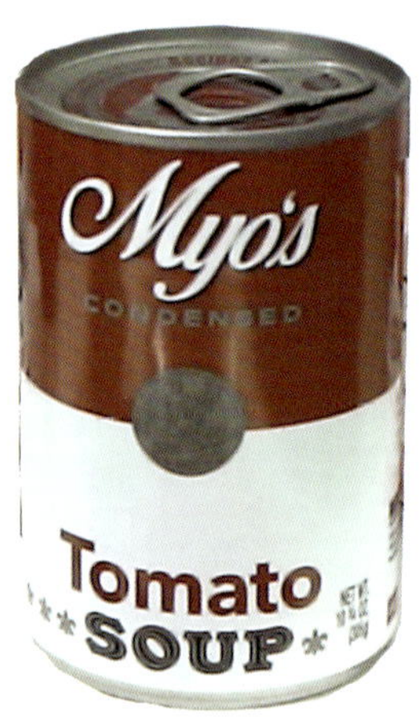

Adam Zaretsky performs *DNA Food Art* with CAM Raleigh's middle-school docents. Jonathan Davis' projected animation visualizes the process of DNA extraction. Photograph by York Wilson.

The *MyoTomato* soup can was created by the SVA's 2016 BioDesign Challenge team: Leman Akpinar, Viktorea Benois, Sebastian Cocioba, Andrew Cziraki, David Hanlon, Marguerite Li, Bo Liu, Steph Mantis, Kirin Pino, Shannon Pollak, Gina Proenza, Tarah Rhoda, Victor Taboada, Darya Warner, and John Wells. Image courtesy of the artists.

our cells. Local scientist and animator Jon Davis of Scientific Studios made a video of the DNA-isolation process to help participants understand what was happening at the molecular level in Zaretsky's lab. *DNA Food Art* brought the techniques of biotech out of the lab and into the household kitchen in an engaging—and delightfully messy—way.

The projects on view at CAM Raleigh included both the analytical and speculative, inquiring about practices and projecting possibilities for the meanings of art and science in different contexts. *MyoTomato*—a bioengineered tomato plant that produces myoglobin, a protein normally found in meat—was the result of student work at the School of Visual Arts by Andrew Cziraki, Victor Taboada, Darya Warner, and John Wells, instructed by bioartist Suzanne Anker and created as part of the GenSpace-sponsored annual Biodesign Challenge, led by director and founder Dan Grushkin. Kirsten Stolle's *Genetically Commodified* brought us into a made world: her aesthetic arrangements are orchestrated from beyond the frame through food systems driven by corporate and governmental concerns. The local musical group *Cyanotype* mixed up our base pairs with innovative improv sounds, along with a piece that was composed to accompany

Stolle's work as it was projected onto the rough surface of a brick wall.

This one-night exhibition aimed to provoke visitors to think about their power in relationship to genetics and how non-scientists can shape debates and intervene in the social and technical processes around biotechnology. In order to encourage visitors to see themselves not just as social participants involved in interactive artworks prepared by artists, moments for reflection were integrated into the exhibition. Visitors to the gallery were asked to contribute their ideas about our genetic futures on a Post-It wall and through informal visitor surveys administered by CAM's middle-school docents, who used an iPad system to collect visitor feedback.

The following day, the NC State University Libraries, led by Exhibits Program Librarian Molly Renda, and NC State's Genetic Engineering and Society Center (GES), led by Co-Director Fred Gould, collaborated with Todd Kuiken, Chris Vitiello, Elizabeth Pitts, Patti Mulligan, and Sharon Stauffer to assemble a day-long workshop. This event brought the artists together with NC State scientists, STS scholars, and humanists with an interest in genetics and biotechnology to discuss the artwork on display at CAM and to engage emerging issues in genetics through

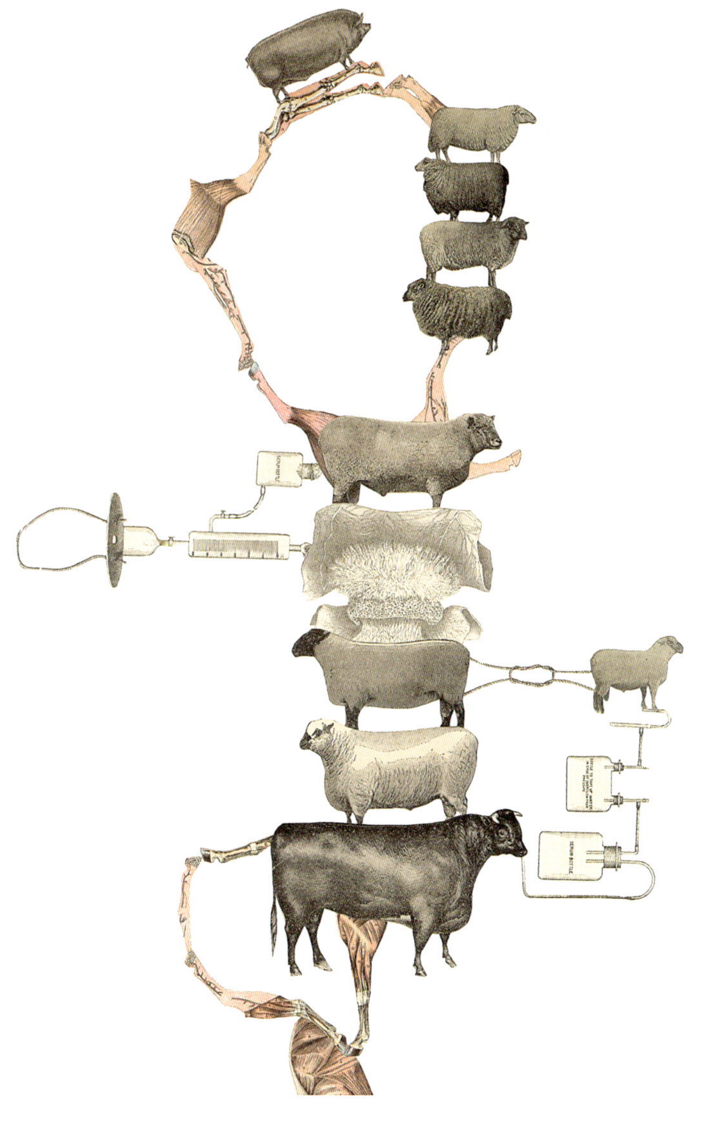

the arts. These groups discussed the show's concept and provided feedback about the artwork, as well as a forum for discussions about how art and biotechnology might be placed in conversation. Together, the pop-up exhibit and the workshop developed ideas about the contributions of artists around genetic engineering and substantially informed this large-scale, multi-site exhibition in fall 2019.

Art's Work/Genetic Futures challenges us to examine what might seem to be the discrete boundary between art and science with boundary-crossing works. Even as bodies are the object of so much of the study of biology, the experience of the body is often left to artists. If we propose to study life, we must insist on visions from both art and science, and it is these categories that *Art's Work* aims to complicate: divisions between bodies and experiences, between the public and experts, and between a belief in a technical and biological deterministic view of our genetic futures and the social choices we are free to make. Accordingly, these artworks were chosen to complicate dichotomous divisions and raise questions about the roles of science and art, and the results of cooperation between these knowledge communities that are not so easy to categorize. Art, or science, is in the eye of the beholder.

Embracing Shared Uncertainties

MEGAN SERR AND JOHN GODWIN

1. https://research.ncsu.edu/
ges/igert/student-research/
island-mice-conserving-
island-biodiversity/

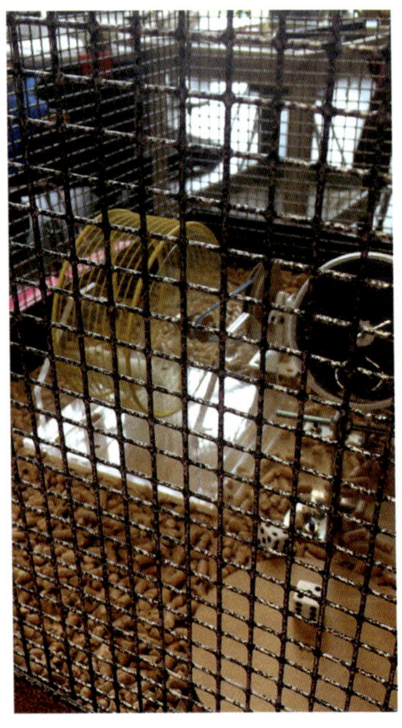

Joe Davis, video still from
Lucky Mice, 2017–19.

Too often science and art are considered to be distinct realms. Today we recognize that there is much more fluidity and interdisciplinarity between the two. We acknowledge that science often requires an artistic lens and that art often requires scientific knowledge. For example, a painter must carefully mix certain pigments to achieve a particular color palette and a scientist must fine-tune their technique and apparatus to achieve the optimum visual field. The exhibition *Art's Work in the Age of Biotechnology: Shaping Our Genetic Futures* highlights the merging of these fields and the realization that human culture is an interwoven tapestry of arts, humanities, and science.

As biologists who focus on genetic engineering and rodents from a conservation perspective, we are interested in art that works with genes, the environment, sex-changing, and behavior. We describe our scientific endeavors in this essay, and how they relate to works in the exhibition. Then we train our scientific lens on several of the artworks that caught our eye in this exhibition and consider their implications for conversations around biotechnology. In particular, we discuss how both the arts and the sciences often rely on uncertainty and the hypothetical and how scientists can benefit from

an exploration of the arts showcased in this exhibition and beyond.

Our research on island rodent population control informs our interests as scientists in this exhibit, particularly with regard to how art and science work with uncertainty and hypotheticals through models and speculative designs.[1] Rodents are often invasive species and can be found on over 80 percent of the world's islands. They can negatively affect plants and animals, causing damage to fragile island ecosystems. Most rodents were unintentionally brought to various islands by human travels, often as stowaways on ships. Once they arrived, they frequently found unlimited resources and island animals that were defenseless against their attacks because they had not evolved with predators present. The traditional method for removal of these invasive rodents is costly, using poisoned bait spread aerially via helicopters. This method is challenging to implement and has several serious drawbacks. The poisons are not species-specific and would be very difficult to use on islands where people reside (80 percent of the islands where invasive rodents threaten biodiversity are inhabited by humans). These baits also require fatal doses of poison, which has raised general animal welfare concerns.

As scientists, we have been exploring the hypothetical use of a genetic technique to sex-bias the population, causing the population to decrease through a lack of mating partners. This might be called a form of "genetic contraception." Our scientific collaborators have been pursuing gene drives in house mice as a genetic technique to control invasive mouse populations. A gene drive is a selfishly inherited gene, inherited the great majority of the time. Unlike the traditional inheritance rate of 50 percent from a mother and 50 percent from a father, these are designed to be inherited from just one parent by almost all offspring (often close to 100 percent of offspring). This should guarantee these genes will spread through a population. The concept is to induce a sex-bias so that all the mice born will be one sex—either all males or all females—depending on which way you sex-bias the population.[2] Importantly, no sex-biasing gene-drive mouse currently exists, so all the research we do is in the hypothetical stage. In the absence of a gene-drive mouse of this nature, we work with non-transgenic mice in semi-natural environments to try to predict how a gene-drive mouse would behave. We also rely on mathematical models to predict how many introduced gene-drive mice would be required to achieve invasive mouse population reduction or removal based on different sex-biasing strategies.

Hence, this project requires several leaps into the unknown: the unknowns of reproductive biology, ecology, genetics, and modeling. However, the greatest unknown for our approach has to do with human society in all its various and diverse parts. It remains to be seen how humans would perceive a gene-drive mouse and whether people, governments, and regulatory agencies would see this as a viable and ethical alternative to poison.

Thus, we live in a world where we may be creating a scientific work that no one wants or that will never be employed. However, as scientists, we embrace the hypothetical. We feel the science is worth pursuing even if the final piece—in our case, the gene-drive mice—never comes to fruition. We get a thrill from exploration and discovery in a world of many unknowns, just as an artist revels in the possibilities for the artworks they create. Science is perhaps a little like art in this way: we undertake these explorations because of the thrill and interest, often not knowing whether they will "work" or if anyone will notice if they do.

Many of the artists in this exhibition rely similarly on the hypothetical for their art. Their works require thinking into the dimension of what could be and ask us to take an imaginative leap into implications and possibilities. Some works in this exhibition show us the here and now by combining cutting-edge science and art. Others prompt us to try and predict our own futures. This exhibition and its catalog provoke us to think about the relationship of art and science to our shared unknown futures.

Joe Davis' *Lucky Mice* stood out to us as scientists working on gene-drive mice. Davis' work also involves house mice and, in this case, the serendipitous inheritance of "luck." Laboratory mice are the most commonly used mammal in research because of their genetic similarities to humans and the ease with which they can be genetically manipulated.

2. https://blogs.
scientificamerican.com/
guest-blog/mice-as-
conservationists/?redirect=1

Laboratory mice are also highly inbred, which allows scientists to test for environmental impacts while ruling out differences in genes. Davis uses domesticated mice that are the same species as those that are invasive on islands and cause harmful environmental effects. Interestingly, wild house mice are quite variable and successful as a "weed" species, perhaps much like humans in this sense. This highlights the many different aspects of mice, in that they can serve as pets, pests, and laboratory models. The human-mouse relationship is an integral part of Davis' work and our own research project. We each rely upon the inheritance of traits for differing aspects and possibilities.

Another piece that relates to our specific scientific perspective is Charlotte Jarvis' *In Posse: Making Female Sperm*, which is an attempt to produce semen from female stem cells. This is a cutting-edge technique and speaks to our project and the transformation from one sex to another. Both the ability to create sperm precursor cells from a female stem cell and the ability to artificially change the sex of an organism rely heavily on novel genetic techniques that were relegated to science fiction just a few years ago. Today, both are possible in the laboratory, which opens possibilities for sex-biasing gene-drive technologies. In fact, scientists have already created a "Y-shredder" mechanism through gene editing that yields only female mouse offspring. As biologists, we have long recognized that there is tremendous diversity in the ways in which animals and plants determine and present their sex. Indeed, some species such as the bluehead wrasse and other coral reef fish are already quite capable of switching sex as adults and even mixing and matching what are sometimes framed as "female" and "male" characteristics. People can learn from biologists, as well as this artist, that there is much more fluidity to sex, which might open people to wider collective conversations about sex and gender in our society.

In this vein, we were intrigued by the depiction of "genetic determinism" in Heather Dewey-Hagborg's *Stranger Visions*. This artwork emphasizes the uncertainty in this field even as its developing technology is being proposed for applications that could impinge upon civil liberties. Certainly biology has made great progress in addressing the question of "genotype-to-phenotype" (how the genetic code translates into the structure and function of organisms), but the often overriding influences of environment and life experience can be inappropriately downplayed within this narrower focus on genetics. An understanding of these environmental influences and their interactions with genetics is key in order to know the limits of new genetic technologies and to maximize their potential benefits. Scientists are beginning to see that the environment has a huge impact on even the structure of our genes. Invasive mice on islands are surely affected by the island landscape just as people in New York City have different environmental exposures than the people of Papua New Guinea. Dewey-Hagborg went into the New York City environment to collect

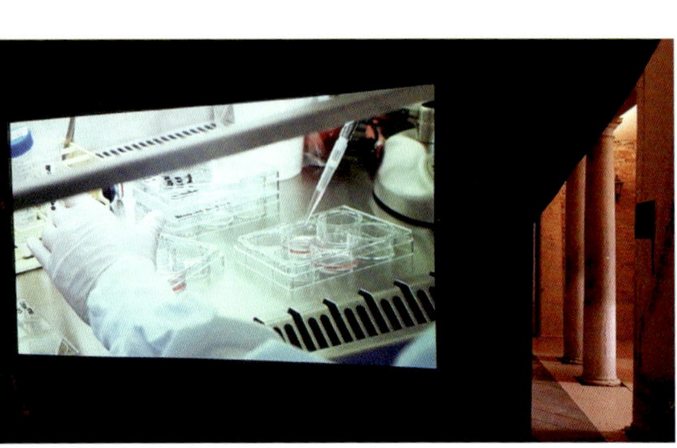

Charlotte Jarvis, video still from *In Posse: Making Female Sperm*, from the series *Corpus*, 2019, multimedia installation. Photographs and HD video by Charlotte Jarvis, Miha Godec, and Eleni Papazoglu. Courtesy of the artist.

these pieces and extract DNA, and then used those DNA profiles and the probability of certain phenotypic characteristics to depict the person. However, what the artist was unable to capture was the impact that a person's environment has had on their DNA (smoking, obesity, tattoos). In the future we might even be able to map these environmental marks on DNA and depict them just as Dewey-Hagborg was able to do.

As scientists working on gene-drive mice, we would be remiss to not also highlight Aaron Ellison and David Buckley Borden's *Novel Ecosystem Generator*. The idea for their project comes from invasive species and the formation of gene-drive organisms and others that have been genetically altered. This work challenges us to think about our interactions with modified organisms and environments. Gene-drive mice released on an island would require just what the artists appear to be aiming for in terms of how these novel environmental situations can be viewed. While we are focused on this project because of the disproportionate impact these invasive rodents have in non-native ecosystems, the artists are touching on an issue that is of concern to scientists and should be of concern to all of us: we are in the midst of a massive, unplanned, and unpredictable experiment due to environmental change. This experiment is already "engineering" the genetics of species with consequences that are very difficult to predict.

Again, many of the works here rely on us to imagine their possibilities, just as scientists often rely on (hopefully) educated guesses and probabilities to predict future outcomes. Many artists use this hypothetical frame to highlight aspects of their work, while scientists, finding this uncertainty "troublesome," often seek to reduce it before we proceed. The future of genetics and what will be possible remains uncertain and, at present, often purely hypothetical, but this uncertainty has also benefited scientists more generally as it makes us consider the wider implications of our research.

Scientists are learning that our work cannot happen in isolation and needs to be shared with others in other fields. Similarly, scientists benefit from viewing artistic works as a way of seeing how science is perceived and reflected in our larger communities. The arts and sciences are presented as entwined across this exhibition, and this opportunity to consider these interrelated realms benefits all of us as we contemplate the unknown future of genetics and life in our modern world.

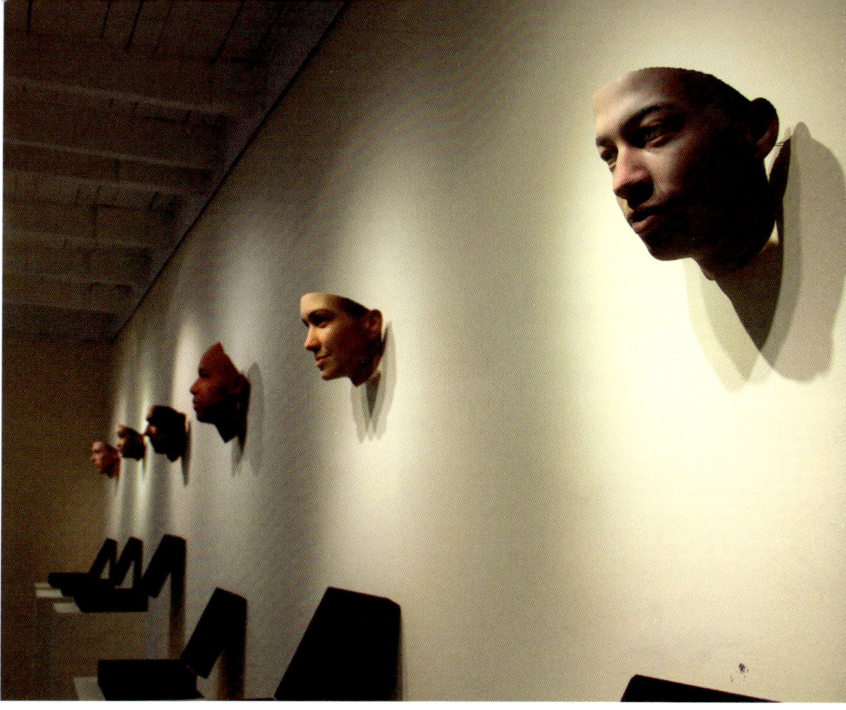

Heather Dewey-Hagborg, installation view of *Stranger Visions*, Saint-Gaudens National Historic Site, September 2014. Courtesy of the artist and Fridman Gallery, New York.

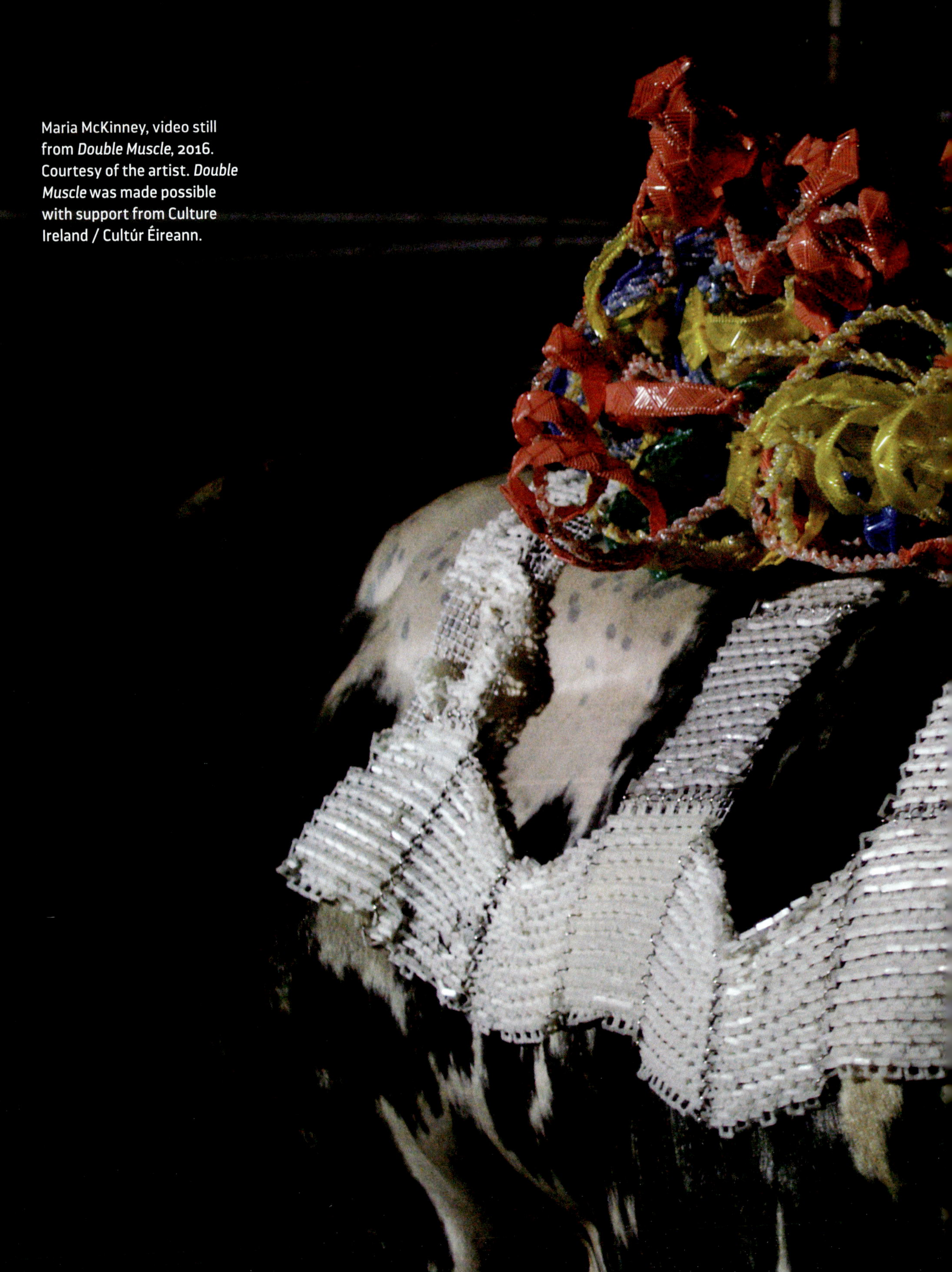

Maria McKinney, video still from *Double Muscle*, 2016. Courtesy of the artist. *Double Muscle* was made possible with support from Culture Ireland / Cultúr Éireann.

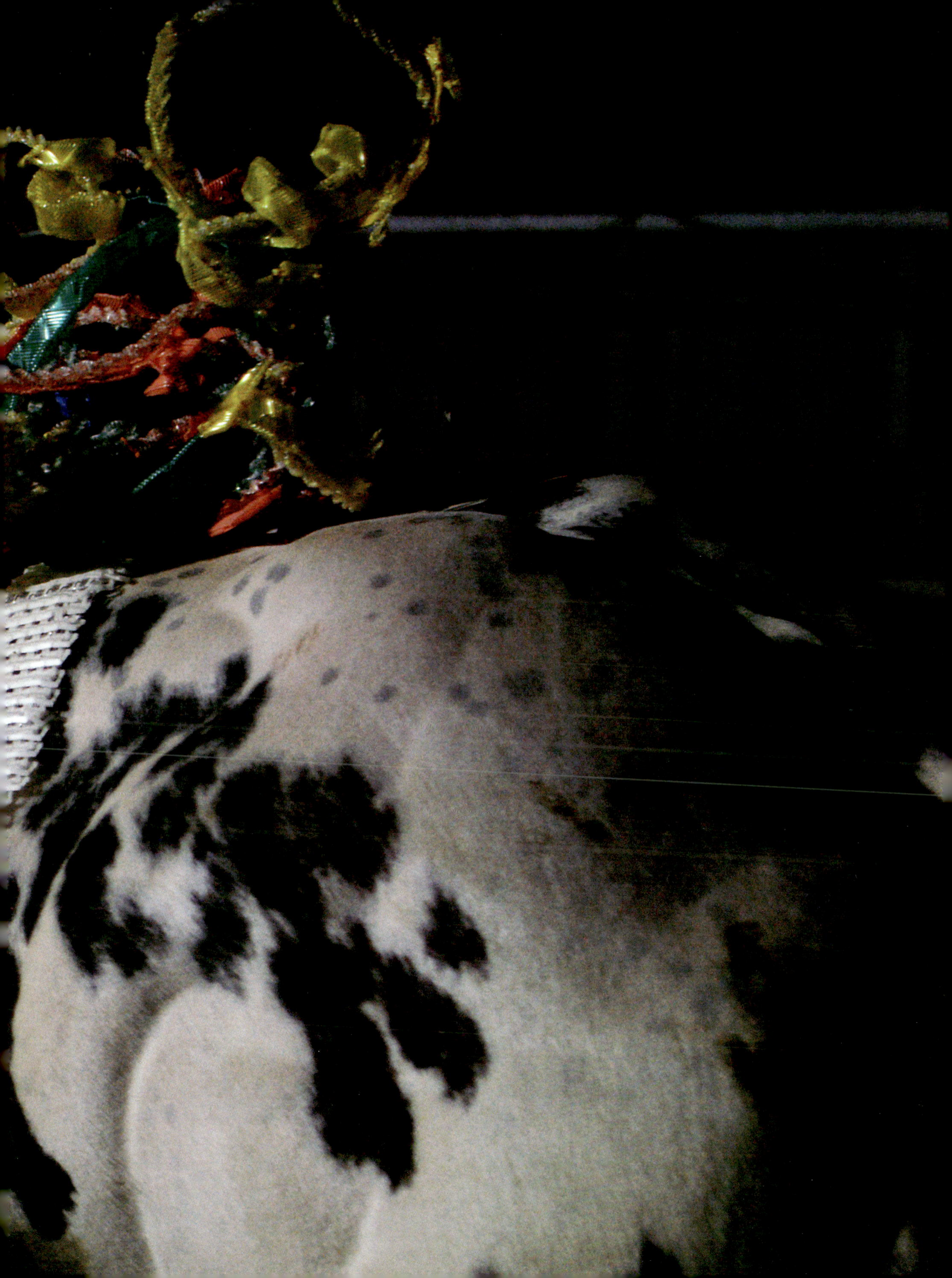

What Artists Offer: Shaping Our Genetic Futures

HANNAH STAR ROGERS

Biotechnology and art are fascinatingly intertwined. From our aesthetic appreciation of plants and animals that brought about breeding regimens, to art about ethics in the genomic age, these artworks invite the public into the conversation about the history, philosophy, politics, and future of biotechnology.

---

1. Durant, J., S. Martin, and J. Tait. 1992. *Biotechnology in Public: A Review of Recent Research.* London: Science Museum Publications. pp. 28–41.

Art's Work in the Age of Biotechnology: Shaping Our Genetic Futures elicits discussion about genetics in society through contemporary art in order to offer viewers new ways of thinking about their roles in potential genetic revolutions. Through their works in this exhibition, artists have addressed questions about biotechnology beyond those typical in scientific conversations, including questions of access, sex and gender, race, the rights and roles of animals, and the involvement of corporations.

The exhibition takes place in North Carolina's Research Triangle (Raleigh, Durham, Chapel Hill), home to major biotechnology firms and many genetic technology startups. But North Carolina was also the home of one of the most notorious and persistent eugenics boards in the United States: it began sterilizations for eugenic science purposes in 1919 and the last law allowing involuntary sterilization was repealed in 2003. It was not until 2008 that Governor Beverly Perdue formed the North Carolina Justice for Sterilization Victims Foundation to begin the task of providing compensation to the victims. Together, that eugenics history and the research and business of cutting-edge biotechnology make North Carolina a fitting place to discuss the future of these technologies. Science offers us the potential to do good and to do harm. It takes on the character society gives it, so it is important to have broad discussions about the way biotechnology can and will be used.

Exhibitions in the area of biotechnology are social and political interventions. As an STS (Science and Technology Studies) scholar and a curator for art and science exhibitions, I have been interested in exploring the potential of an exhibition on biotechnology that raises complex social and political ideas, while also considering the way that artworks, particularly those that involve scientific expertise or technical materials, are understood by visitors. The projects on view are both analytical and speculative, asking about practices and projecting possibilities for the meanings of art and science in different contexts. This exhibition aims to engage the public about the social uses, familiar and new, that biotechnology might offer through artworks that deal directly with biotechnologies or offer new ways of contextualizing them.

Soliciting conversations with the public about emerging technologies like biotechnology often creates a tension between how much information and detail to provide versus how to encourage visitors to value what they already bring with them to the exchange.[1] Science communication scholars have argued that it is important to avoid the "deficit model,"[2] where it is presumed that, if the public disagrees or expresses ideas that are not in concert with the reaction scientists or science communicators expect, then there has been a "deficit" in communication. The usual response is that more communication, in the form of additional information, is needed. In this model, there is no route by which the public may legitimately disagree or even raise serious issues with the science presented to them.

For curators, this can create a roadblock: how much information should we provide to visitors? At what point may we be distracting from the conversations we want visitors to have by adding details that may be unapproachable or even alienating to the very people we hope to draw into dialogue? There will, after all, always be technical unknowns, particularly in the case of emerging technologies. Art finds ways around this inclusion conundrum: rather than emphasizing technical details that audiences are meant to master before becoming part of the conversation as lay experts, art challenges us to think about the effects of these technologies, starting from the big picture of social, political, and ethical context. Rather than the small picture of, for example, precisely how CRISPR-Cas9 can be used, how *Trifolium repens* might be bred to produce more four-leaf clovers, or how hox genes affect embryonic development, artists begin by asking what people will or should do with the power to edit their own genomes and what it could mean culturally if we could create mermaids or make all clovers have four leaves. Maria McKinney's *Double Muscle* film and sculpture made of colorful bovine semen straws asks about the traditions of cattle breeding that have been altered through new biotechnological processes. The work implicitly asks visitors to consider what we have already done with these new technologies.

Our society needs to grapple with these social, political, economic, and cultural effects. Asked these questions by these artists, we may all have an informed opinion shaped by our individual daily experiences and fueled by our interpretations of artworks that address these subjects. Our scientists are specialized enough to handle the details: we need artists to help us imagine our futures. Along the way, visitors learn about biotechnologies, but in ways that are relevant to the choices we collectively and individually face. The expertise that artists provide offers a way into important conversations about biotechnology that are not so much technical as social. Artistic expertise expands the conversation in an accessible way—not absent of technical details, but open to the values and concerns of the public who are experiencing their art.

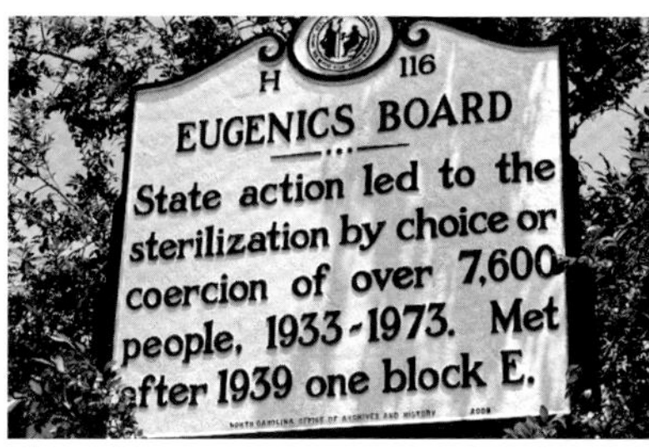

North Carolina highway historical marker located on US 401 in Raleigh.

2. Allum, Nick, P. Sturgis, D. Tabourazi, and I. Brunton-Smith. 2008. "Science knowledge and attitudes across cultures: a meta-analysis." *Public Understanding of Science* 17: 35–54.

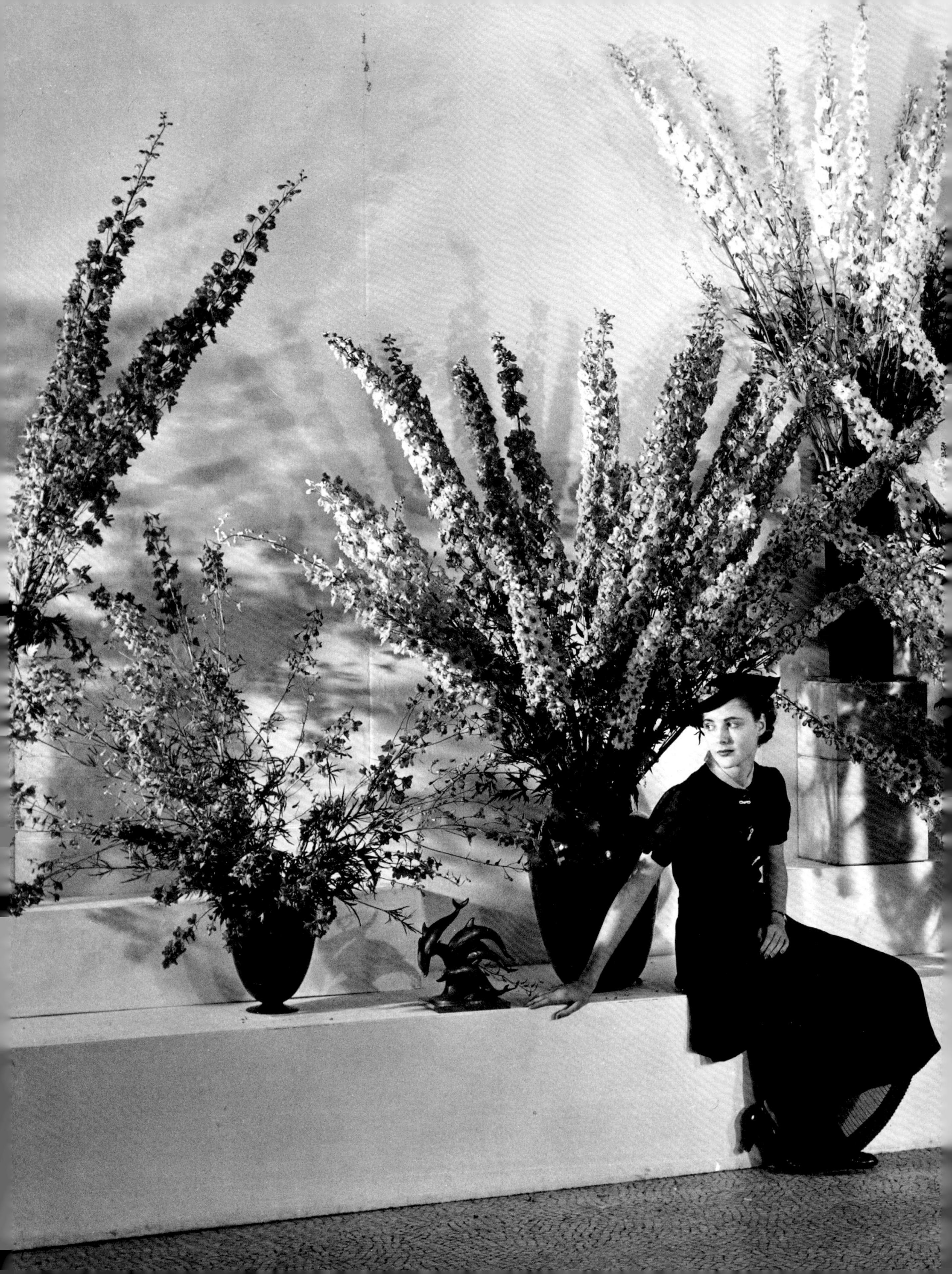

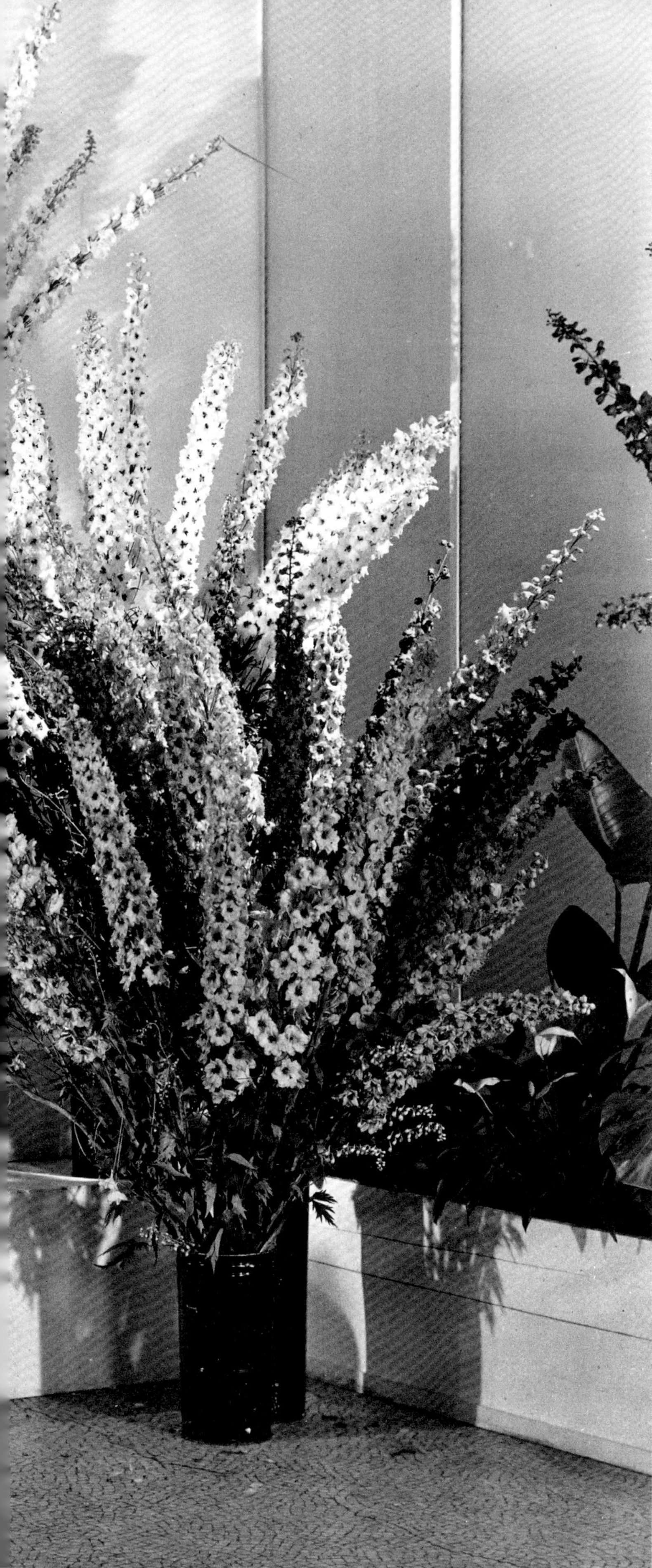

Edward Steichen, (1879–1973) © ARS, NY. Installation view of the exhibition, "Edward Steichen's Delphiniums," The Museum of Modern Art, New York, June 24, 1936 through July 1, 1936. Photograph by Edward Steichen. (IN50.2) The Museum of Modern Art Digital Image © The Museum of Modern Art/Licensed by SCALA/Art Resource, NY.

This exhibition has been created to engage the public about the social uses, both familiar and new, that this technology might offer through provocative art that deals directly with these technologies or offers new ways of contextualizing them. Dimensions of both biotechnology and art are on display through *Art's Work/ Genetic Futures*. Viewers' perceptions of art and science will shape the politics of meaning ascribed to the pieces in the exhibition.

The Intertwined History of Aesthetics and Genetics

Biological and aesthetic selection have always been intertwined. This relationship is evident in everyday things like our food, pets, and household objects. Genetic archeologists have shown that ten thousand years ago, teosinte,

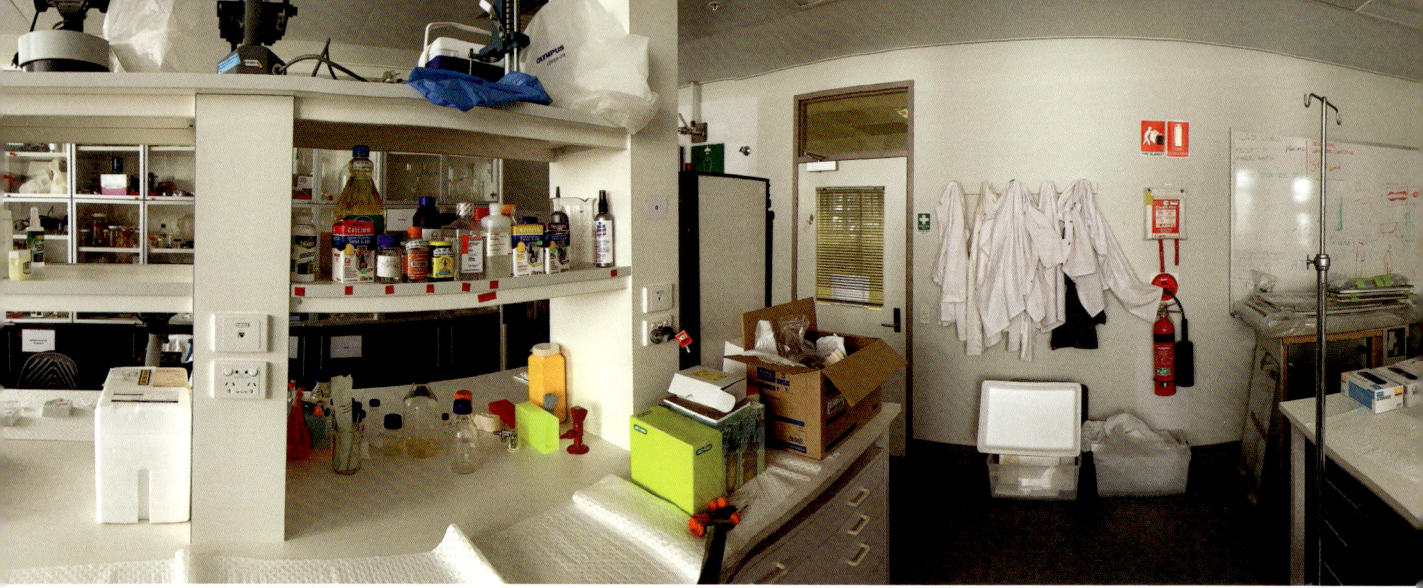

3. Carroll, Sean. 2010. "Tracking the Ancestry of Corn Back 9,000 Years." *New York Times.* May 24. https://www.nytimes.com/2010/05/25/science/25creature.html

4. Dalley, Stephanie. 1993. "Ancient Mesopotamian Gardens and the Identification of the Hanging Gardens of Babylon Resolved." *Garden History* 21 (1): 1-13 doi:10.2307/1587050.

5. Malek, Jaromir. 2006. *The Cat in Ancient Egypt.* London: The British Museum Press.

6. Hartmann, Celia. "Edward Steichen Archive: Delphiniums Blue (and White and Pink, Too)." MoMA/MoMA PS1 Blog. March 8, 2011. https://www.moma.org/explore/inside_out/2011/03/08/edward-steichen-archive-delphiniums-blue-and-white-and-pink-too/.

7. Gedrim, Ronald J. 1993. "Edward Steichen's 1936 Exhibition of Delphinium Blooms." *History of Photography* 17 (4): 352-363. doi:10.1080/03087298.1993.10442317.

8. Curry, Helen Anne. 2016. *Evolution Made to Order: Plant Breeding and Technological Innovation in Twentieth-Century America.* Chicago: University of Chicago Press.

the genetic predecessor to maize, was already under cultivation in what is now Mexico.[3] Written evidence of gardening practices and artistic cultivation of cultivars by the Mesopotamians at Court of Palms dates back to 1800 BCE.[4] In ancient Egypt, two main cat breeds were developed around 2000 BCE. Dogs had already been domesticated for over a thousand years by this time.[5] In China, the world's first paper was being created from cultivated hemp during the height of the Eastern Han dynasty (25–220 CE). Preferences for food and fiber, gardens, and even pets led to selection for preferred traits that themselves changed over time. Yet, whatever their aesthetic value, few of these breeding programs have been positioned as works of art.

To find the roots of contemporary art and genetics, however, we need only look as far back as Edward Steichen (1879–1973), painter, photographer, and delphinium breeder. From 1947 to 1961, Steichen served as director of the Department of Photography at New York's Museum of Modern Art and, in 1936, he installed the first live plants in the galleries.[6] Steichen was an avid plant breeder whose massive delphinium inflorescences drew crowds, but what made his display crucial to the history of art and genetics was that his plant breeding techniques involved direct genetic interventions, including the use of the medication colchicine, which created mutations in the plants and, therefore, new varieties. Two years later, Steichen would retire from commercial photography to create more time to pursue his delphiniums. His "Connecticut Yankee," named for Mark Twain's novel *A Connecticut Yankee in King Arthur's Court*, was brought to market in 1965 and remains available to the present day.[7]

Steichen's work is also notable because of its timing. As historian Helen Curry writes, the mid-1930s marked the beginning of what would turn out to be a period of considerable scientific interest in creating new cultivars through genetic interventions with a variety of poisons, x-rays, and radioactive substances.[8] These mutation-making practices would continue through the early 1950s as scientists, farmers, and home gardeners sought to see what new possibilities atomic science might bring to their botanicals. Though it is often suggested that the recent developments in genomics like at-home DNA testing for ourselves, and even for our furry pets, is a

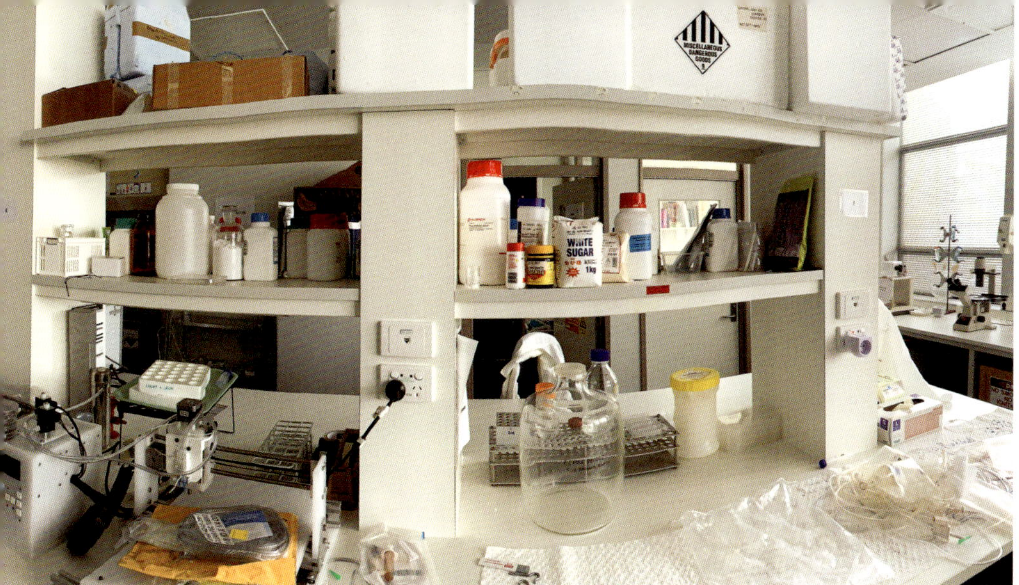

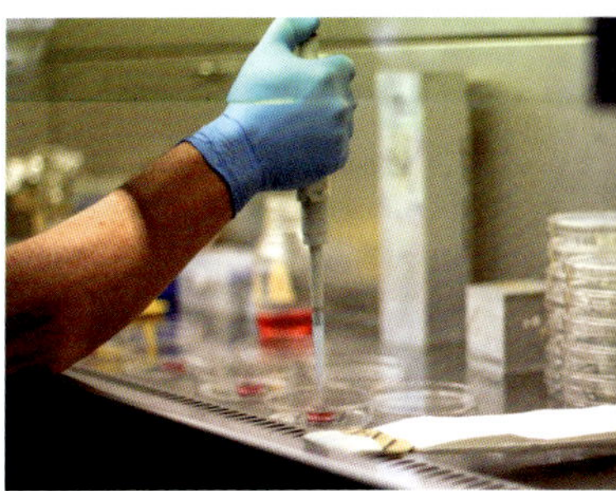

LEFT and ABOVE: SymbioticA laboratory space and bench work, The University of Western Australia, 2019.

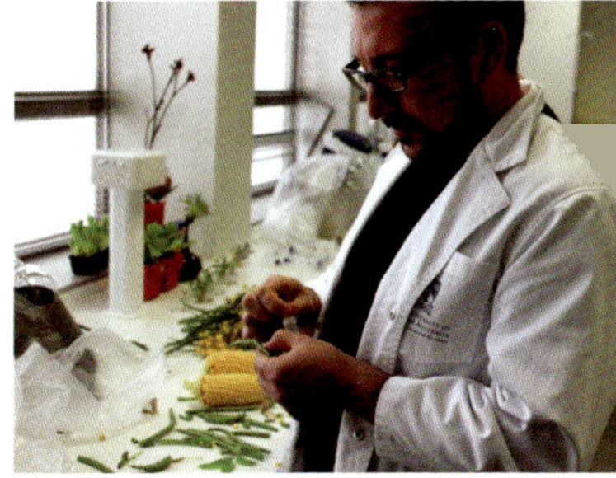

ABOVE: Artist Mike Bianco, Plant Tissue Culture Workshop participant, SymbioticA Lab, 2016.

new degree of availability of biotechnology, a look back at this period of amateur or citizen science experimentation with plant breeding reveals the long, rich history of non-scientists working with what we now think of as biotechnology. Understanding the history of genetics can help to enrich our interpretations of artworks about these technologies. Steichen's interest and work shows that rather than following scientific advances and celebrating and making use of them in due measure, artists are often at the vanguard of conversations about science, particularly genetics.

Influences and Inspirations: Bioart, Tactical Media, and Speculative Design

Much of the work in the area of art science, and perhaps particularly in the area of art and emerging technoscience, tends to be situated as novel. In fact, a great deal of work has taken place in this area. While it is important to recognize new artworks and streams of thought in art, emphasizing their novelty tends to remove them from their context and, as a consequence, mute some interesting interpretations of the work. The artists represented in *Art's Work/Genetic Futures* draw on a number of artistic and design traditions to produce their work. In various measures, many of the artists have engaged with bioart, worked with performative interventions, or produced projects influenced by speculative design. Prominent among the many types of artworks that have engaged genetics in the last twenty-five years has been the practice of bioart, or art that involves working with living things including live tissues, bacteria, living organisms, and life processes.

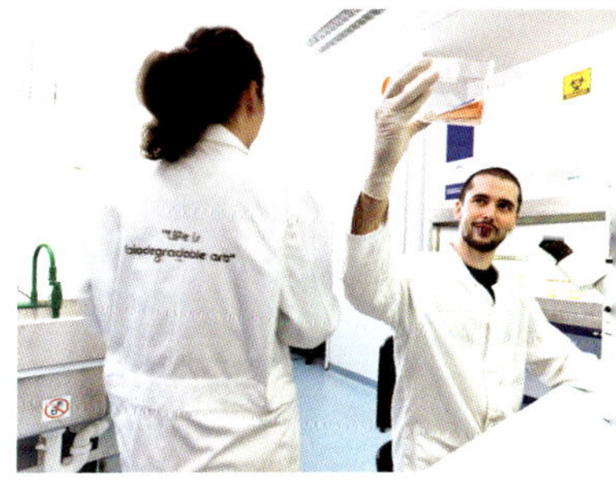

Resident artists Benjamin Forster (right) and Nora Vaage (left), 2013. Photograph by The University of Western Australia.

The term "bioart" was coined by Eduardo Kac in 1997 in relation to his artwork *Time Capsule*, though many artists like Joe Davis, Suzanne Anker, and George Gessert already constituted a community that had been working in this area for at least a decade. A marked feature of the last three decades of bioart work has been the emergence of artistic laboratory spaces, which have afforded artists the opportunity to work in biological labs and enabled new kinds of artworks. Such spaces are the site

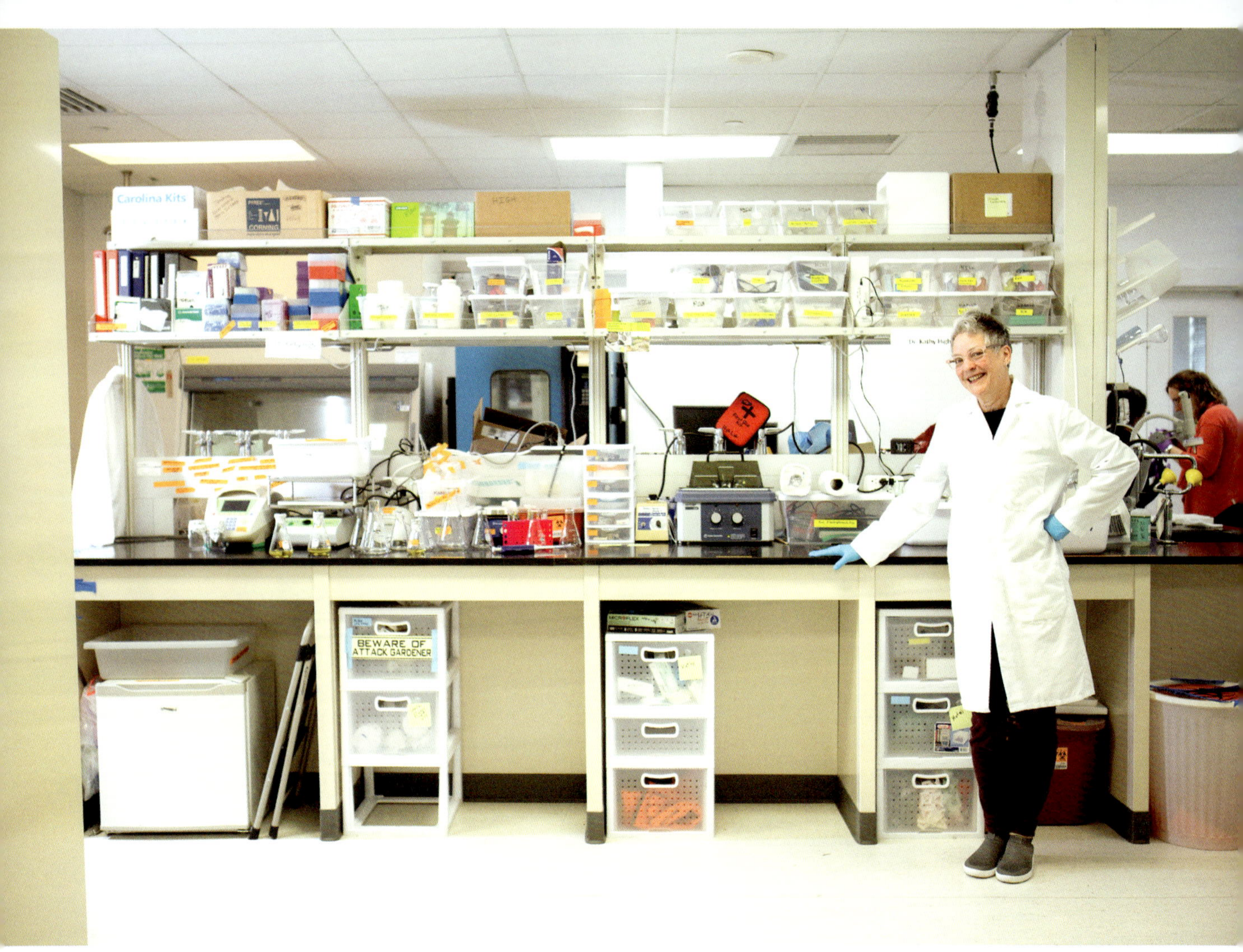

Artist and professor Kathy High in her laboratory at the Center for Biotechnology and Interdisciplinary Studies, Rensselaer Polytechnic Institute, Troy, New York, 2019. Photograph by Eleanor Goldsmith.

of both physical laboratory resources and practical protocol know-how. They include the University of Western Australia's SymbioticA (2000) led by Oron Catts and Ionat Zurr; Rensselaer Polytechnic Institute's The BioArt Initiative (2007) founded by Kathy High, with Rich Pell, Daniela Kostova, and Boryana Rossa; the University of Windsor's Incubator founded by Jennifer Willet (2009); Brooklyn-based GenSpace (2010), which sponsors the Biodesign Challenge for which kerasynth was developed; the School of Visual Arts' (SVA) Bio Art Lab (2011) established by Suzanne Anker; and the University at Buffalo's Coalesce (2016) initiated and directed by Paul Vanouse.

Many artists represented in this exhibition have founded, trained in, or contributed to these growing institutions. Paul Vanouse was an early SymbioticA resident who, as mentioned above, went on to found Coalesce. Joel Ong received an MSc at SymbioticA and recently held a residency at Coalesce. Heather Dewey-Hagborg performed the DNA analysis for *Stranger Visions* at the early GenSpace lab, and GenSpace sponsored the Biodesign Challenge that occasioned the creation of *Kerasynth* (Diana Eusbio, Erin Kirchner, Grace Kwon, Rachel Rusk, and Sydney Sieh-Takata). Rich Pell collaborated with Kathy High and others on the BioArt

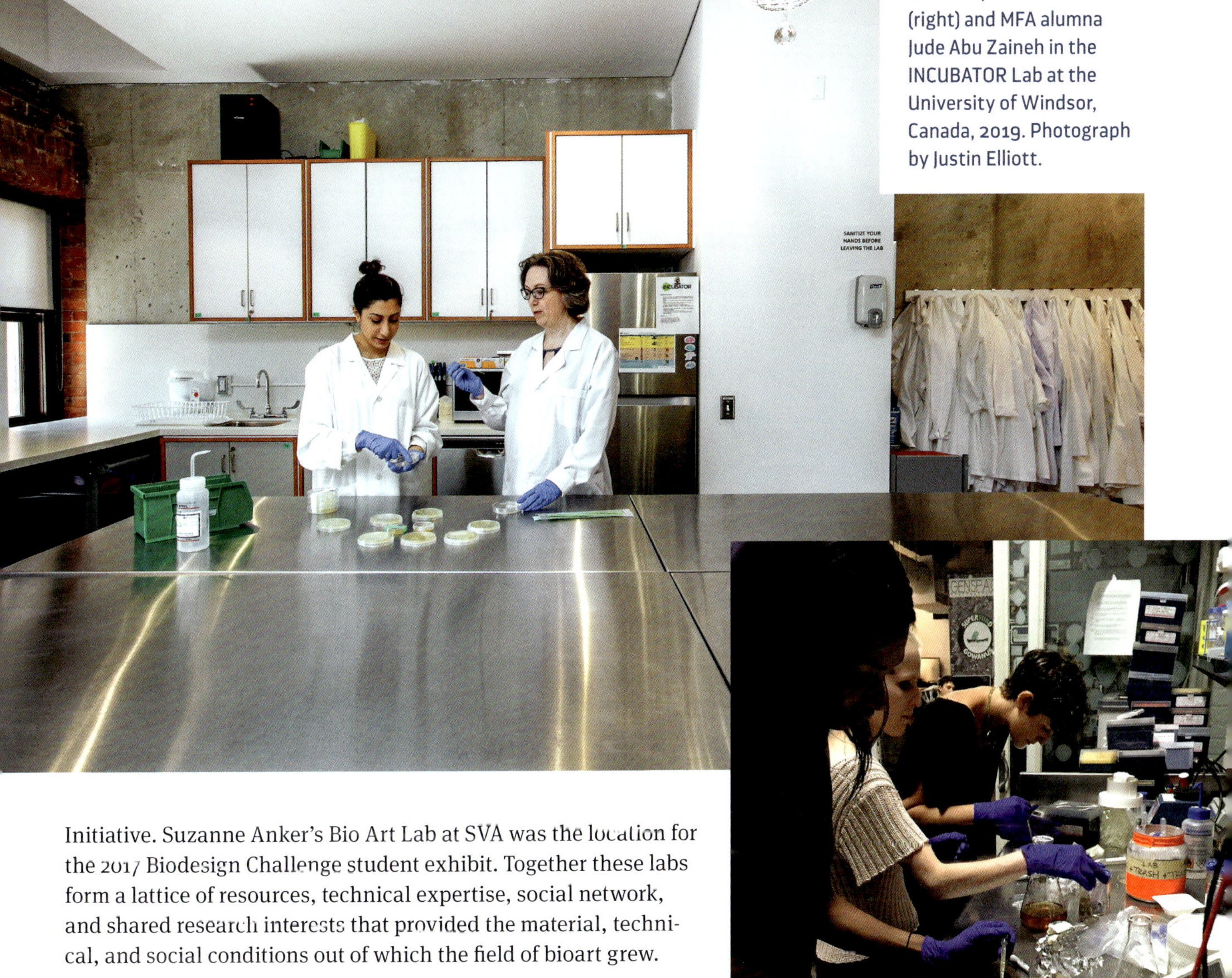

Director Jennifer Willet (right) and MFA alumna Jude Abu Zaineh in the INCUBATOR Lab at the University of Windsor, Canada, 2019. Photograph by Justin Elliott.

Members of Genspace, Brooklyn, working in the lab.

Initiative. Suzanne Anker's Bio Art Lab at SVA was the location for the 2017 Biodesign Challenge student exhibit. Together these labs form a lattice of resources, technical expertise, social network, and shared research interests that provided the material, technical, and social conditions out of which the field of bioart grew.

Tactical media was a 1990s online culture-jamming movement in which practitioners posed as official organizations like regulatory bodies and companies under the guise of newly available websites. Tactical media drew on the Situationist idea of détournement and combined it with the newly available yet still low-tech websites that were appearing on the internet. The Yes Men are the most recognizable tactical media group. They created performative social interventions based on their tactical media creations. Through numerous satirical projects, The Yes Men purported to be a myriad of organizations including DOW Chemical, WHO, BP, and the US Chamber of Commerce. The artists produced press releases, websites, and media appearances to ridicule and expose the motives of these organizations. Recent art and genetic projects have used some of these same tactics.

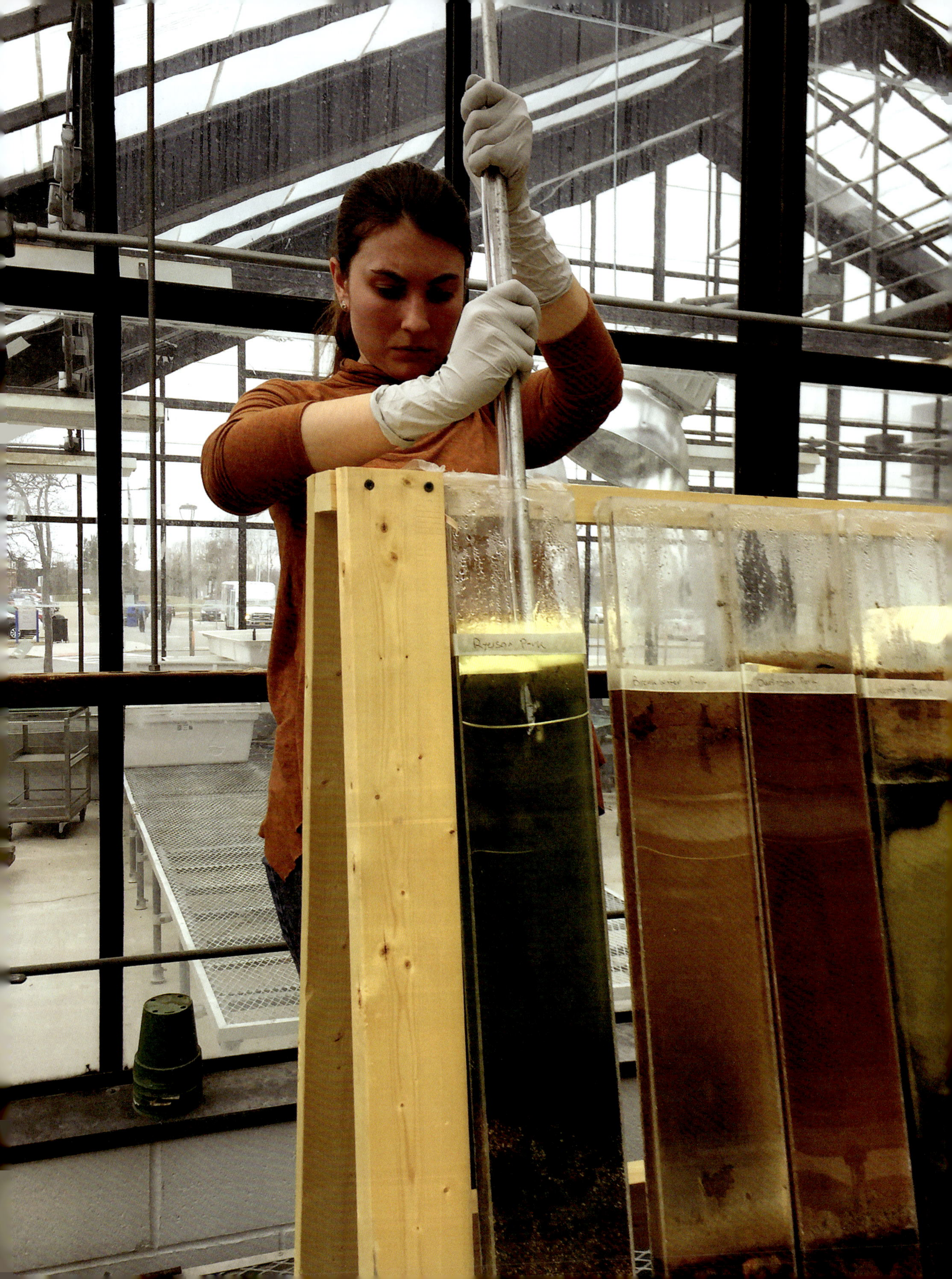

Ryerson Park

OPPOSITE: Coalesce artist-
in-residence, Nicole Clouston,
working on her project "Soil"
in the University at Buffalo's
greenhouse.

BELOW: The School of Visual
Arts' Bio Art Lab, New York.
Photograph by Jung Hee Mun.

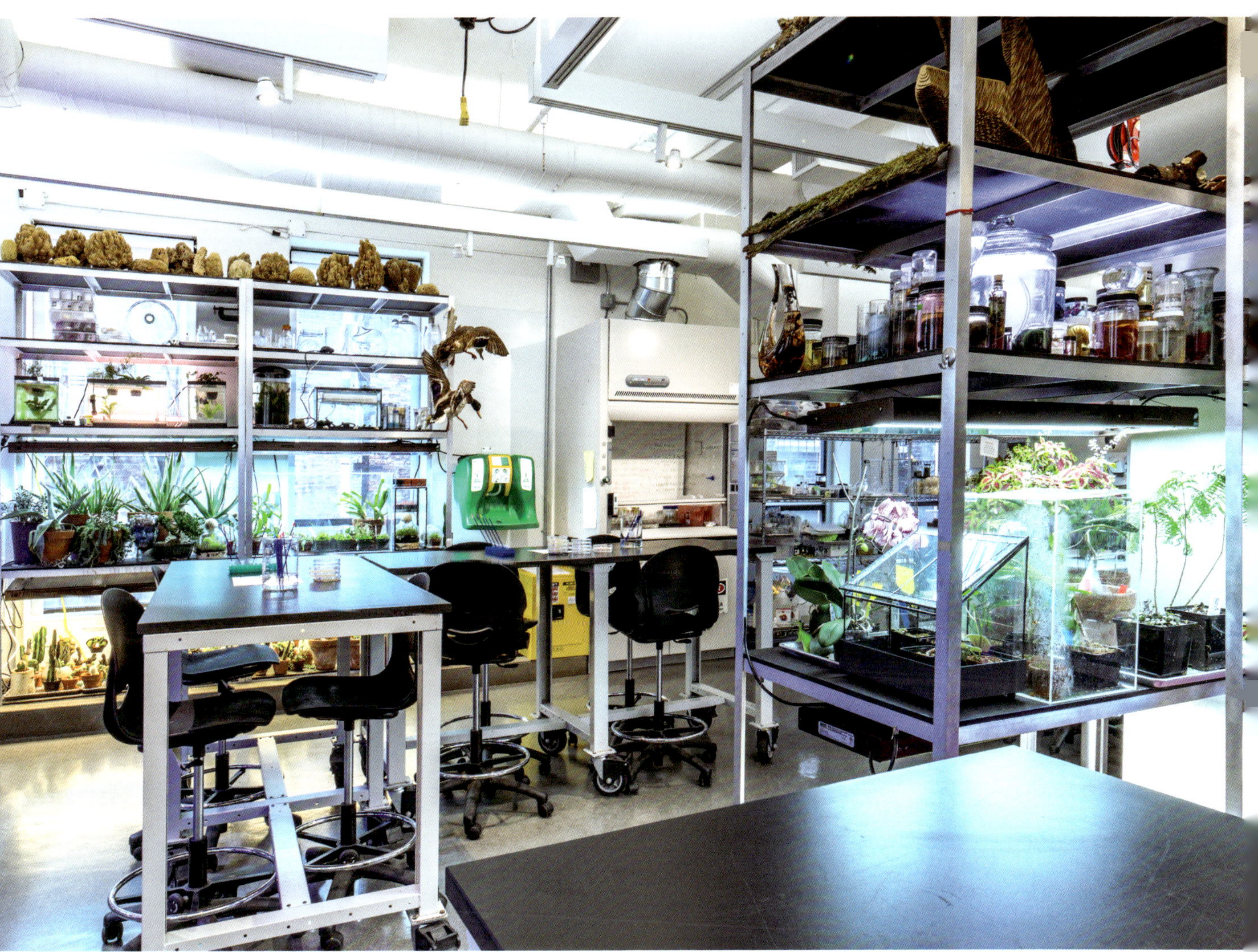

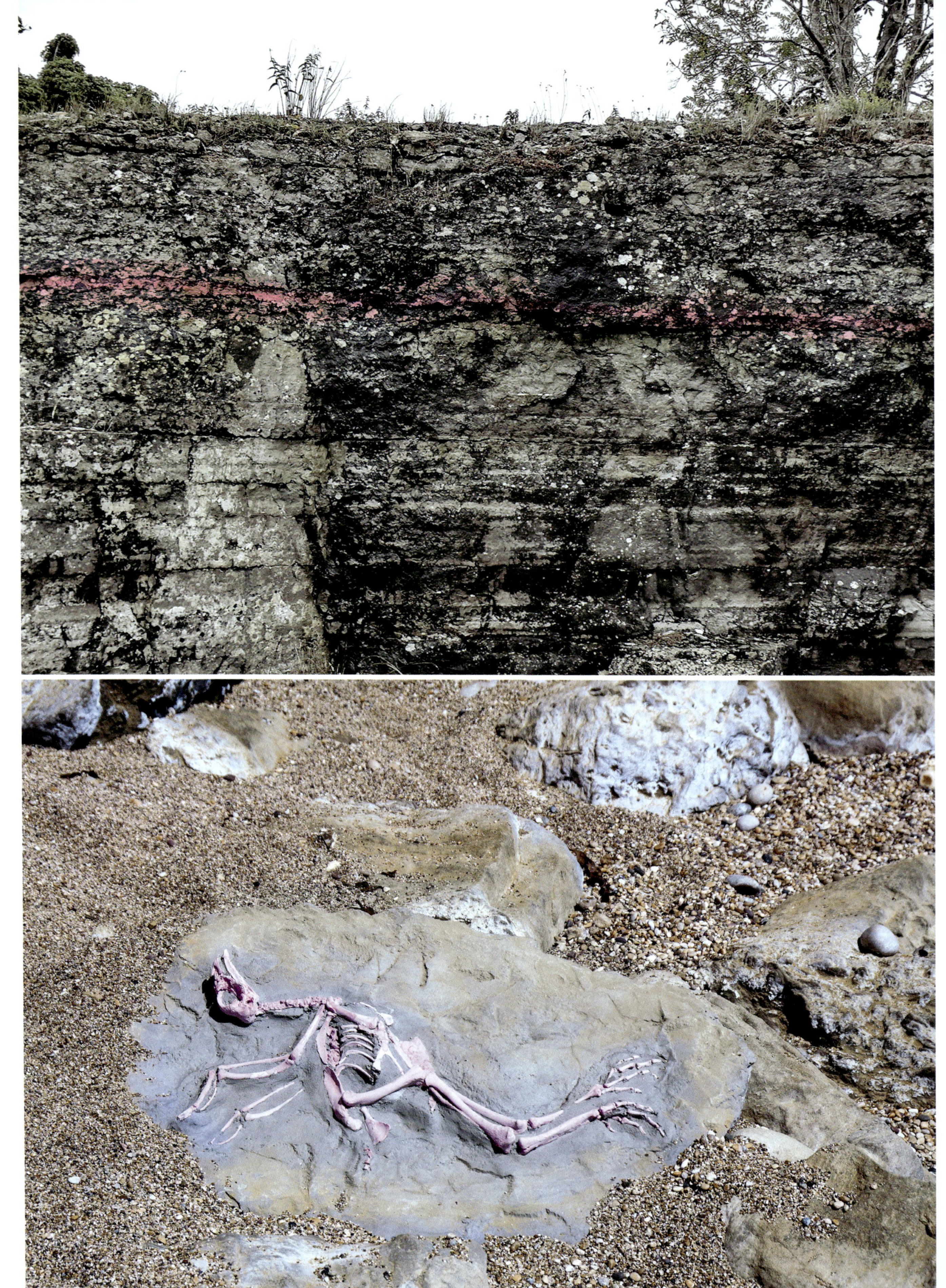

The Pink Chicken Project (2018) was an online media campaign that proposed "using a 'Gene Drive' to change the colour of the entire species *Gallus gallus domesticus* to pink" in the interest of creating a pink Anthropocene geological marker. In *Art's Work/Genetic Futures*, a number of pieces make use of possibilities brought forward by tactical media practitioners. The use of the concept of a company—and all of its strengths and potential concerns—is something that artists employ for their own purposes. Richard Pell offers a look into the history of mermaids and research toward creating modern mermaids by manipulating hox genes. Even as Pell raises questions about the cultural means of mermaids and how they might be imagined scientifically, and Kirsten Stolle's *Miracle Grow* reminds us of a history of problems produced by capitalistic interventions into agriculture and food systems, some exciting aesthetic projects like the creation of kerasynth are precursors to companies created from art world ideas. These similarities and contradictions offer an opportunity to reflect on the power dynamics of corporate biotechnology and the roles that corporations and individuals are playing in our genetic futures.

Other pieces in the exhibition, like Emilia Tikka's film and object *EUDAIMONIA —Biotechnologization of the Soul?,* hail from the field of speculative design. They offer not just the objects for an imagined future—in this case injectors with personality-related gene-editing technology—but well-developed scenarios about how, why, and by whom those objects might be used. This form of design shows us new technologies currently in our own society's hands, rather than in a utopian future where people face choices made easier by technology or are themselves better people such that the choices are made more clear. Tikka's film gives us people very much like ourselves facing a radical new technology.

Speculative or critical design was developed by designers Anthony Dunne and Fiona Raby at the Royal College of Art's Design Interactions programme.[9] Many people are accustomed to thinking about design from a modernist perspective: that is, understanding design primarily as a problem-solving tool. However, Dunne and Raby propose speculative design as an activity that imagines the world differently by envisioning possible scenarios and investigating them through methods like designing artifacts for that scenario or researching potential users' reactions to a created situation.[10]

Rather than seeking to solve an already-given problem, speculative designers consider the role of designers without the notion that each problem has a best design solution, usually presented in the form of a new or improved product. Instead, speculative designers have moved away from the designer's service position in which their profession works to fill in gaps or solve problems with designs. This way of thinking re-situates the designer and offers the possibility of new types of interactions with other professionals in a multidisciplinary peer capacity rather than as a consultant or troubleshooter. This tendency toward collaborative scenario creation may account for the highly interdisciplinary work that has resulted from the use of this method.

Just as Tikka's exploration of future home-use gene editing technology has roots in discoveries around genetics and personality, *Kerasynth* offers a future where a wool

9. Dunne, Anthony, and Fiona Raby. 2013. *Speculative Everything: Design, Fiction, and Social Dreaming.* Cambridge: The MIT Press.

10. Dunne, Anthony, and Fiona Raby. 2001. *Design Noir: The Secret Life of Electronic Objects.* London: August.

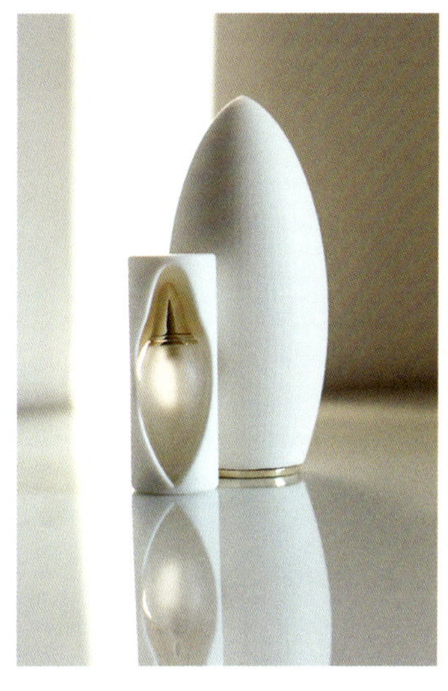

Emilia Tikka, object from *EUDAIMONIA— Biotechnologization of the Soul?,* 2018. Courtesy of the artist. Glasswork by Wiebke Matthes, Technische Universität Berlin.

OPPOSITE, TOP: The Pink Chicken Project, Nonhuman Nonsense, *Stratum of the Anthropocene*, Cumbria, UK, ca. 400 million years in the future, 2018. BOTTOM: *Pink Chicken Fossil*, Scunthorpe Poultry Processing Site, UK, ca. 80–83 million years in future, 2018.

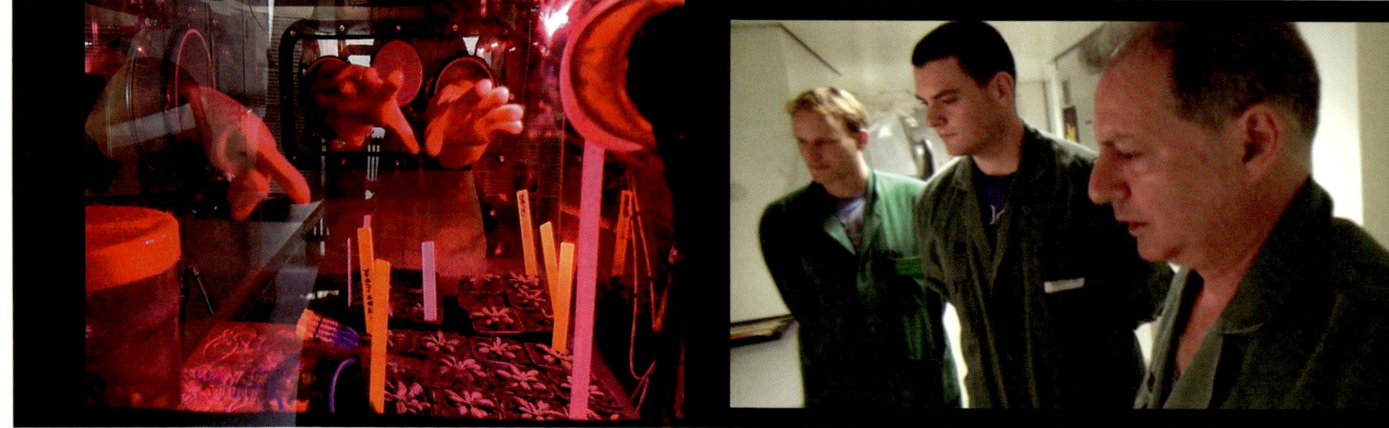

fiber that does not require sheep brings massive changes to the fashion industry. The 2018 Biodesign Challenge Team *Kerasynth* offered a future scenario in the tradition of speculative design. In this future, the team imagines that the technical problems with lab-grown wool are overcome and the product becomes a fashion-must. Artifacts, including fashion shoot images, a production process film, and prototyped clothing, helped the designers explore the possibilities for what this change to the industry would mean. There are many more influences and traditions displayed across *Art's Work/Genetic Futures* and attention to the interplay of these strands can help us to situate art about genetics in the lineage of art history to which it belongs.

Scientific Collaborators: Art-Science Projects

Many of the artworks in this exhibition were created in consultation with scientists. In the same way that scientists make use of graphic and image expertise in their work, many artists make use of scientific materials and ideas. But the artists in this exhibition who are engaged with biotechnology take this a step further by working with scientists in a range of ways. Sometimes a scientist's work is an inspiration or even a muse for an artist; other scientists provide resources or technical information on an individual basis. Yet other projects are the result of partnerships between artists and scientists who work together in a collaborative manner.

Adam Zaretsky's *Errorarias* is an example of a piece that involved scientists in several ways. The piece is a video game console that houses a containment and growth chamber for genetically altered plants. The controls of the console allow visitors to introduce stimuli including light and sound. These variables have the potential to affect the growth and development of the plants. The artwork raises questions about predictability in genetic expression and how we should understand the work of scientists in changing genomes and the possibilities and limitations of the resulting phenotypes. Zaretsky's process involved discussing his ideas and learning the genetic intervention protocol by working in a lab at the University of Leiden with scientist Bert van der Zaal (in collaboration with David Lourier and Neils van Tol) and collaborating with Carole Saravitz at NC State's Phytotron—a

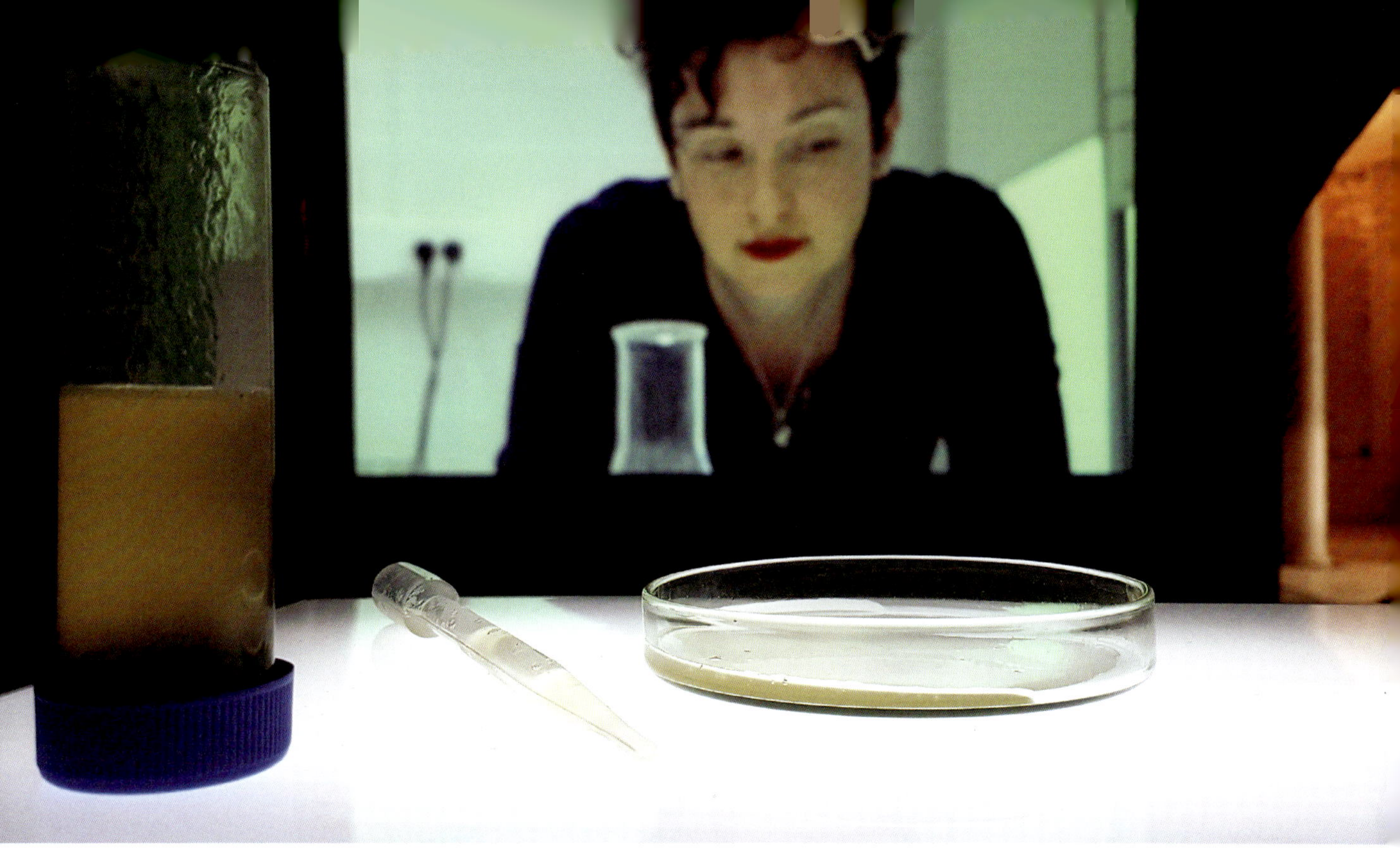

facility for growing plants under various combinations of strictly controlled environmental conditions—to propagate the plants on site for the artwork.

Some of the collaborations between artists and scientists unfold on a longer scale. Artist Charlotte Jarvis, creator of *In Posse: Making Female Sperm*, is working in a long-term collaboration with scientists to produce a female sperm. Jarvis is at the cutting edge of what is often considered science's domain. The leading edge of discovery and experimentation is, however, not a new place for artists to be. Edward Steichen's experiments with delphinium mutations or The Tissue Culture & Art Project's ironic work *Disembodied Cuisine* (2003), the first production and consumption of laboratory meat, also placed artists at the forefront of areas now usually associated with science. Jarvis' collaborator, Susana Chuva de Sousa Lopes of the Leiden University Medical Center, has received the Netherlands-based five-year Vici science grant to pursue the project of creating spermatozoa cells that will push the project of creating female sperm forward.

Both parties are continuing their shared work, which meets their individual interests and is fitted into the separate areas of art and medicine. Many artists and scientists are involved in these kinds of ongoing relationships, like the creative team of evolutionary ecologist and artist Aaron Ellison and architect and multidisciplinary artist David Buckley Borden, who present the playful but provocative sculpture *Novel Ecosystem Generator* (2019). Both art and ecological expertise are on display as the work asks viewers to consider the ways that

Charlotte Jarvis, video still from *In Posse: Making Female Sperm*, from the series *Corpus*, 2019, multimedia installation. Photographs and HD video by Charlotte Jarvis, Miha Godec, and Eleni Papazoglu. Courtesy of the artist.

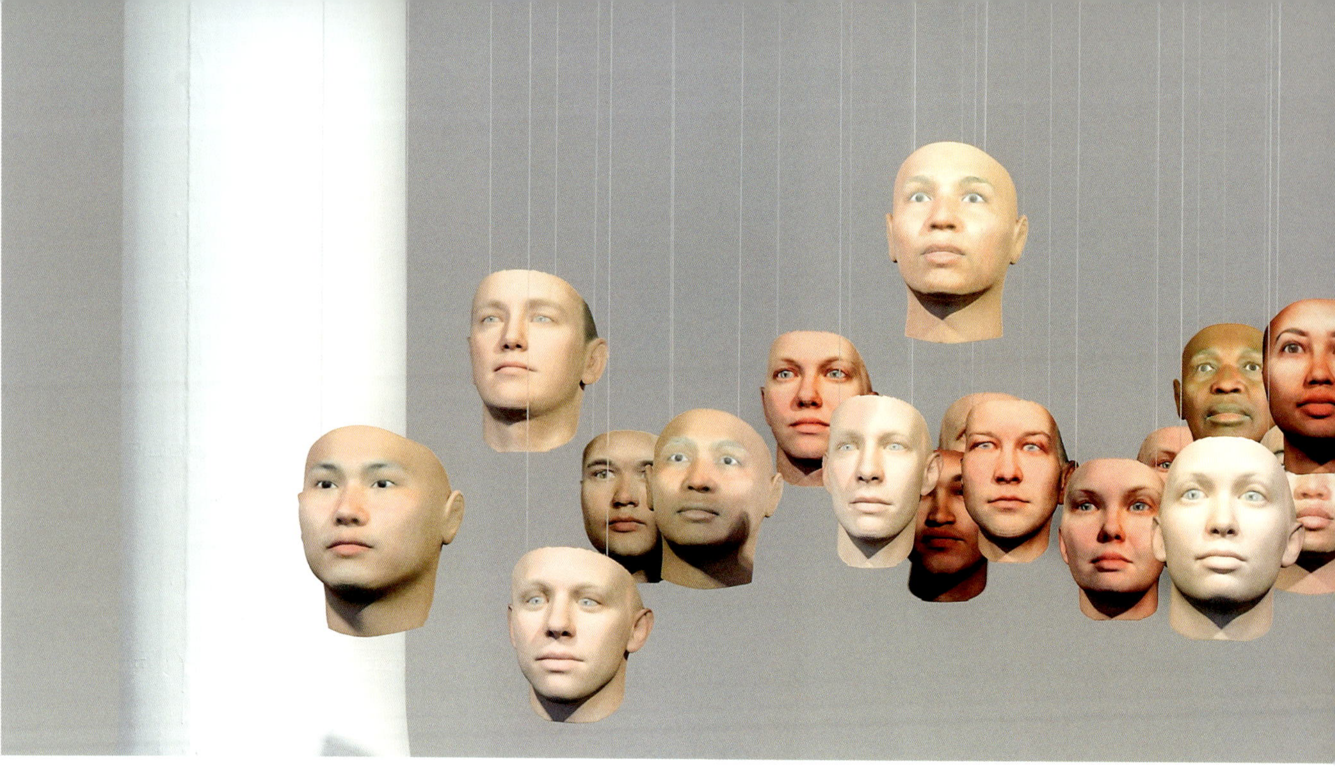

Heather Dewey-Hagborg and Chelsea E. Manning, *Probably Chelsea*, 2017, genetic materials, custom software, 3D prints. Thirty portraits, each portrait 8 x 6 x 8 in. (20.3 x 15.2 x 20.3 cm), overall dimensions variable. Courtesy of the artist and Fridman Gallery, New York.

human intervention is leading to the production of wholly new ecosystems as part of the ecological changes that are part and parcel of the Anthropocene.

Artists and Biotechnology: Using Versus Critiquing

Joe Davis' *Lucky Mice* (2018) is an installation of mouse-operated dice-throwing machines that asks the question: what if luck is heritable? To test this possibility, the artist proposes the idea of using a dice-casting apparatus that is controlled by a mouse, selecting mice who have the best outcomes, and breeding those mice together for successive generations to create lucky mice. The artwork is, on the one hand, a critique of the idea that contemporary biotechnology puts forward about what is heritable. On the other hand, the piece necessarily uses protocols from animal breeding practices to create the artwork. To make his point about how science treats luck and what gets to count as scientific research, Davis uses scientific apparatus and protocols in order to raise his critique of modern understandings of genetics and heritability. Perhaps as a result of the way in which artists have wanted to participate in conversations often reserved for scientists, artists have tended to use scientific materials as their mediums. This tension between using and critiquing biotechnology is present in many of the works in this exhibition.

The commercial potential and capitalistic uses of biotechnology have made the area fraught for some left-leaning artists. Many of the earliest bioart pieces resisted potential enrollment in the commercialization of life or critiqued the influx of funding and resources being made available to biotech companies throughout the 1990s. Second-wave bioart has emphasized the role of the non-human, including an influx of work around animals and microbes, and particularly those that function as part of the systems of the human body. At the same time, more work has

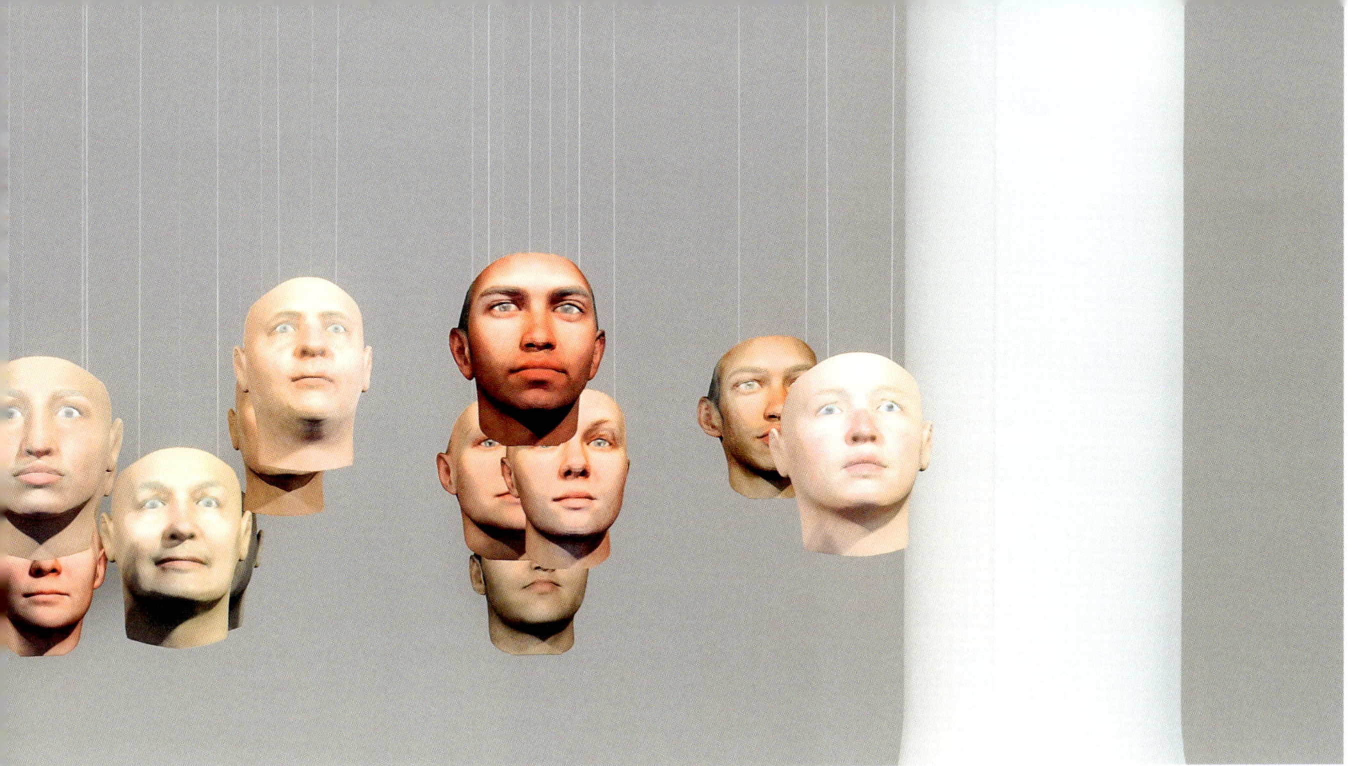

focused on new life forms as artworks—an idea made possible through advances in synthetic biology. Irony and humor are still crucial bioart tools for critically examining the potential of developing sciences. Bioartists continue to focus on concepts like Oron Catts and Ionat Zurr's "genohype"[11] or the genetic privacy issues that catalyzed Heather Dewey-Hagborg's classic work on view in the exhibition, *Stranger Visions*, while also taking on subjects that might not seem immediately related to art about life as a biological process. New artworks are as likely to take aim at issues in climate change, labor, and gender, even as the more traditional interests in fragmented bodies, the "semi-living,"[12] and animals continues.

Many of the artworks position themselves as moments of tension between the use of biotechnology and its critique. The affordances and possibilities of these new technologies are on display but are, at the same time, the subject of questions, reflections, and critical analysis. In Dewey-Hagborg's *Stranger Visions*, viewers encounter a series of portraits made possible by the artist's analysis of DNA she recovered from other people's discarded items, such as hair, cigarettes, and chewing gum. The piece includes 3D-printed portraits, which Dewey-Hagborg produced from the DNA on the found objects. These discarded source items are displayed and labeled in black boxes. Yet even as these faces stare back from the wall, loaded with the suggestion of a future where privacy is fundamentally changed by the genetic information we each constantly shed, viewers are aware of the artist's choices in selecting what traits to test for and to emphasize in the portraits. The DNA analysis only offers probabilities, not certainties.

Issues of possibility and probability surface again in the case of Joel Ong's *Terra Et Venti* (2018), which engages synthetic biology. His speculative futures piece is a research-creation project that explores the role that synthetic biology might

11. Zurr, Ionat and Oron Catts. "Big Pigs, Small Wings: On Genohype and Artistic Autonomy." *Culture Machine* 7 (2005). https://culturemachine.net/biopolitics/big-pigs-small-wings

12. Catts, Oron, and Ionat Zurr. 2002. "Growing Semi-Living Sculptures: The Tissue Culture and Art Project." *Leonardo* 35 (4): 365–370.

play in planetary-scale geoengineering and weather modification practices in the near future. The computational system presented in the gallery generates text for insertion into the genome of the *Pseudomonas syringae*. The bacteria, a plant pathogen, are involved in atmospheric biological ice nucleation and the formation of clouds. *P. syringae* are ubiquitous in the soil, on plants and in the air, travel freely on planetary circulation systems, and are literally rainmakers themselves.

Ong's piece connects with a long tradition of artists involved with genetics as an information code. In the late 1980s, artist Joe Davis' pioneering work in this area included *Microvenus*, carried out with molecular geneticist Dana Boyd at Jon Beckwith's laboratory at Harvard Medical School and at Hatch Echol's laboratory at the University of California, Berkeley. The piece used coded visual information for extraterrestrial intelligence, including a visual icon representing the external female genitalia (the same icon as an ancient Germanic rune representing the female earth) and a short decoding primer into a 28-mer DNA molecule. Ong's piece builds on this tradition of treating the genetic sequences as a medium for artistic expression.

Like Dewey-Hagborg's *Stranger Visions*, Emeka Ikebude's *Fragments* also plays on the concept of the portrait by suggesting multiplicity rather than singularity. The image is a portrait made from reclaimed toothpicks that the artist dyed and arranged in bundles, but the artist's imposition of the image of a single individual belies the complications of its process. The discarded toothpicks each contain the DNA of its individual user in tiny amounts of blood, tissue, and the microbes that help process what we eat. While the individuals who used those toothpicks will never be known, the image that the discarded toothpicks create together raises questions about the relationship between identity and this biological information that we each so easily discard. Each toothpick in this composition represents a unique human being—a contributor and unaware participant in this project of rethinking the bacterial and viral genomes of the human body.

This impulse toward exploring our shared genetic material is the subject of Paul Vanouse's *America Project*, which received the Ars Electronica Prix Ars Hybrid Prize in 2017. The project makes use of a relatively common genomic technology to make a point about our shared DNA. The artwork consists of a spittoon where participants may offer a DNA sample by gargling a cup of saline, which is then run as a single-gel electrophoresis tray. Vanouse has created specialized software that inverts the process typically used so that the artist can cut the DNA with known enzymes in specific locations to create a pattern. The fact that it is possible to use the mixture of DNA in the spittoon to create an image selected in advance (for example a flag or a crown) demonstrates that humans have much more shared DNA than they have differentiating sequences. Everyone's spit is mixed together, making individuation impossible. All collected samples are, as the artist puts it, "promiscuously commingled." Rather than emphasizing genetics as a marker for individuality, Vanouse visualizes our shared identity in these images.

Imagining Genetics with Art

When we think of art and genetics together, we reach toward understandings about the human condition, the materiality of our bodies, and the consequences of biotechnology in ways that are uniquely possible through the combination of bench science and contemporary art. These analytical and speculative works comment on the social implications of genomic technologies and consider the factors that will shape the future designs of these technologies. They can help us imagine the implications of modern biotechnology practices, encourage us to reflect on historical and contemporary methods of genetically modifying organisms, and implicate us in the choices around the ethics, politics, and social practices of genomics.

Art's Work/Genetic Futures challenges us to examine what might seem to be the discrete boundary between art and science through these boundary-crossing works. As these works collectively show, the categories of art and science are determined not by universal axioms or through practices that circumscribe bodies of knowledge. Their meanings are shaped by the conversations the pieces participate in and our interpretations of the works. The artworks in this exhibition and others like them expand conversations about how art and science—in this case genetic engineering and biotechnology—are shaped by the work of artists, scientists, and the public. This exhibition aims to provoke visitors to think about their power in relationship to genetics and how non-scientists can shape debates and intervene in the social and technical processes around biotechnology.

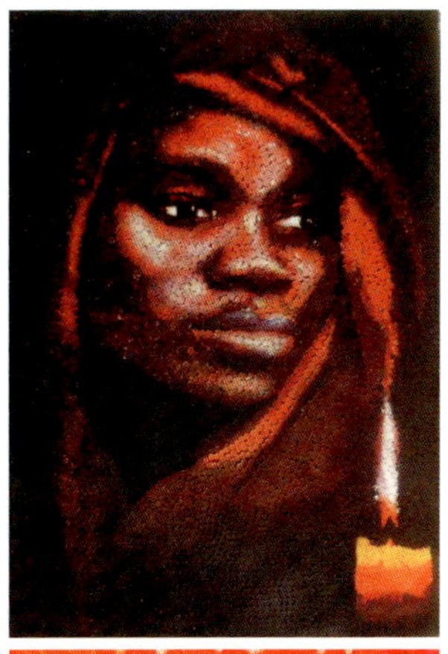

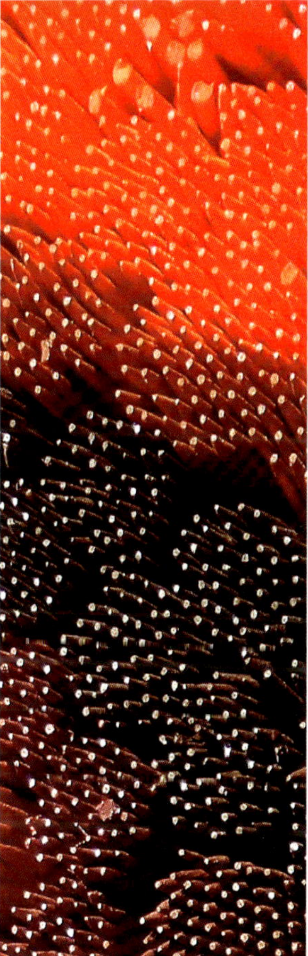

TOP: Emeka Ikebude, *Fragments*, 2016, toothpicks, natural dyes. Courtesy of the artist. BOTTOM: Detail.

It was a miracle! We had finally done it: found a reliable way to plant seeds, to change empty land into fields of fruits and grains. It was no longer necessary to start every day with a long walk to find food and hope there was water nearby. We could dig wells and erect houses. It was a glorious time . . . until the flood. First it was slow, then it seemed to happen all at once. It must have been the will of the Gods, a punishment. The elder men said it was so. The water inundated the very lands we had first planted with seeds. We had perverted the will of the Gods by making fruit where there was none. We were cast from the garden for our sin, of making nature bend to our will![1]

May Matriarchal Mayhem Manifest

WILLIAM MYERS

Approximately 11,000 years ago, a combination of alterations in Earth's orbit with biological activity on land and in the oceans brought an end to the last ice age, causing vast glaciers to melt and prompting a sea level rise of several feet.[2] One of the results of this change was the flooding of land that today is the seafloor of the Persian Gulf, likely one of the most fertile places on Earth at some point, and possibly the location of one of civilization's most important first steps: the Neolithic Revolution, which brought the domestication of crops. It is hard to imagine what the experience of seeing these lands flooded by sea level rise might have been like for people of the time, or what myths and explanations might have arisen from it.

As the floods of the twenty-first century grow in number and severity, as crops fail and temperatures soar, we are prompted to face the unintended consequences of global industrialization, what will in hundreds of years perhaps be thought of as a profound, original sin. We also find ourselves in the peculiar position of wishing that new technologies will address the problems we have caused through our embrace of technology in the first place. At such a moment, we can turn hopefully to the wisdom that emerges from the field of Science and Technology Studies (STS), from a critical evaluation of technoscience, and the social constructions that both shape and are shaped by it. We also call on artists to help us see the dimensions of the darkened room in which we find ourselves, unsure of where we are or what to do about it. In sum, while the important works of scholarship in STS help us define dysfunctions arising from technology's genesis and deployment, artists wield aesthetic experience as a language to grasp the cultural meaning of our shifting reality, often helping to define our role in it.

The work *Novel Ecosystem Generator* by Aaron Ellison and David Buckley Borden takes a step in this direction by illuminating the human activity causing these changes, what lies beyond the immediate present, and the complex interconnectivity between species and environment. The before and after conditions in the artwork tell a story of dramatic change while challenging the notion of the pristine, undisturbed, human-less landscape. Indeed, such a project helps deromanticize the chaotic symphony of growth and destruction that is continually played, with or without a human conductor.[3] This way of thinking is perhaps a necessary step in taking responsibility for our collective impact, realizing also that we have always

1. This is a fictional imagining of how ancient peoples might have interpreted sea level rise. For nonfiction exploration into how the Garden of Eden was thought of and searched for throughout history, see Brooke Wilensky-Lanford, *Paradise Lust*, Grove Press, 2012.

2. See Jeffrey I. Rose, "New Light on Human Prehistory in the Arabo-Persian Gulf Oasis," *Current Anthropology* 51(6), 2010.

3. For an introduction to the human microbiome and recent research, see Ed Young, *I Contain Multitudes*, Ecco, 2018.

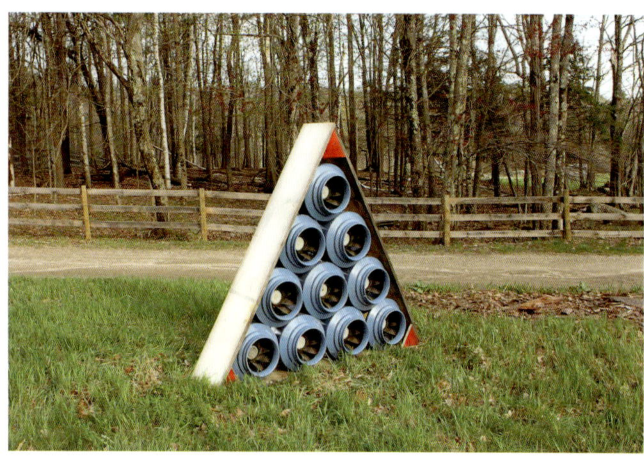

4. The evolving concept of "next nature" is analyzed at length via the writing and projects of the philosopher and artist Koert van Mensvoort. See in particular *Next Nature: Why Technology is Our Natural Future*, Maven, 2019 (original in Dutch, English edition forthcoming). See also the work of the Center for Genomic Gastronomy. http://genomicgastronomy.com/

been biohackers and are amidst a "next nature" wherein we ought to, in earnest, deliberately design the biotechnosphere with the mandate that all must benefit.[4]

Terra Et Venti is a work by Joel Ong that continues on the trajectory of the climate crisis and human activity, exploring aspects of how we might geoengineer on a planetary scale to modify the weather. The focus of the work is the alteration of the DNA of *Pseudomonas syringae*, adding both practical and poetic content to its sequence of base pairs. The bacteria, which can act as cloud condensation nuclei, may play a role in such a future where the weather is designed by people. Ong pirouettes on the borderline between rational utilitarianism and the ethical quandaries that attend environmental engineering. It is akin to stamping a floral pattern on the bridle of a workhorse—a gesture of appreciation for aesthetic pleasure all the more potent in its unlikeliness and invisibility.

The concept of alteration is explored on a very different scale in *We Make Our Own Luck Here*, a work by Ciara Redmond that glows with an aura of whimsy. Its deceptively simple appearance is one that even a child can appreciate, with a plenitude of "lucky" four-leaf clovers that is at once charming and uncanny. Do engineered symbols in the living world retain their power? How necessary are rareness and realness to our definition of beauty? Such a work of art suggests that our biotechnical future—the biodesigned landscape that may both cause and prevent extinctions—may contain a modicum of joy. Balancing this presentation of carefully-bred beings that seem to wish luck to our future selves (who will surely need it) are explanations of the science that supported their creation. Our understanding of plant breeding, the technique used here, stretches back to the beginning of human history; it can even be thought of as the first of all the arts, and that which gave rise to all else we consider the trappings of civilization.

The work of Charlotte Jarvis titled *In Posse: Making Female Sperm* is less focused on the possible biotech-laden future and more on the fantastical present and our ancient, dystopian past with regard to sexuality, power, and reproduction. The work involves semen and world history's problematic male domination, which recalls a joke by the comedian Louis C. K.: that as a white male he could time-travel to the past at ease, even back to the year 2 CE, confident he would be

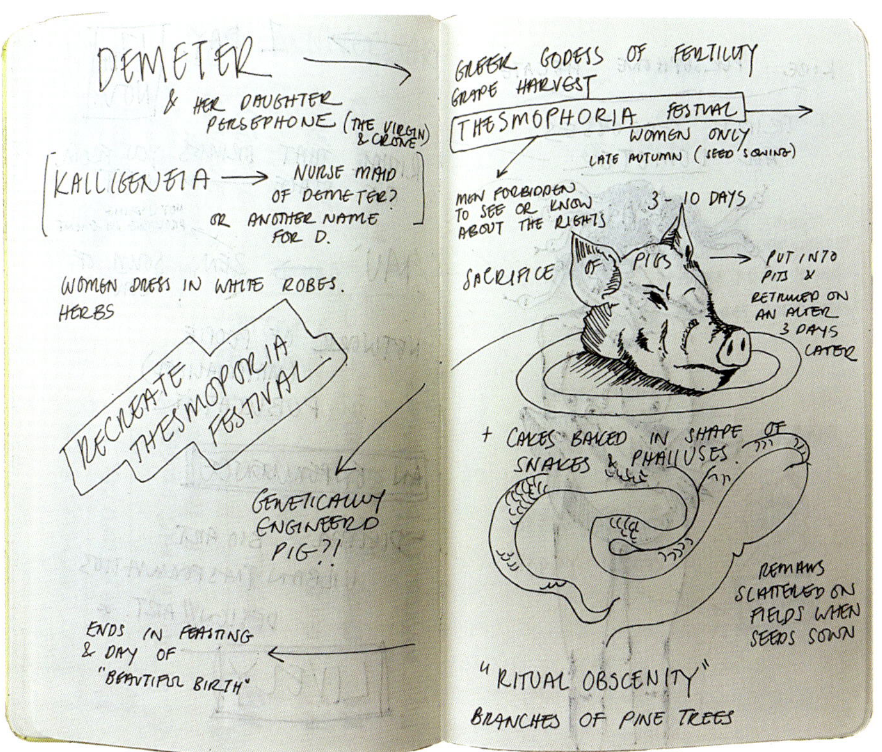

Charlotte Jarvis, notebook from *In Posse: Making Female Sperm*, from the series *Corpus*, 2019, multimedia installation: human cells, HD video. In collaboration with Dr. Susana Chuva de Sousa Lopes and Kapelica Gallery/Kersnikova Institute with support from MU Gallery Eindhoven.

welcomed and safe. The humor arises from the self-deprecating quality of the confessional and its contradictory nature, declaring his privilege undeserved while simultaneously savoring it. In this case art would imitate life, as the world would later learn that the comedian abused his power with acts of sexual misconduct that were concealed, tolerated, or endured for years. A consideration of the rhetorical nature of comedy helps unveil one of the more pernicious ways that women have been abused.

Throughout much of history, semen has been upheld as a sacred substance in patriarchal societies, referred to by Jarvis as *a drop of the brain*, a *life force*, even *that which sows the seeds of virtue in the female soul*. In contrast, the uterus and vagina have been labelled as inert vessels—the latter as a sheath, or that which houses the all-important sword. The hierarchy implied in these and other examples plainly shows how language perpetuates male ascendancy.[5] But as the title *In Posse*—a Latin term for having the potential to exist—implies, a new and different set of conditions for the gender and genital power balance can be brought into being. A potent, symbolic means to this end is to remove the exclusivity of semen as a male-made substance.

Within *In Posse*, this is achieved by producing possibly the world's first spermatozoa from a human female. The realization of this work will include presenting evidence of the process, as well as a series of artifacts and rituals that constitute a creative reenactment of the ancient Greek festival of Thesmophoria, widely celebrated in honor of the goddess Demeter and her daughter Persephone, and intended to bring about female and agricultural fertility. While little is known about how the women-only festival took form (Aristophanes aimed his wit at parodying it in *Thesmophoriazusae*), the performance of *In Posse* will include and expand on scant

5. For in-depth yet accessible analysis of these issues and how they connect to language usage, see Natalie Angier, *Woman*, Mariner, 2014. Also see Inga Muscio, *Cunt*. Seal Press, 2018 edition.

6. On the significance of
this development, a concise
summary can be found in
Megan Scudellari, "How iPS
cells changed the world."
Nature News, June 15, 2016.

elements passed down through surviving commentary, including the burial of a pig, the use of pine branches, and the making of serpentine and phallic offerings.

With the collaboration of Susana Chuva de Sousa Lopes at the University of Leiden and the Kapelica Gallery in Ljubljana, Slovenia, Jarvis is converting stem cells from her own blood into sperm-producing cells found in adult testes. This will be combined with seminal plasma, the basis of which is blood collected from several women including the artist. The other substances to be added include proteins, fructose, lactic acid, and cellulose, representing in total a collective act and a rejection of hierarchy. The science behind this work has been rapidly advancing, particularly since the achievements of Shinya Yamanaka, the Nobel Prize–winning researcher who found in 2006 how adult cells could be converted to induce pluripotent stem cells which, in turn, can be prompted to become sex cells, or cells of any other type.[6] This is helpful for the development of the field of regenerative medicine, which had been slowed by the limited availability of stem cells from fetal tissue (a topic for another essay), as well as for fertility treatments. It suggests the possibility, although perhaps still years away, that any couple, regardless of their sexes, could create an embryo that blends their genetic material.

An important step in this process, which is being supported by a Vici grant made to de Sousa Lopes, is to utilize CRISPR-Cas9 technology. This gene-editing tool is used to make the artist's pluripotent cells produce male sex cells, despite not having a male Y chromosome to begin with. They must be modified, replacing genetic instructions for female sexual development with those for a male.

A project like this stands out in contemporary art for its depth and direct involvement with what is actual pioneering research into reproductive technologies. The title and content lead to an inevitable comparison to *The Cremaster Cycle* (1994–2002) by Matthew Barney, a series of films that makes numerous visual references to the stages of human embryonic development when the sex appears undetermined. Notably, the protagonist of the film series ascends to his destiny, becoming Master Mason, but only after performing ancient rituals, enduring trials, and bludgeoning his female double, in the form of Aimee Mullins.

The *Cremaster* films have been compared with *Un Chien Andalou* by Salvador Dalí and Luis Buñuel, the 1929 Surrealist film known for its early scene in which a man apparently cuts a woman's open eye with a razor. There are certainly many more details and layers of meaning readable in these films, and they are not the first or last pieces of art that feature the act of physically hurting a woman, but they help to situate us in the context of art on women's bodies and thereby identify why Jarvis' work is unique. She is bringing into being what was just a few years ago a science fiction or speculative scenario. Further, she is linking possibly the world's first example of human sperm generated by a female with rituals from antiquity that are rich with symbolism about collective female power. While ancient Greece was no panacea, evoking that era with its mysterious and embryonic character can lead us to wonder about civilization's birth, and how things might have developed differently if matriarchal societies had become the norm thousands of years ago.

If organized society began with agriculture and the act of planting seeds where Nature had not naturally planted them, a kind of violation of God's will, perhaps it will reach a new stage with yet another leap of transgressive biotechnology. What is "natural" and what is "perverse" are, of course, socially constructed and forever in flux. The first "test tube" babies in the 1970s were controversial, just as the early works of Stelarc and Eduardo Kac, featuring alterations to the body or connections of an evolutionary process to the early internet, were met with skepticism. Similarly, there is some repulsion today to work by artists such as Julia Lohmann and Sonja Bäumel, who incorporate microbes in their art. Their work adds new dimensions to the concept of portraiture in light of the microbiome. Such artistic acts invite us to relish the immensity of what the future will hold and of how differently we might regard our bodies, the environment, and what is deemed "natural" as biotechnology advances.

To paraphrase two talented artists, Susan Hiller and Jenny Holzer, whose work does not involve the sciences directly but points to the significance of the works in this exhibition with regard to power and the evolution of society: the role of the artist is to unveil phenomena not yet articulated within a society, and to use aesthetic experience to communicate that for which words may not exist. And if it is a new type of world you wish to see, consider using what is dominant in a culture to change it quickly.[7]

7. This line from Holzer's *Truisms* appears on multiple works: "Use what is dominant in a culture to change it quickly." It was first screen-printed in red on brushed aluminum in 1990. For the phrasing from Susan Hiller, see *Thinking about Art: Conversations with Susan Hiller*, edited by Barbara Einzig, Manchester University Press, 1996.

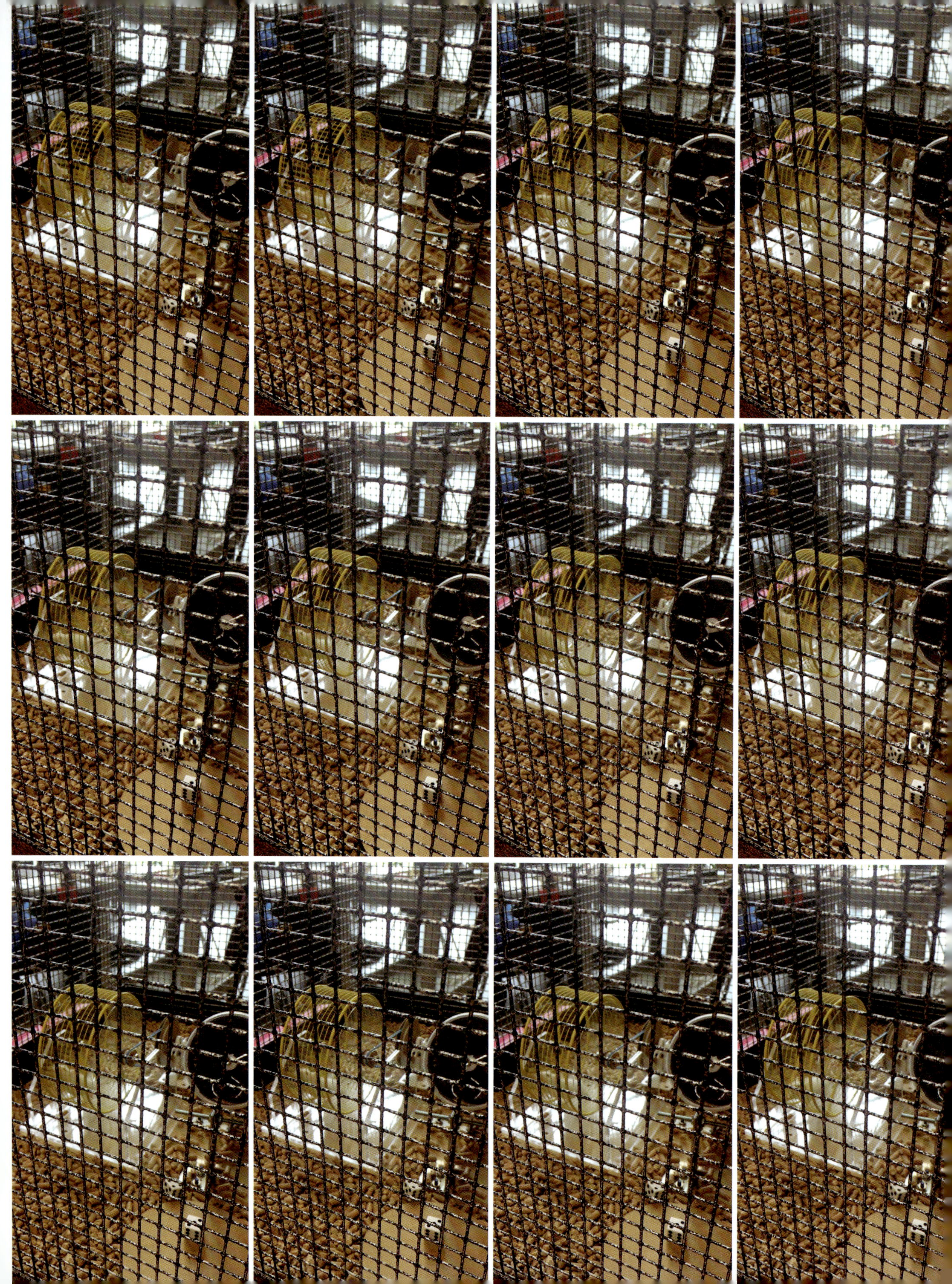

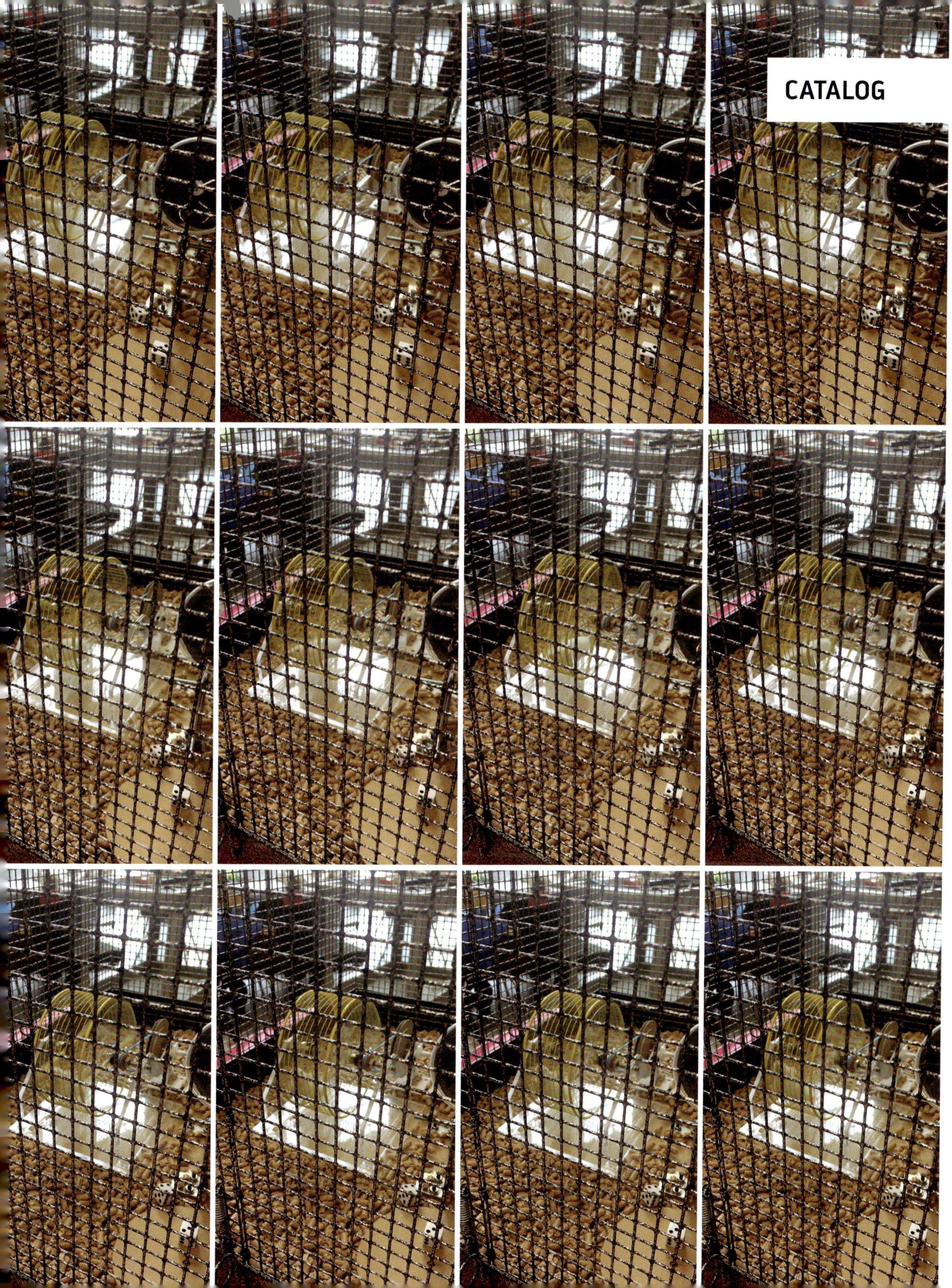
CATALOG

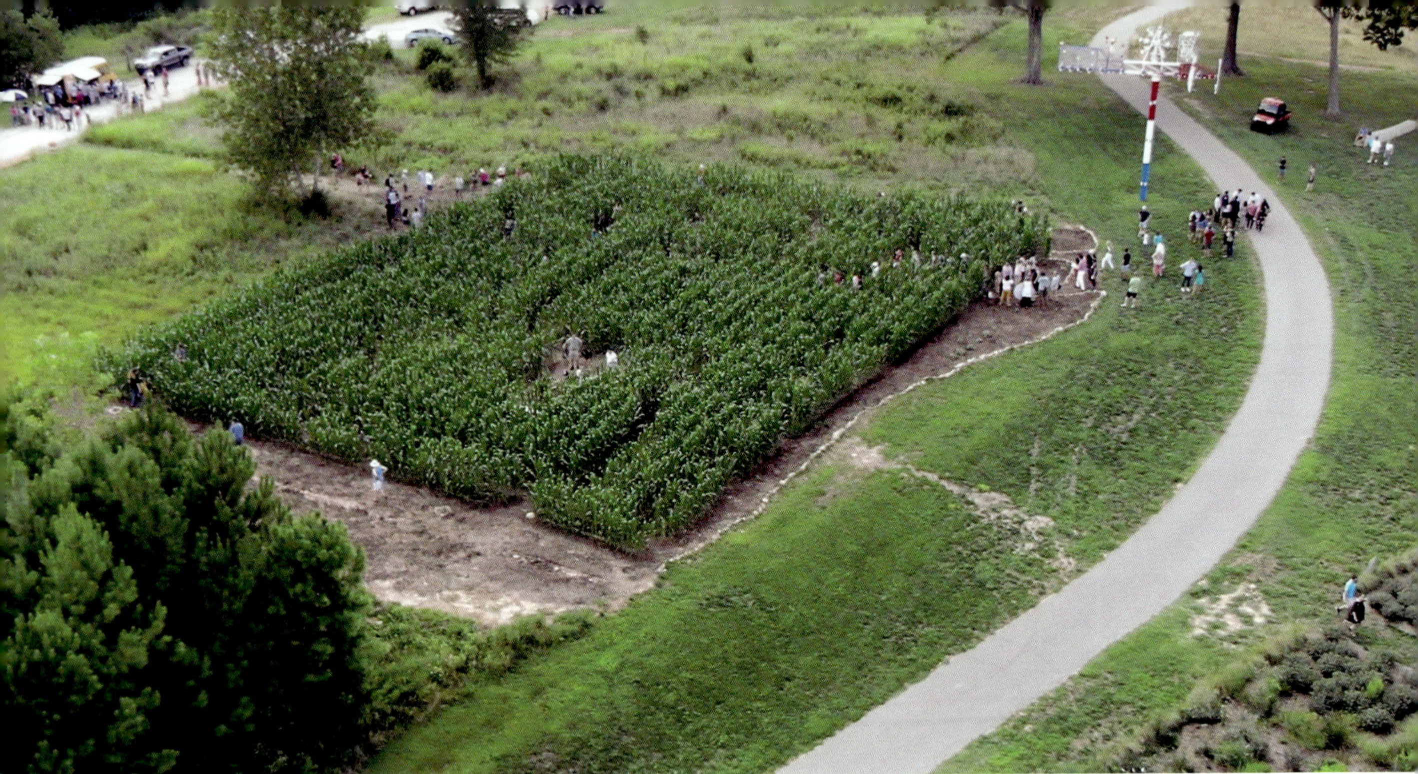

Pages 49–50: Joe Davis (American), video stills from *Lucky Mice*, 2017–19, cage, enrichment wheel, dice-casting device. Courtesy of the artist.

ABOVE: Video still from the public opening of *From Teosinte to Tomorrow*, corn maze at the Ann and Jim Goodnight Museum Park, North Carolina Museum of Art (NCMA), August 11, 2019. Drone footage by Luke Mehaffie, courtesy of NCMA.

OPPOSITE: Diana Eusebio, Erin Kirchner, Grace Kwon, Rachel Rusk, Sydney Sieh-Takata (American), *Kerasynth*, 2018, synthetic fiber prototype garment. Courtesy of the Kerasynth, Baltimore.

The exhibition's creators invited artists to offer work that provides novel insights and awareness about genetic science and the role of genetics in our society. Through their work, these artists ask questions and raise challenges about those roles. *Art's Work in the Age of Biotechnology: Shaping Our Genetic Futures* places the work of contemporary artists in historical and cultural contexts from the perspectives of both art and science. The exhibition attempts to give visitors a sense of the rich community of artists working across lines of artistic traditions including performance, bioart, and speculative design, and mediums including sculpture, image-making, and film. These pieces display a variety of ways of working with scientists, designers, and artistic collaborators. Among the many artistic approaches to these subjects are works that explore individual perspectives on these issues, aimed at broad publics or specialist audiences. Some artists want to extend conversations with scientists about the technical aspects of their work and its social implications through material means, while others seek to draw audiences into aesthetic,

emotional, and philosophical experiences. Artworks, including Joe Davis' *Lucky Mice* and Paul Vanouse's *America Project*, reflect on the rituals of the lab as performances that can be recorded and reconsidered as artwork. In Adam Zaretsky's *Errorarias*, sound has a potential direct effect in his containment console, while Joel Ong uses sound to represent bacteria in *Terra Et Venti*. Emeka Ikebude's *Fragments* and Heather Dewey-Hagborg's *Stranger Visions* use found objects to create new forms of portraiture, while others, like Jennifer Willet's *Baroque Biology (Paper Theater)* and Maria McKinney's *Sire*, take stock of the role of craft in relation to science as well as art. McKinney's film *Double Muscle* is displayed along with its accompanying bovine semen straw sculpture seen harnessed to the animal's back. Charlotte Jarvis' *In Posse: Making Female Sperm* is experienced both as sperm in a petri dish and through the film of her process and investigation of the Thesmophoria festival. Emilia Tikka offers her film *EUDAMONIA—Biotechnologization of the Soul?* with an accompanying injector object that is used as a prop in the film. The tension between the energy and specific interpretation of the use of the object in the film and the materiality of the objects themselves situates these works as representing both the authenticity of the object as a presence in the gallery and the energy of both the people who use the objects and the animals that are affected by them.

The exhibition is an example of the immense variety of artwork that engages with science and social issues with scientific dimensions. Through this engagement, artists are producing new visual languages, new forms of audience participation, and new philosophies of knowledge. Many exhibitions on other subjects could be formulated to create conversations about issues of relevance related to a wide variety of contemporary issues in science and technology.

Art's Work/Genetic Futures asks visitors to participate as witnesses, donors, or interlocutors in the nuanced conversations around genetics. Some of these artworks are rooted firmly in the past, while others raise scenarios about near-future and far-future possibilities for our society. Yet each is radically present-centered, since they reflect on our current social, political, and technical conditions. The artists in this exhibition generally avoid utopic or dystopic futures. Emerging biotechnology has allowed some of the artists to imagine futures where human behaviors have been altered or new affordances have been made possible. They assume that the social world as we know it would not be radically transformed, even as new technologies enter into our interactions. Instead these artists suggest that many things we know from our own context of human behavior and social value will remain constant. Individuals and our society are influenced by these technologies, which themselves are influenced by our social values.—HANNAH STAR ROGERS

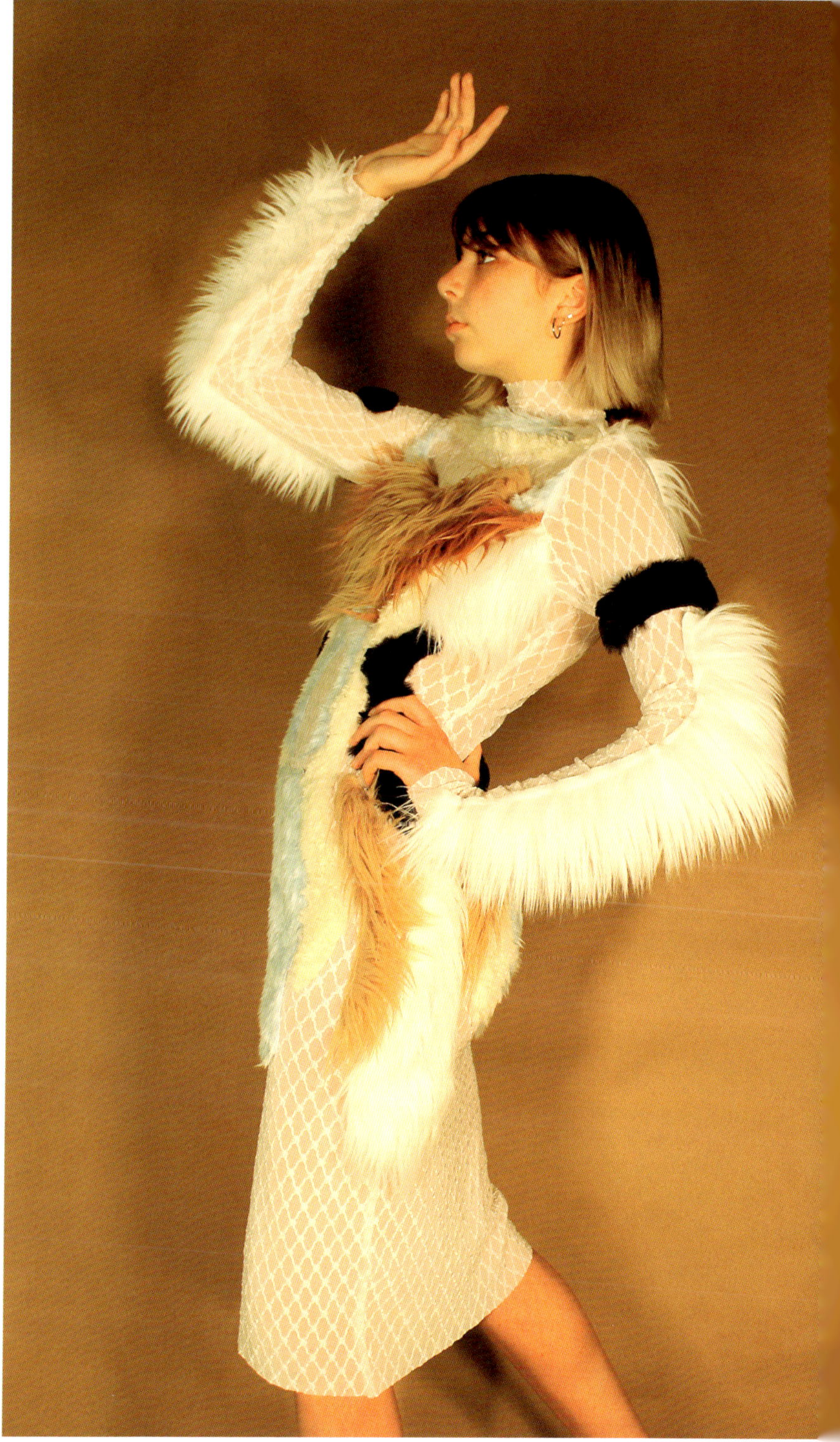

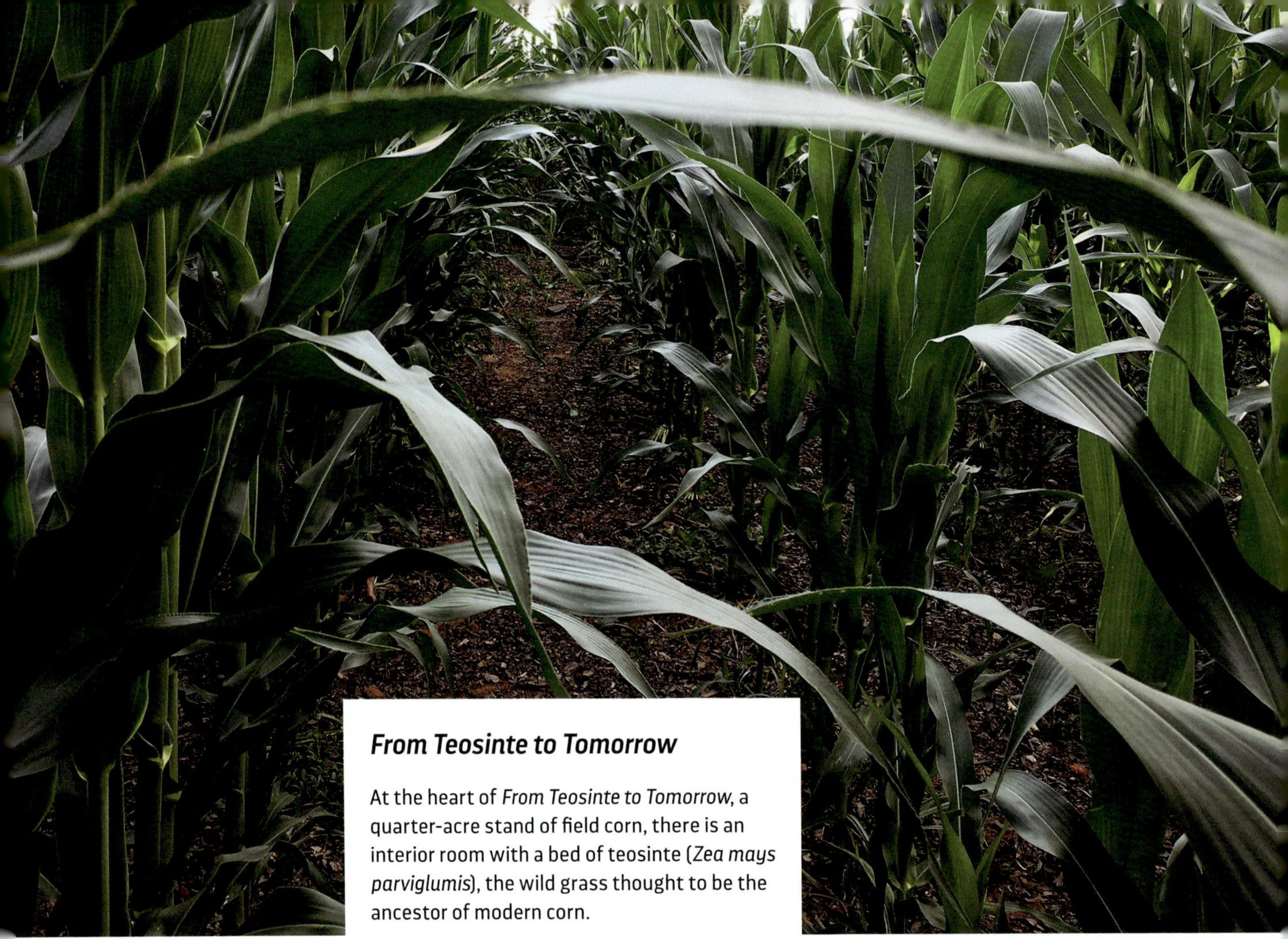

From Teosinte to Tomorrow

At the heart of *From Teosinte to Tomorrow*, a quarter-acre stand of field corn, there is an interior room with a bed of teosinte (*Zea mays parviglumis*), the wild grass thought to be the ancestor of modern corn.

The maze forms the symbolic entrance to *Art's Work in the Age of Biotechnology: Shaping Our Genetic Futures.* Rooted in the earliest form of biotechnology, selective breeding, it offers multiple pathways to solve a puzzle. And the short ground covered to the teosinte plants represent thousands of years of agricultural history.

As humanity struggles with challenges like population growth and climate change, there is a growing disconnect between first-world populations, the sources of our food, and the people who labor to grow it and deliver it. As one of the earliest cultivated grains in the western hemisphere, the cultural significance of maize (*Zea mays*) invites conversations about these issues as well as issues of class, identity, community, and genetics in society.

The maze design was inspired by artist Josef Albers and based on his drawing, *Sanctuary*, made during the years he and Anni Albers traveled extensively in Mexico (1930s–60s).

Molly Renda and William H. Dodge (American), *From Teosinte to Tomorrow*, 2019, corn maze, 90 x 120 ft. (27.4 x 36.6 m). Ann and Jim Goodnight Museum Park, North Carolina Museum of Art. Photograph by Molly Renda.

From Teosinte to Tomorrow is funded by the NC State University Libraries' Goodnight Educational Foundation Endowment for Special Collections with additional support from the Genetic Engineering and Society Center, and in-kind donations from the College of Agriculture and Life Sciences, the JC Raulston Arboretum, Hanbury, and the North Carolina Museum of Art.

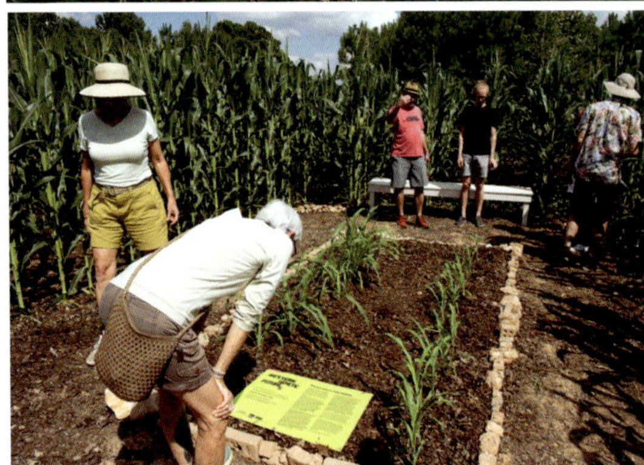

Visitors examine young teosinte plants. Photograph by Christopher Ciccone.

RIGHT: Field in early August with *Wind Machine* by Vollis Simpson, 2002. NCMA.

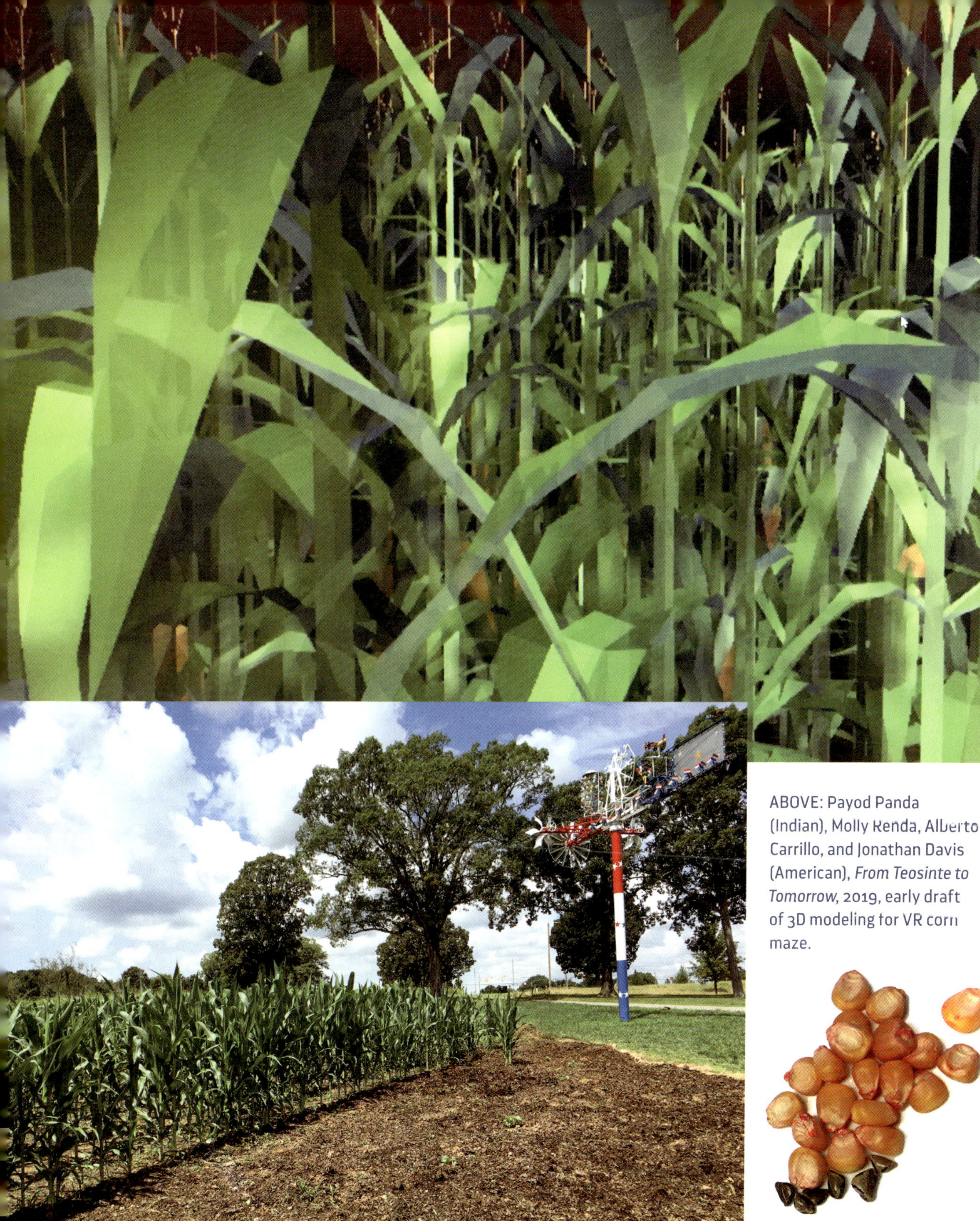

ABOVE: Payod Panda (Indian), Molly Renda, Alberto Carrillo, and Jonathan Davis (American), *From Teosinte to Tomorrow*, 2019, early draft of 3D modeling for VR corn maze.

Pioneer field corn (*Zea mays*) and teosinte seed (*Zea mays parviglumis*).

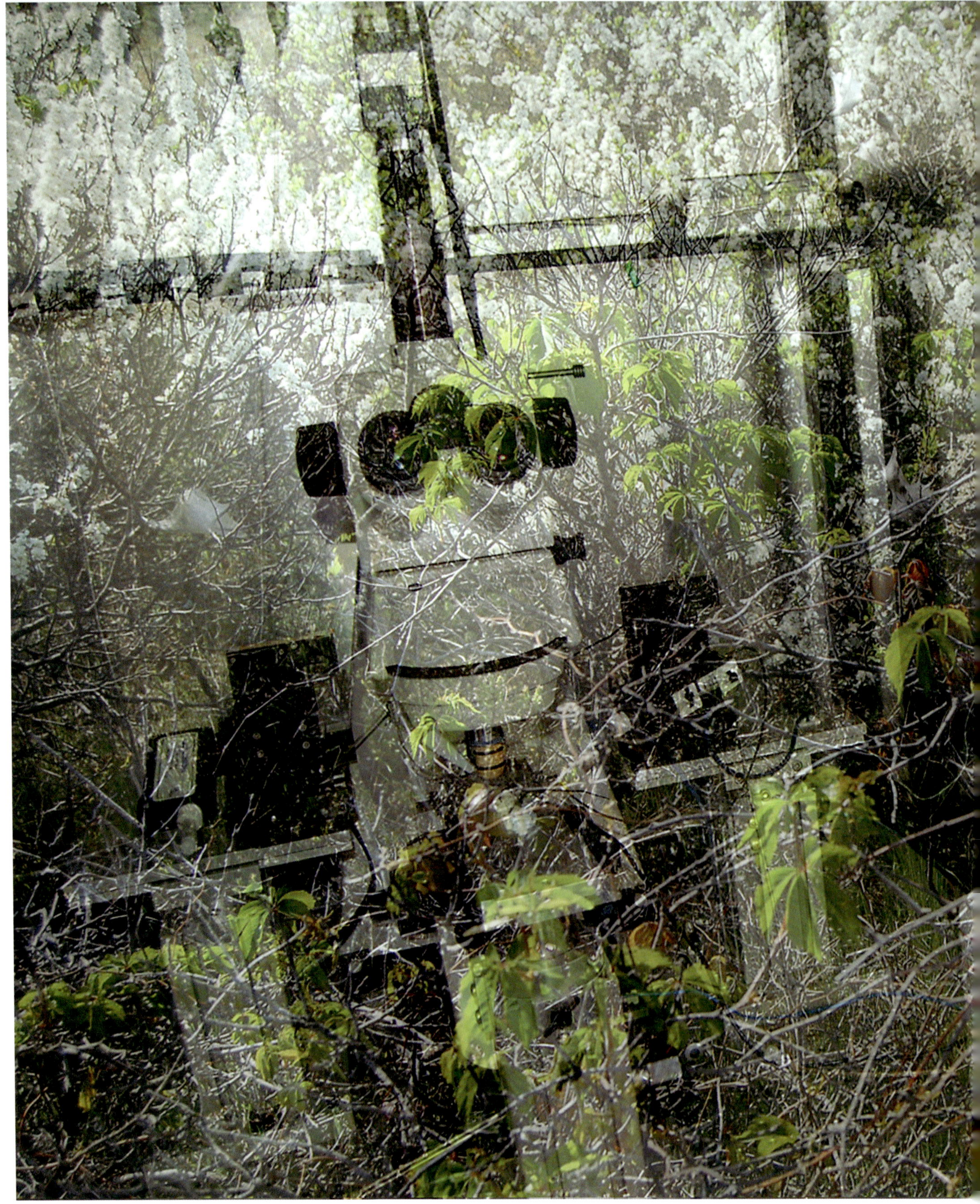

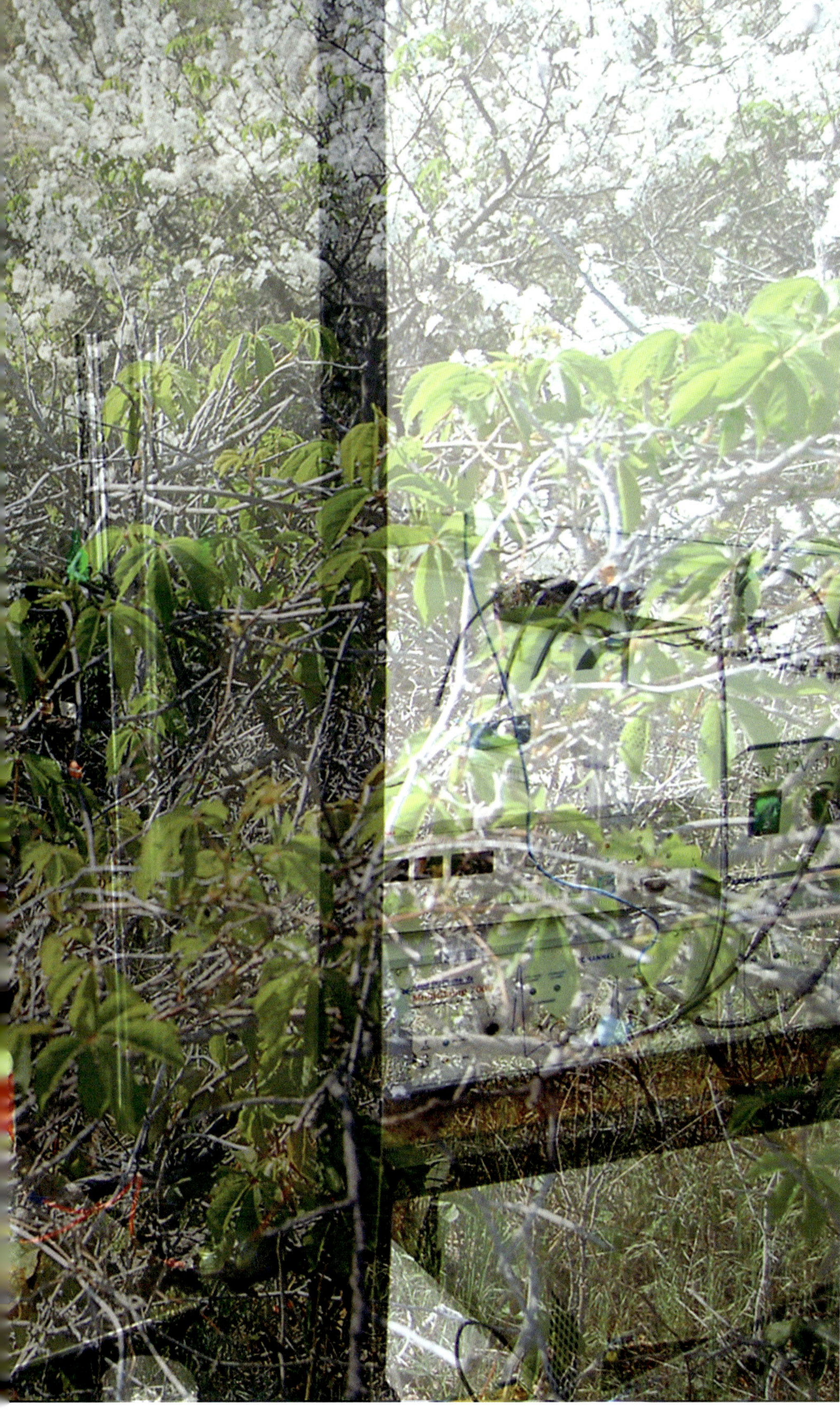

Suzanne Anker (American), *Snowman*, from the series *Laboratory Life (for Oryx and Crake)*, 2007, pigmented ink-jet print on archival paper, 24 x 36 in. (61 x 91 cm). Courtesy of the artist.

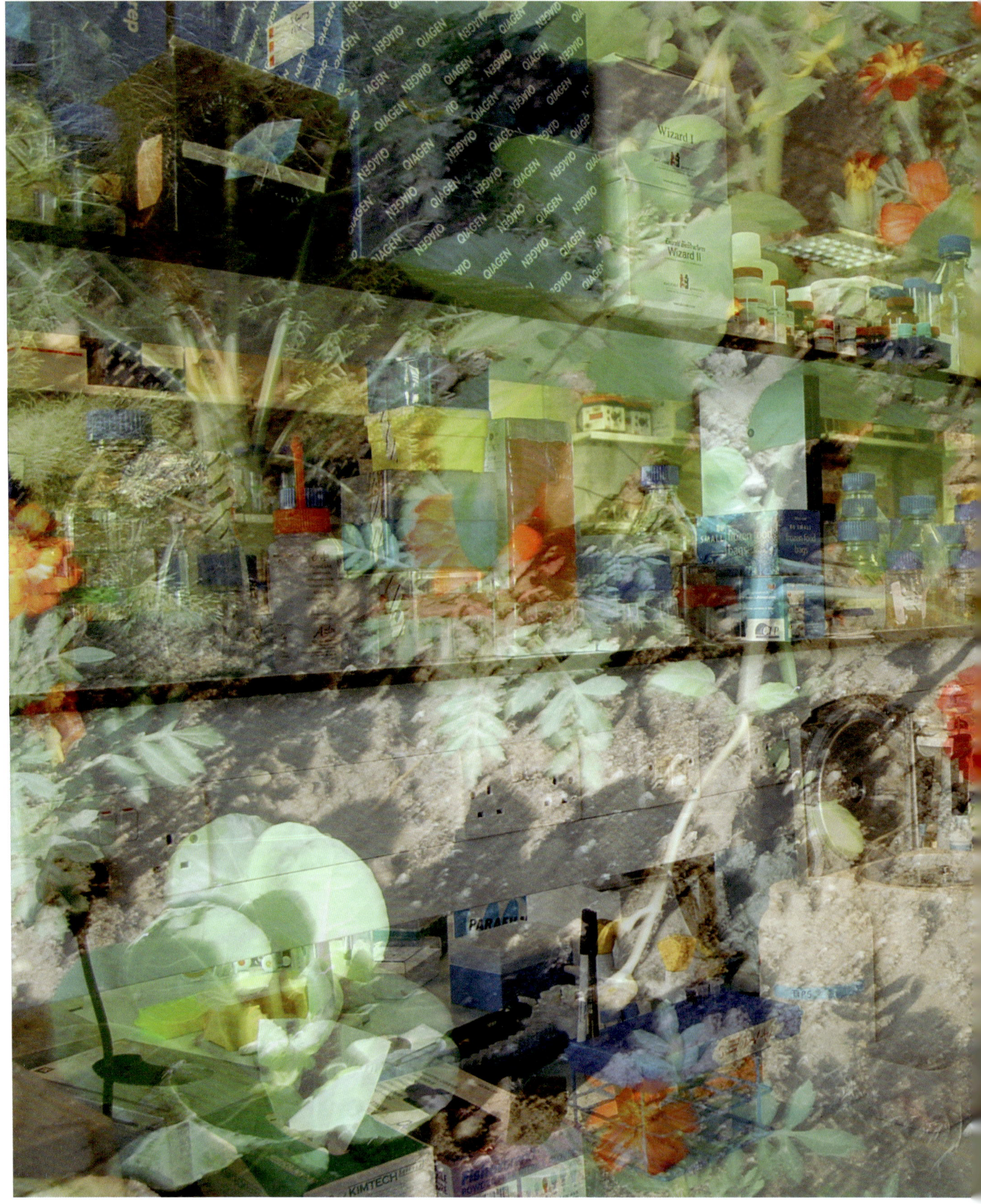

Wizard I
Wizard II
QIAGEN
PARAFILM
KIMTECH

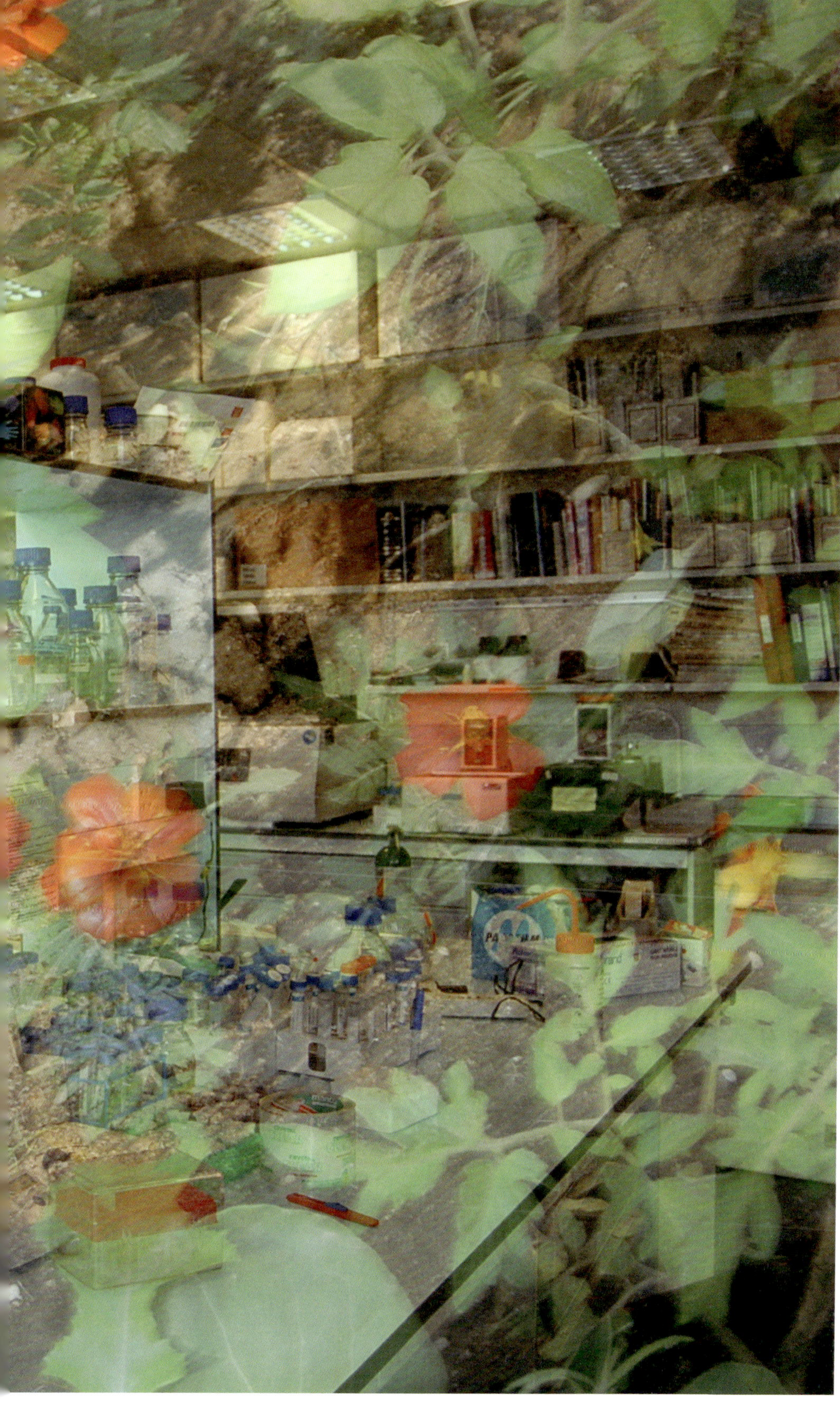

Suzanne Anker (American), *Vanishing Point,* from the series *Laboratory Life (for Oryx and Crake),* 2007, pigmented inkjet print on archival paper, 24 x 36 in. (61 x 91 cm). Courtesy of the artist.

Laboratory Life (pages 54–57)

OPPOSITE and pages 60–61: Suzanne Anker (American), *Remote Sensing*, 2013–18, rapid prototype sculptures; plaster, pigment, resin, glass petri dish, glass containers 4 x 4 x 2 in. (10.2 x 10.2 x 5.1 cm) each. Photographs by Raul Valverde.

In the series *Laboratory Life (for Oryx and Crake)*, Anker investigates the visual, geographic, and spatial world of the scientist. Her layered images, with their palette of places, repeated colors, and familiar yet non-domestic forms, implicitly ask what the material cultural context of science does to the life of the scientist and the potential knowledge being created. Anker's evocative title references two books: one from the social sciences and the other from literature.

The first is *Laboratory Life: The Construction of Scientific Facts* (Latour and Woolgar 1979), which offers a sociological account of how scientific knowledge is created. It follows scientists through routine lab practices, the publication of papers, scientific prestige, research finances, and other elements of laboratory life. The second book that Anker's work references is *Oryx and Crake*, Margaret Atwood's 2003 novel, which the author refers to as "speculative fiction." The novel follows a post-apocalyptic character called Snowman. Among the twists pertinent to Anker's artwork, another character named Crake attends the highly respected Watson-Crick Institute for advanced bioengineering, while Jimmy ("Snowman") studies the humanities at the Martha Graham Academy, but the education is only seen as useful for its propaganda applications.

Anker's images show us the world of scientists at renowned institutions but avoid the documentary style of Latour and Woolgar's foundational science studies text by complicating it through the filter of point of view and consequences as depicted in Atwood's novel. The scientists who populate this laboratory bring with them perspectives that Anker's images continuously invoke.

Selections from *Remote Sensing*

An assemblage of thirteen of Anker's sculptures 3D-printed from her *Remote Sensing* series explores environmental degradation and its landscape-level effects. The works use the tiny scale frame of petri dishes to reference our cultural imagination of biology and our relationships to other living things. This series uses petri dishes to reference our cultural understanding of experimentation, but in this case the experiments are taking place on our landscapes. Anker's miniature landscapes are rapid prototype extrusions simulating satellite data that reference polluted regions, or what Anker terms areas of "self-inflicted toxicity."

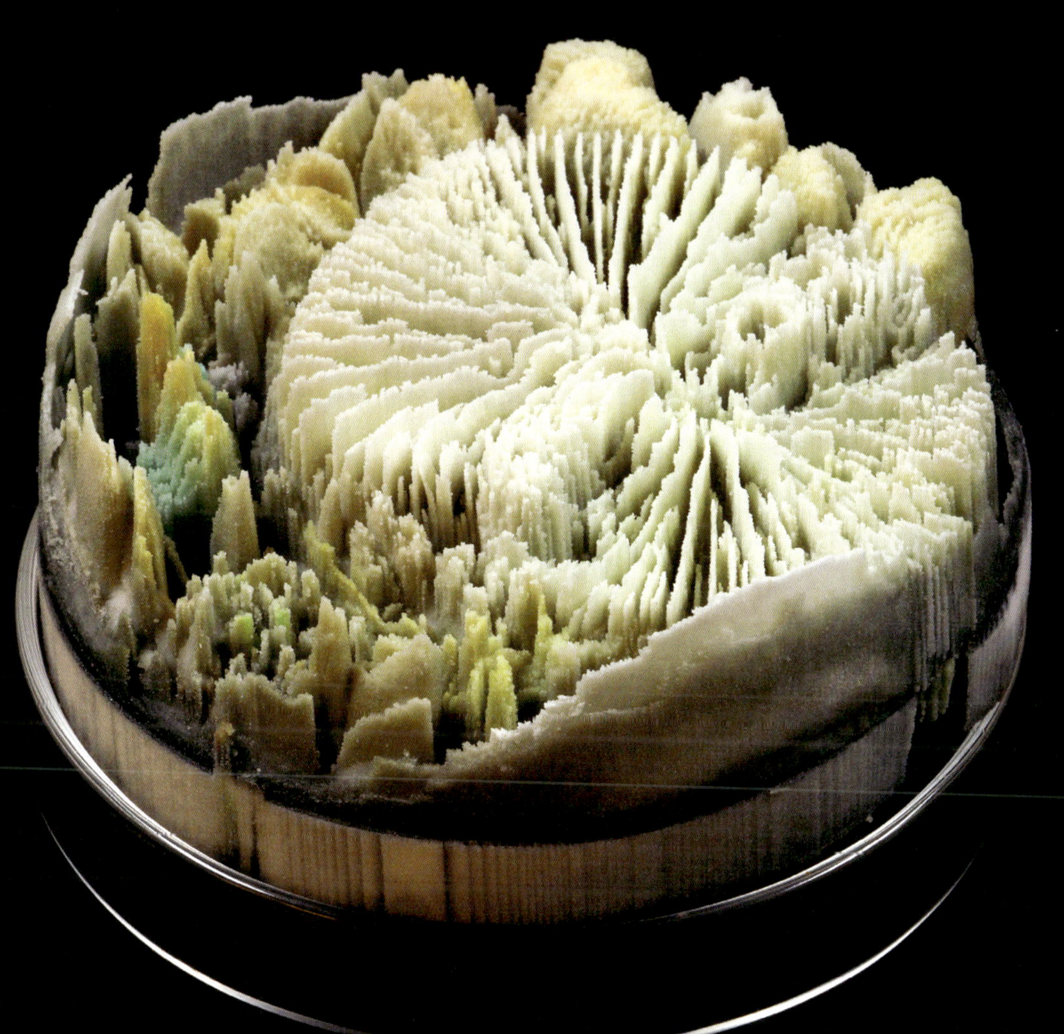

#28

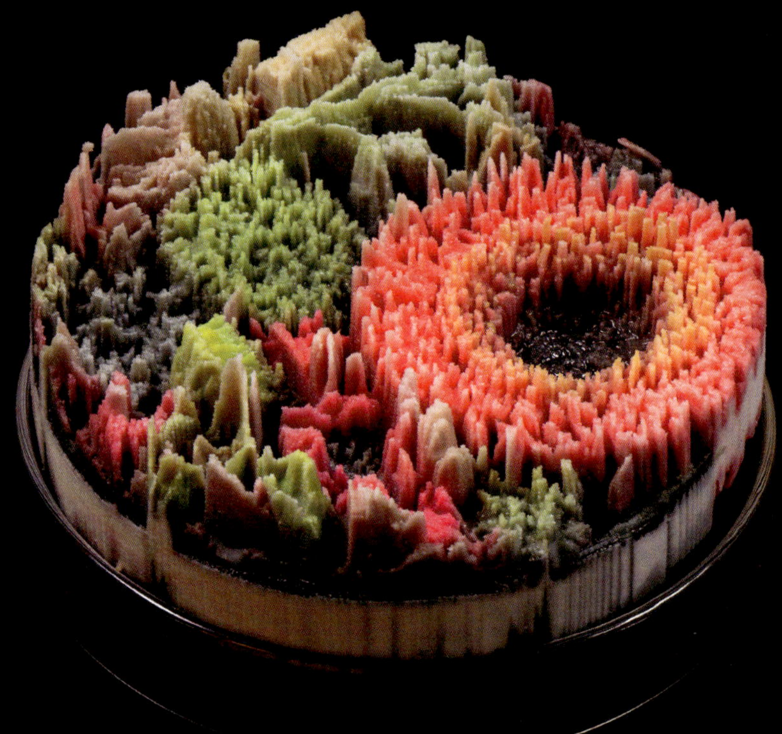

#42

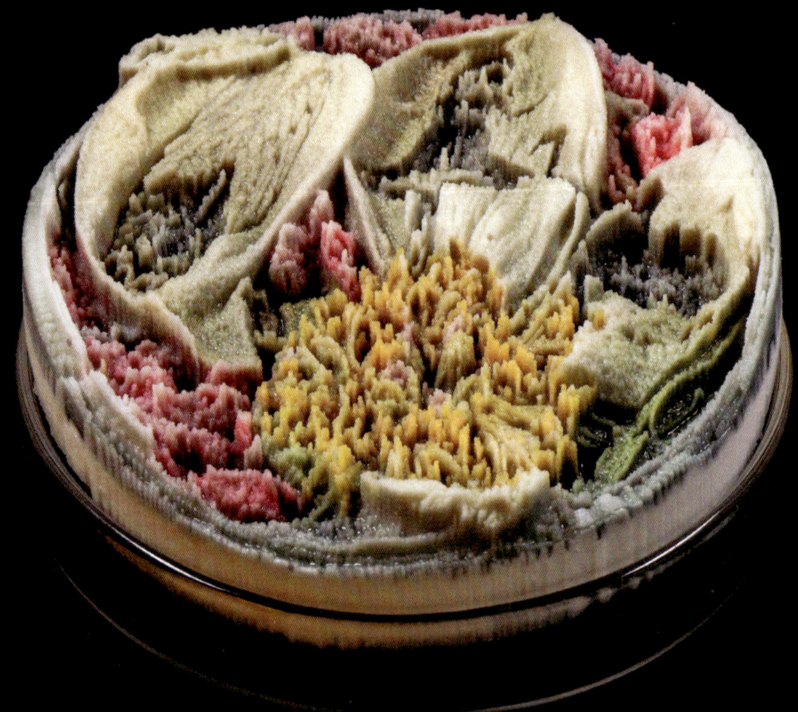

#15

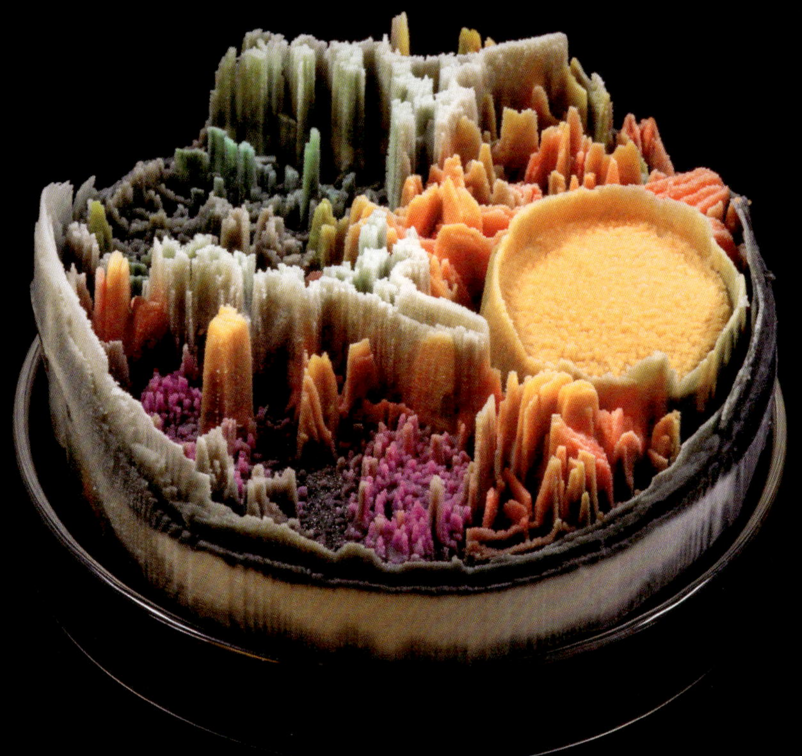

#38

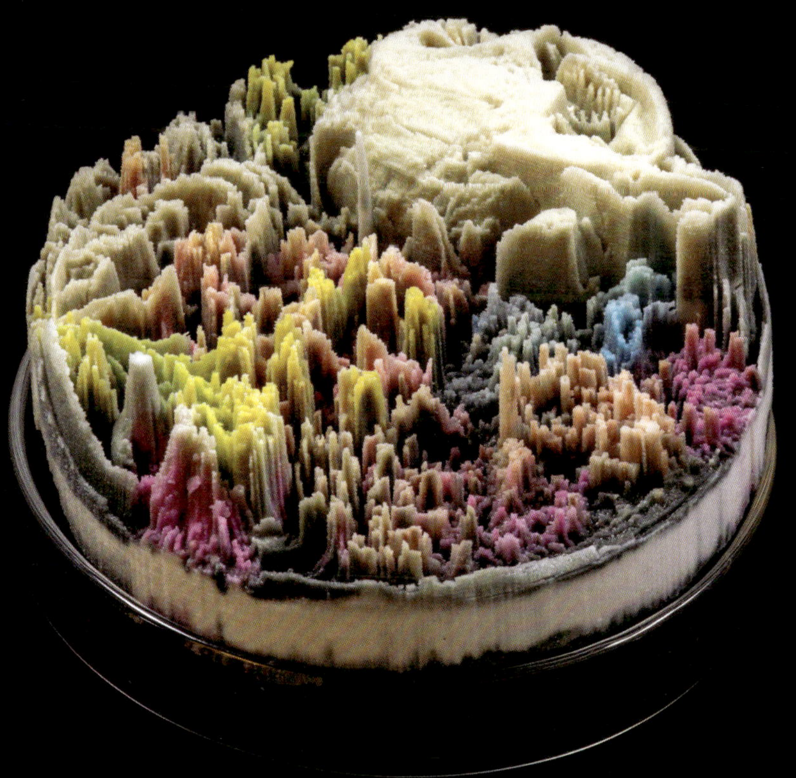

#35

JOE DAVIS

Joe Davis (American), video still from *Lucky Mice*, 2017–19, cage, enrichment wheel, dice-casting device, dimensions variable. Courtesy of the artist.

Lucky Mice

Lucky Mice explores the possibility that luck is heritable—a notion with ties to folktales and science fiction—by offering a mouse rolling dice and tabulating the results for comparison. The experiments observe serendipitous behaviors with a mouse-operated dice-throwing apparatus and pursue selective breeding of "lucky mice." Davis was inspired by Larry Niven's fictional *Ringworld* novels in which aliens carry on secret experiments to enhance good luck through human breeding. Davis explains that, while serendipity might be ascribed to chance, closer examination suggests it is chance coupled with coincidence. Serendipitous discovery comprises both the ability to accommodate unexpected events and a kind of judgment in recognition. History recounts many accidents that, through reasoning and deduction, become transformed into opportunity. Investigations of luck have been undertaken in psychology, cognitive science, information science, and economics, but correlations of serendipity and genetics have never been studied.

Production of enhanced traits in *Homo sapiens* would take centuries, but a single generation of mice can be produced in only about twelve weeks. *Lucky Mice* is part performance, part installation. The installation includes a film of the performance in which a single mouse completes a dice-throwing trial. This artwork attempts to participate in a scientifically rigorous approach by using protocols for ethical research and humane treatment of laboratory animals. The artist is collaborating on the project with Ashley W. Seifert of the University of Kentucky, whose research focuses on developmental biology and regenerative medicine. Davis' use of live mice highlights human-animal relationships and examines regulations underlying the use and care of laboratory animals. The work implicitly questions the social status of art and science. Since different people place different values on the knowledge produced by these two communities, there are different restrictions and freedoms on the use of animals for art, science, or other cultural contexts.

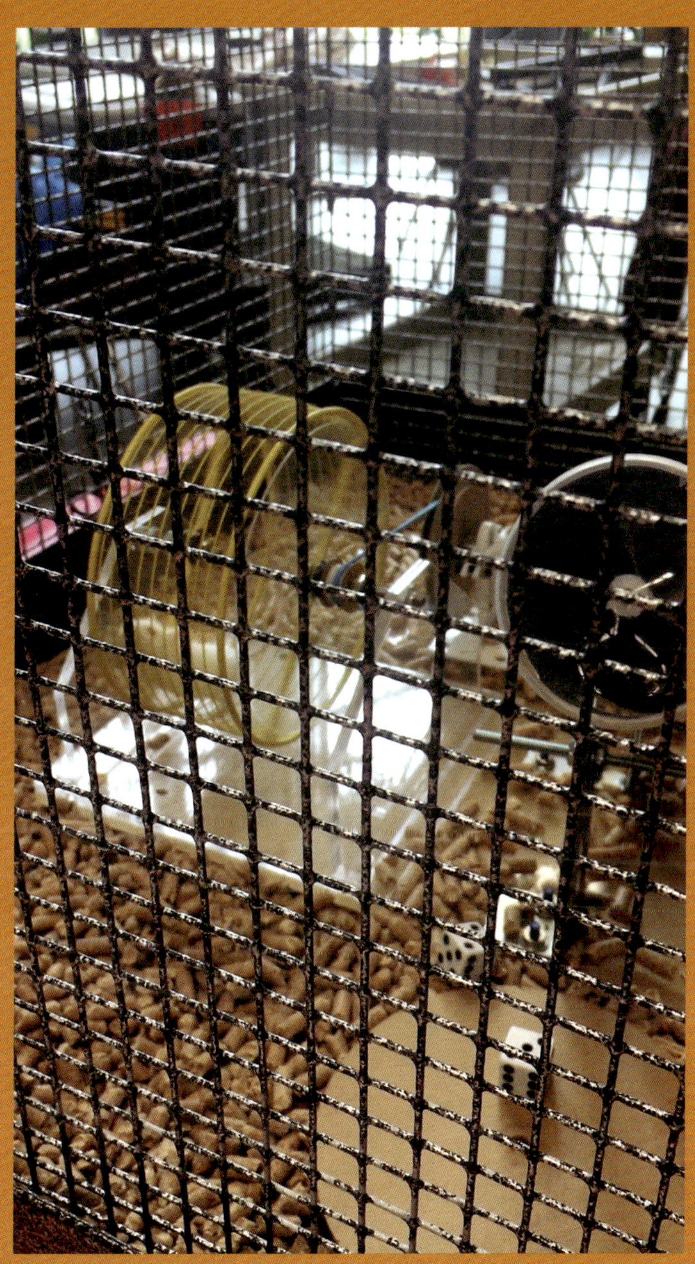

JONATHAN DAVIS

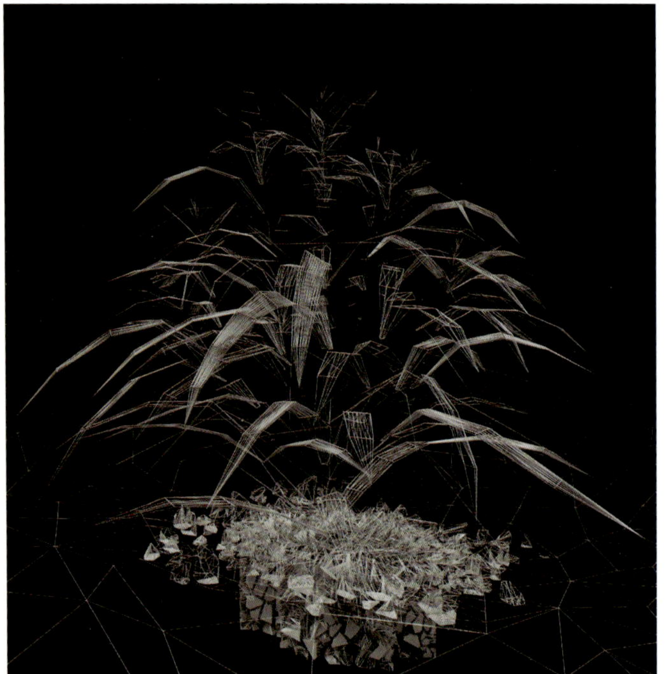

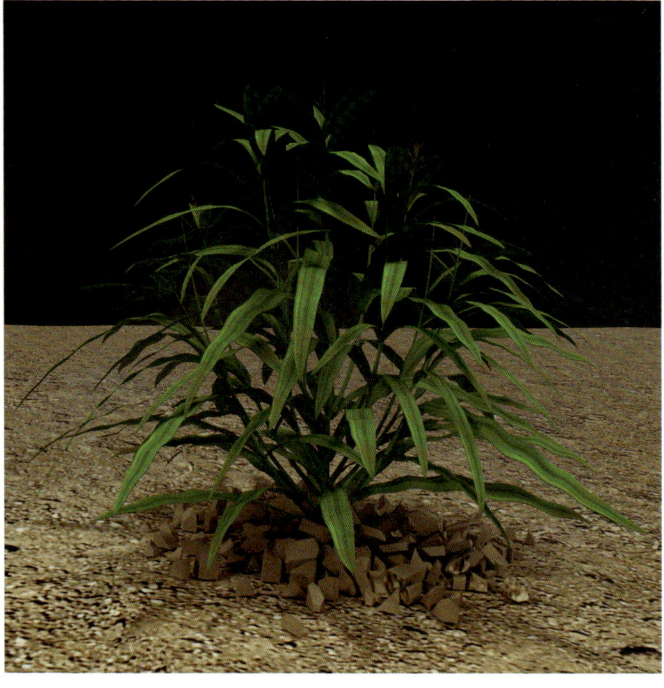

Jonathan Davis (American), wireframe for 3D simulated time-lapse animation of teosinte growth; the fully textured model; and underlying structure of the model revealed in wireframe, fading into the fully textured model on the right.

3D Teosinte Animation

As they reach the end of the virtual corn maze in the *From Teosinte to Tomorrow* VR experience, the visitor sees a teosinte plant emerge and grow to maturity in a few seconds. The computer-generated 3D animation was created using time-lapse videos of real plants as guides and inspiration. Each leaf blade is animated independently, reflecting the daily and seasonal movements plants make as they track the sun during growth. The compression of an entire growing season into less than a minute references our perception of time, intersecting with the theme of how we understand the passage of time in the historical context of the development (via human intervention) of corn from teosinte, and currently, as new technologies are applied in agriculture and other aspects of human experience.

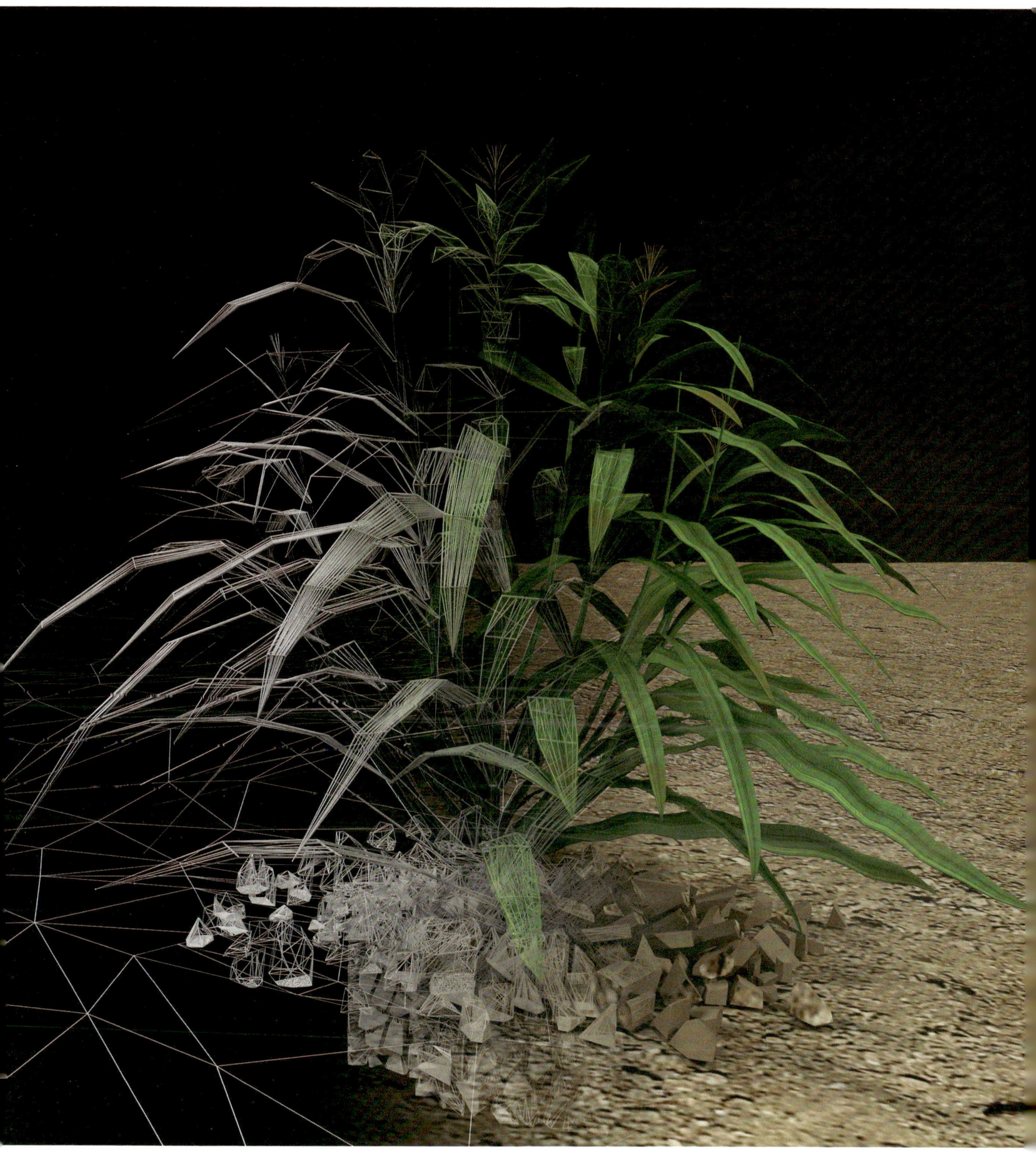

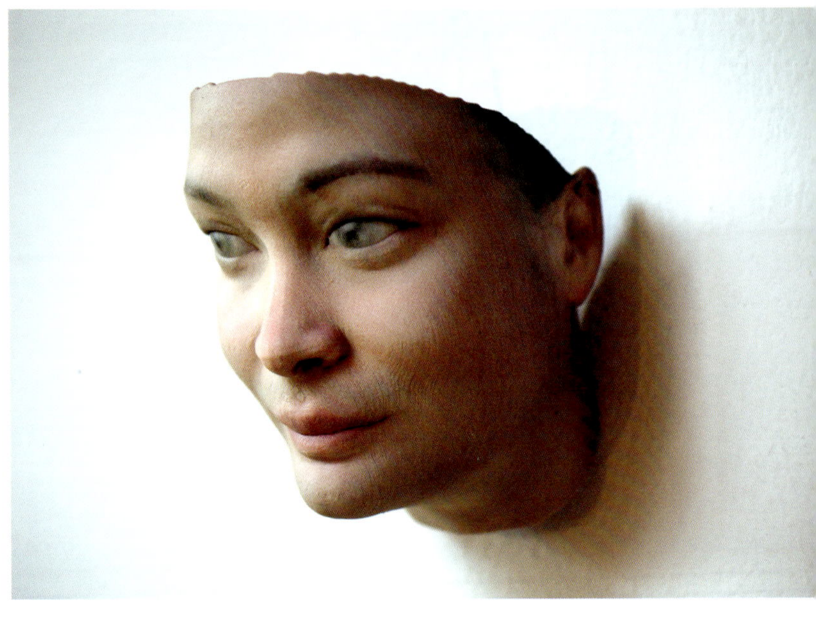

Stranger Visions

ABOVE: Heather Dewey-Hagborg (American), *East Hampton: Sample 7*, from the series *Stranger Visions*, 2012–13, found genetic materials, custom software, 3D prints, documentation, 8 x 8 x 6 in. (20.25 x 20.25 x 15.25 cm). Courtesy of the artist and Fridman Gallery, New York.

OPPOSITE: Heather Dewey-Hagborg (American), *New York: Sample 7*, from the series *Stranger Visions*, 2012–13, found genetic materials, custom software, 3D prints, documentation, 8 x 8 x 6 in. (20.25 x 20.25 x 15.25 cm). Courtesy of the artist and Fridman Gallery, New York.

Heather Dewey-Hagborg creates portrait sculptures from analyses of genetic material collected in public places. Working with the traces that strangers unwittingly leave behind, Dewey-Hagborg calls attention to the developing technology of forensic DNA phenotyping, the impulse toward genetic determinism, and the potential for a culture of genetic surveillance. To create the sculptures, Dewey-Hagborg collected hair, chewing gum, and cigarette butts from the streets, public bathrooms, and waiting rooms of New York City. She extracted and analyzed each sample's DNA to computationally generate 3D-printed, life-size, full-color portraits representing what those individuals might look like, based on genomic research. More recently, in her new work *Probably Chelsea* (2017), Dewey-Hagborg created thirty different possible portraits of Chelsea Manning algorithmically generated by an analysis of Manning's DNA. The artist writes that this shows that an individual's DNA can be interpreted as data and demonstrates how subjective the act of reading DNA really is.

Dewey-Hagborg's work raises questions about legal, social, and ethical implications for surveillance and privacy with the advent of reliable genetic tests. Her work asks what can be revealed and what remains hidden when DNA testing is employed on found cells—those constantly shed into our shared world. The artist has devoted critical efforts to discussing the limitations and bias in phenotyping technology, which she (and many scientists) do not consider accurate or impartial enough for use in criminal investigations. *Stranger Visions* was created with the support of Eyebeam and the mentorship of Genspace and New York University's Advanced Media Studio. It is in the collection of the Centre Pompidou and private collections worldwide. Soon after this work was produced, Paradon Snapshot, a private company, began offering a commercial product to police departments for suspect identification. This project received international press on *CNN*, and in the *Wall Street Journal*, the *Times* (UK), and the *Daily Mail* (UK), and won the Ars Electronica honorary mention in 2015.

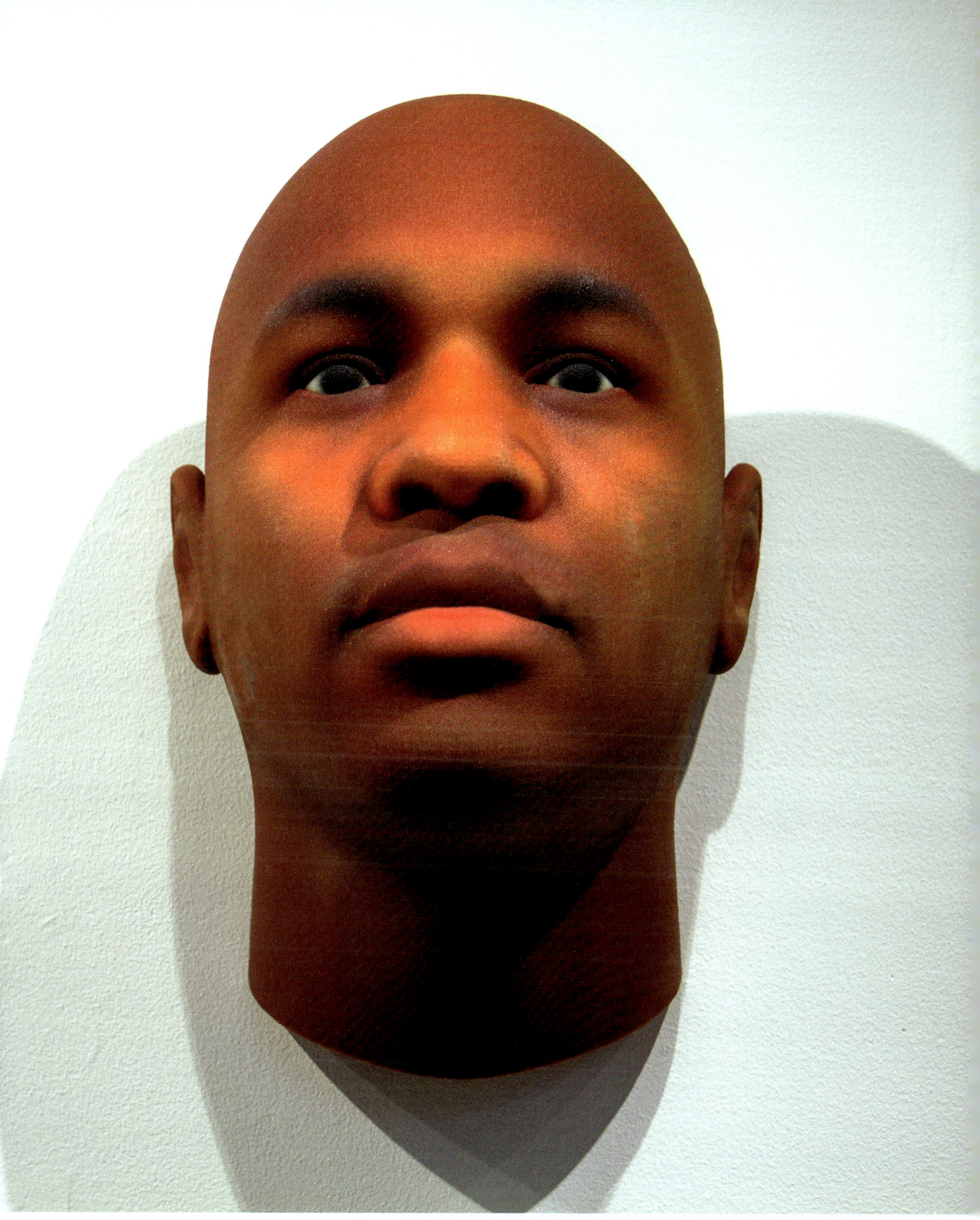

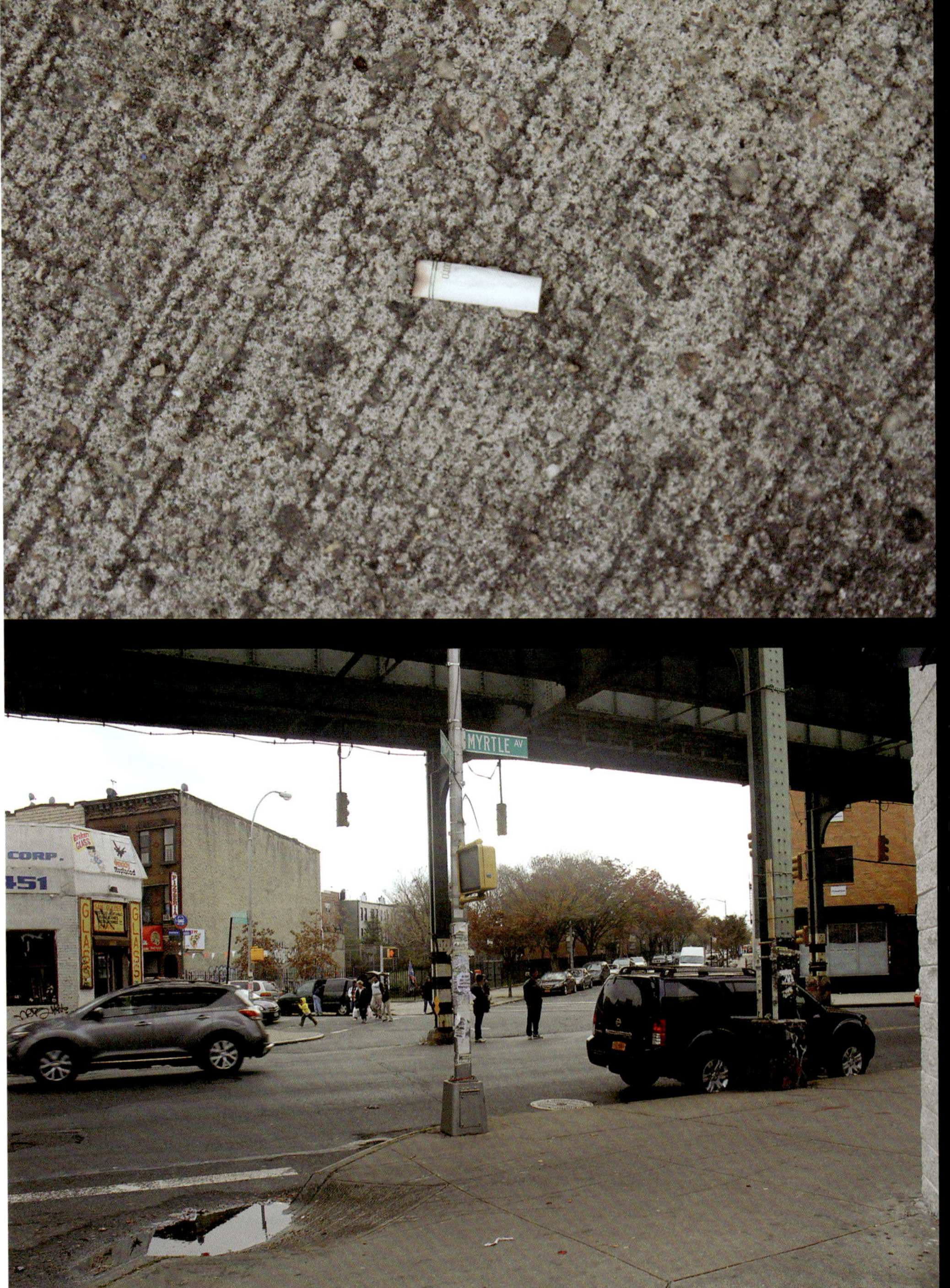

Heather Dewey-Hagborg (American), *New York: Sample 4*, from the series *Stranger Visions*, 2012–13, found genetic materials, custom software, 3D prints, documentation, 8 x 8 x 6 in. (20.25 x 20.25 x 15.25 cm). Courtesy of the artist and Fridman Gallery, New York.

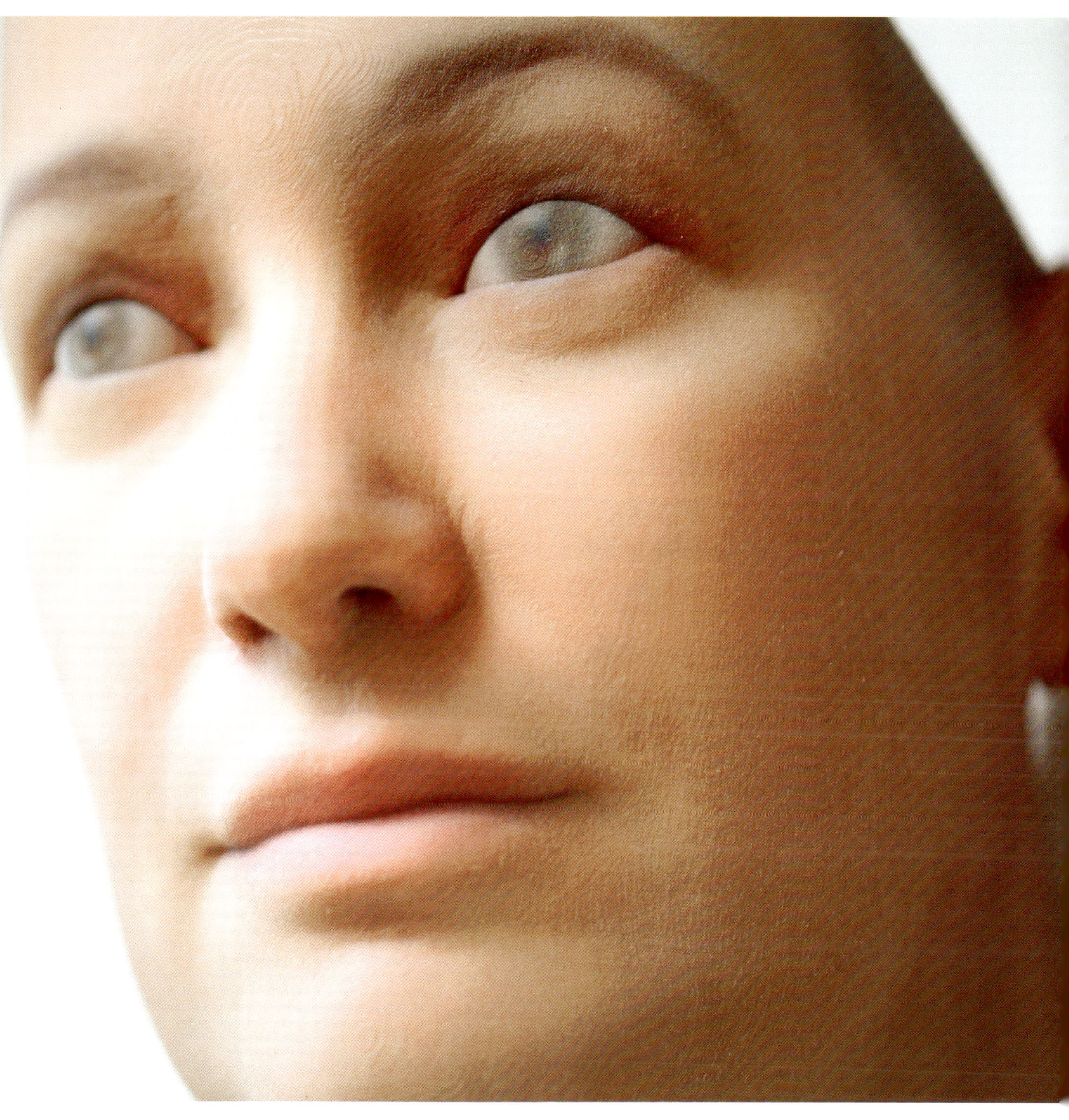

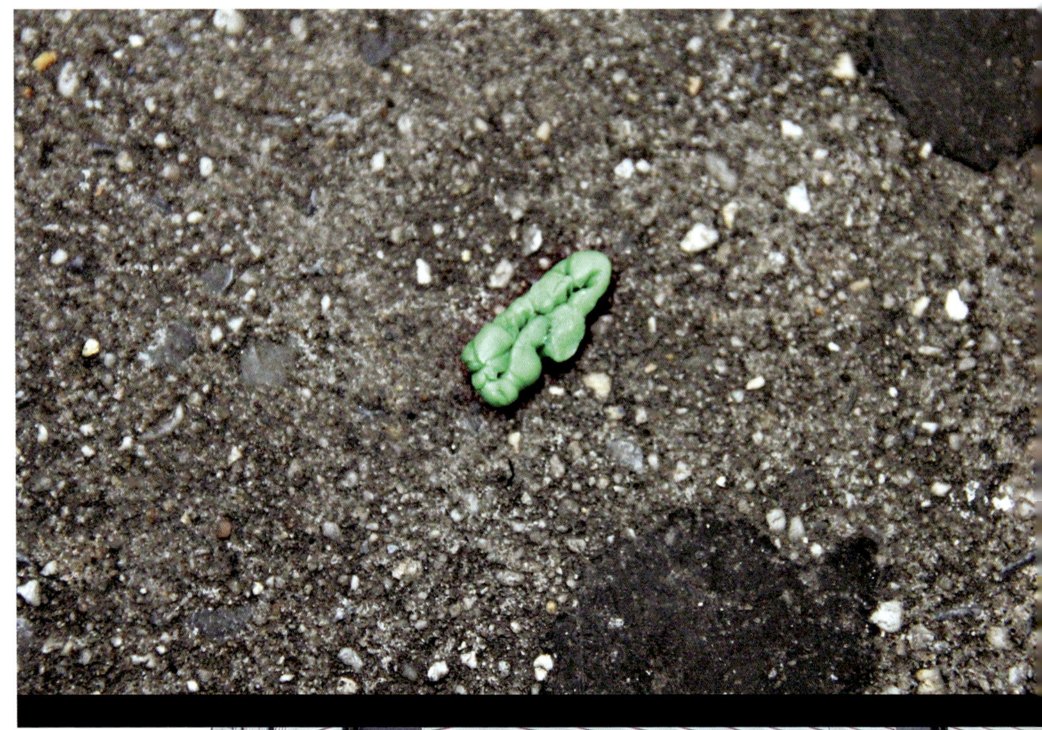

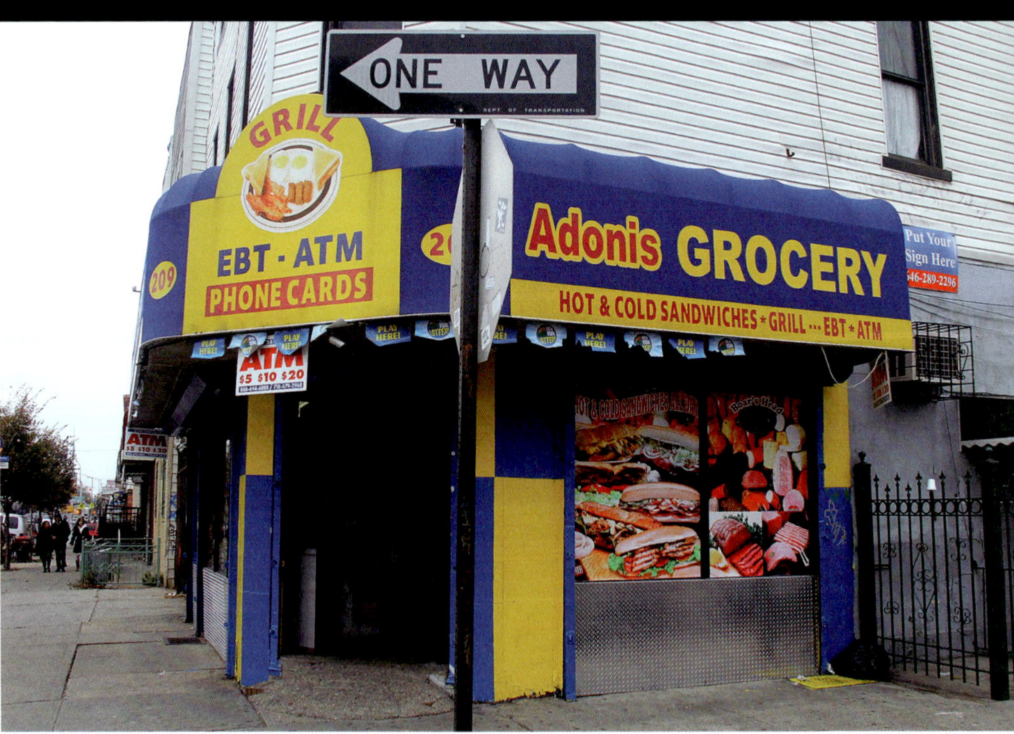

Heather Dewey-Hagborg (American), *New York: Sample 6*, from the series *Stranger Visions*, 2012–13, found genetic materials, custom software, 3D prints, documentation, 8 x 8 x 6 in. (20.25 x 20.25 x 15.25 cm). Courtesy of the artist and Fridman Gallery, New York.

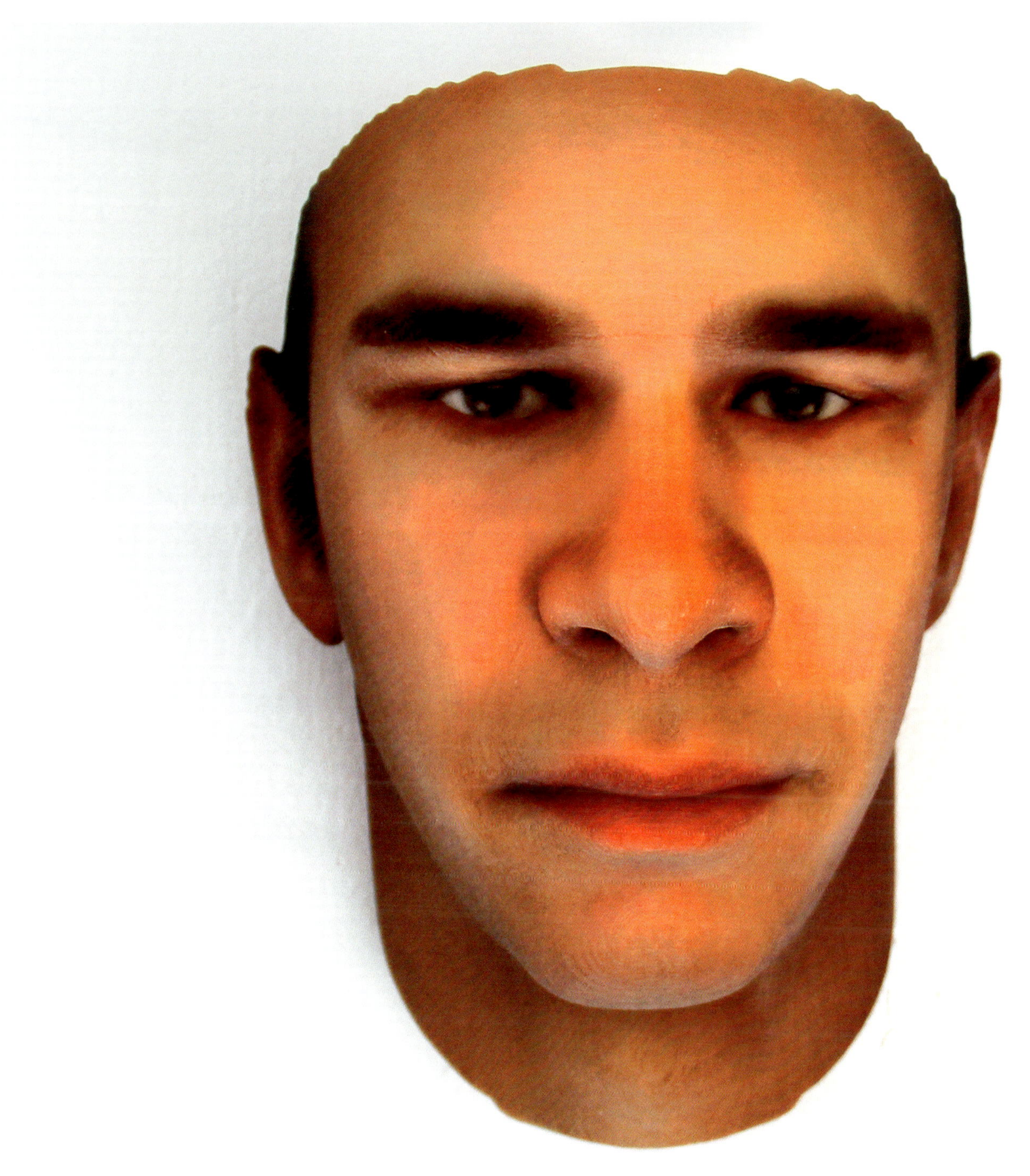

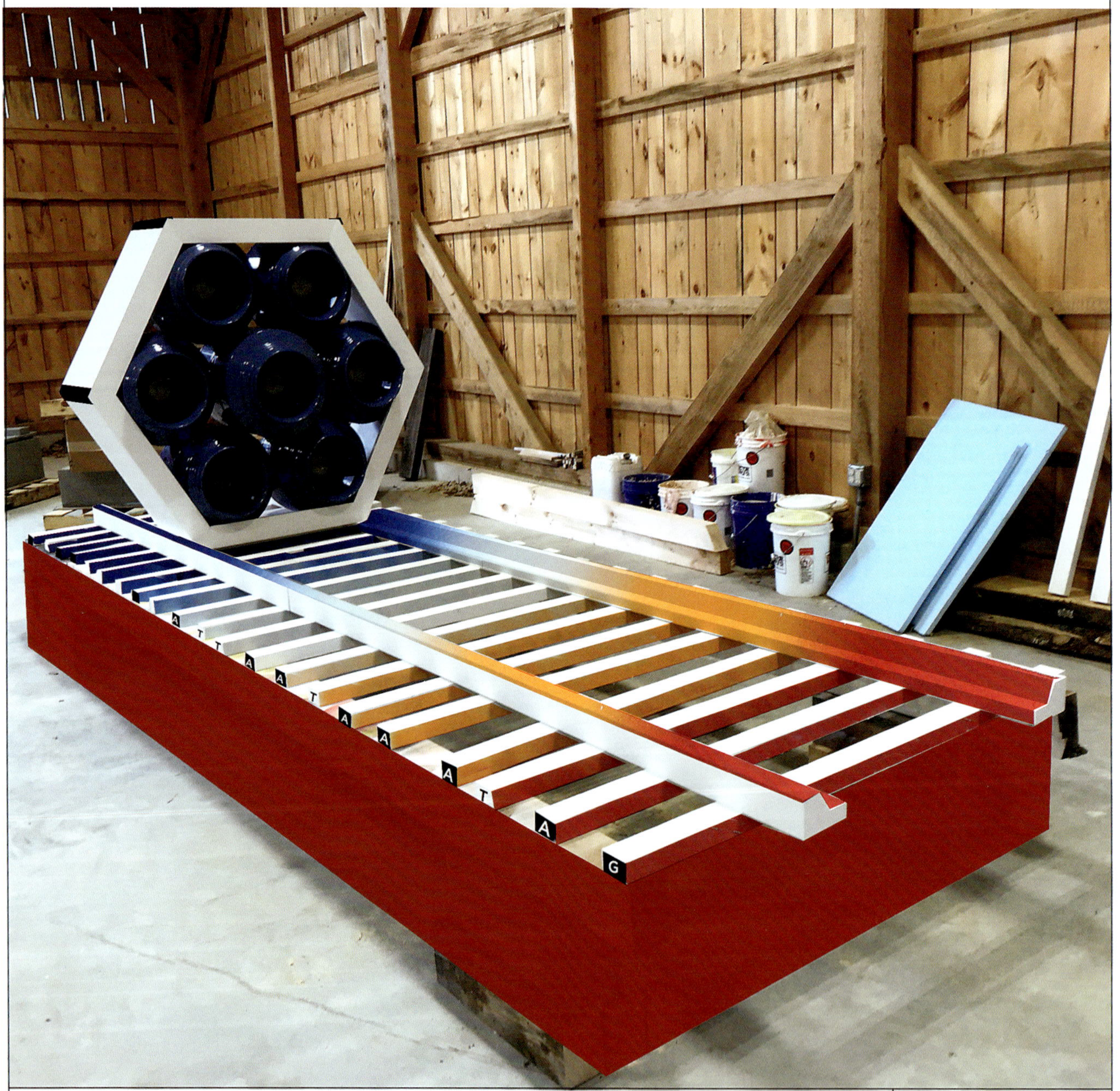

NEG Colorway Study 1

A A R O N   E L L I S O N

D A V I D   B U C K L E Y   B O R D E N

Novel Ecosystem Generator

This playful, kinetic public art installation is designed to represent a process engine that takes in existing genes, organisms, or entire ecosystems, restructures and rearranges them, and outputs new biological systems. The sculpture physically enacts this idea that new ecosystems are generated by inputs through a machine: it points out that whether or not we intend the creation of a new ecosystem, there are a set of processes that shape them. The before and after conditions represented in the artwork challenge viewers to consider profound examples of this Anthropocene phenomenon.

People are constantly disassembling, rearranging, and restructuring genes, organisms, ecosystems, and the environment. This process of creating novel ecosystems occurs both deliberately and unintentionally, creating consequences that range from the predictable to the unimaginable. Deliberate cross-breeding, production of genetically modified organisms (GMOs), introduction of "gene-drives" for mosquito control, or gene splicing using CRISPR all result in the introduction of new kinds of plants and animals. These intentional introductions engender new interactions in ecosystems that may have been in place for millennia.

Similarly, people transport species from state to state and between countries, leading to the arrival and spread of introduced species in new places. These movements of species

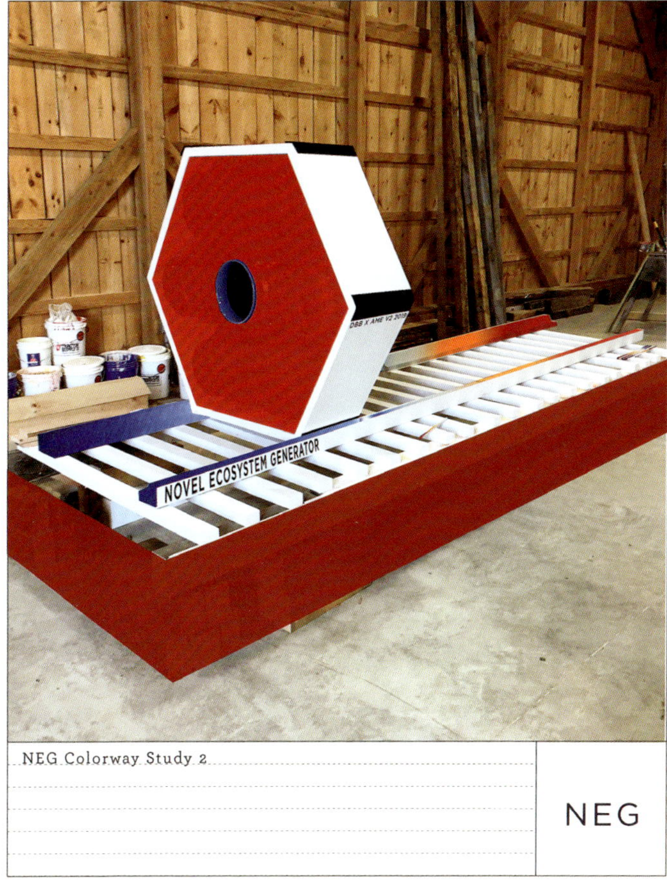

and their interaction with native organisms, coupled with ongoing, human-caused changes to the land, sea, and climate, together lead to unexpected and unintended consequences. Such "unintentional genetic engineering" is happening continuously and, like its intentional counterpart, has great potential to generate new and unexpected ecological relationships. Ellison and Borden's sculpture prompts us to think about our individual and collective responsibility for the environmental changes we have created—and continue to create.

Aaron Ellison and David Buckley Borden (American), *Novel Ecosystem Generator*, 2019, wood, metal, salvaged industrial fans, fabric, acrylic paint, vinyl, and miscellaneous hardware, 65 x 60 x 180 in. (165 x 152 x 457 cm). Additional collaborators: Lucas Griffith, Matthew Hickler, Roland Meunier. Courtesy of the artists.

EMEKA IKEBUDE

Emeka Ikebude (Nigerian, lives in Dallas), *Fragments*, 2016, toothpicks, natural dyes, 70 x 52 x 4 in. (178 x 132 x 10 cm). Courtesy of the artist.

Fragments

In *Fragments*, the artist creates an imposing portrait made from discarded toothpicks, each of which potentially contains the DNA of its individual user. The image of the woman created by the toothpicks is described by the artist as a "a revolutionary black woman. . . . This woman comes with her own light/fire to interrogate the epistemologies that frame her condition and burn things down if necessary." The toothpicks were mainly collected in restaurants where they had been discarded. The artist dyed them in bunches with organic dyes that are harmless to the environment and painstakingly arranged these bundles into a single large image. The piece plays on conventions of found and community art since the piece is produced by an organizing artist but would not have been possible without the collecting of these found toothpicks from many individuals who unwittingly contributed them.

While the identities of these toothpick users will never be known, the collective image their discarded toothpicks create raises questions about their biological information, which potentially includes a tiny amount of blood, tissue, and digestive microbes, all of which we each so easily discard. The anonymity of the toothpick users settles into the universality of our bodies—distinguishing details yet erasing differences. The artwork inquires about our understanding of the complex relationship with our microbial community, which would help inform a better understanding of the human body, foster healthier habits, and improve well-being. Each toothpick in this composition represents a human being—a contributor and participant in this project of rethinking the bacterial and viral genomes of the human body.

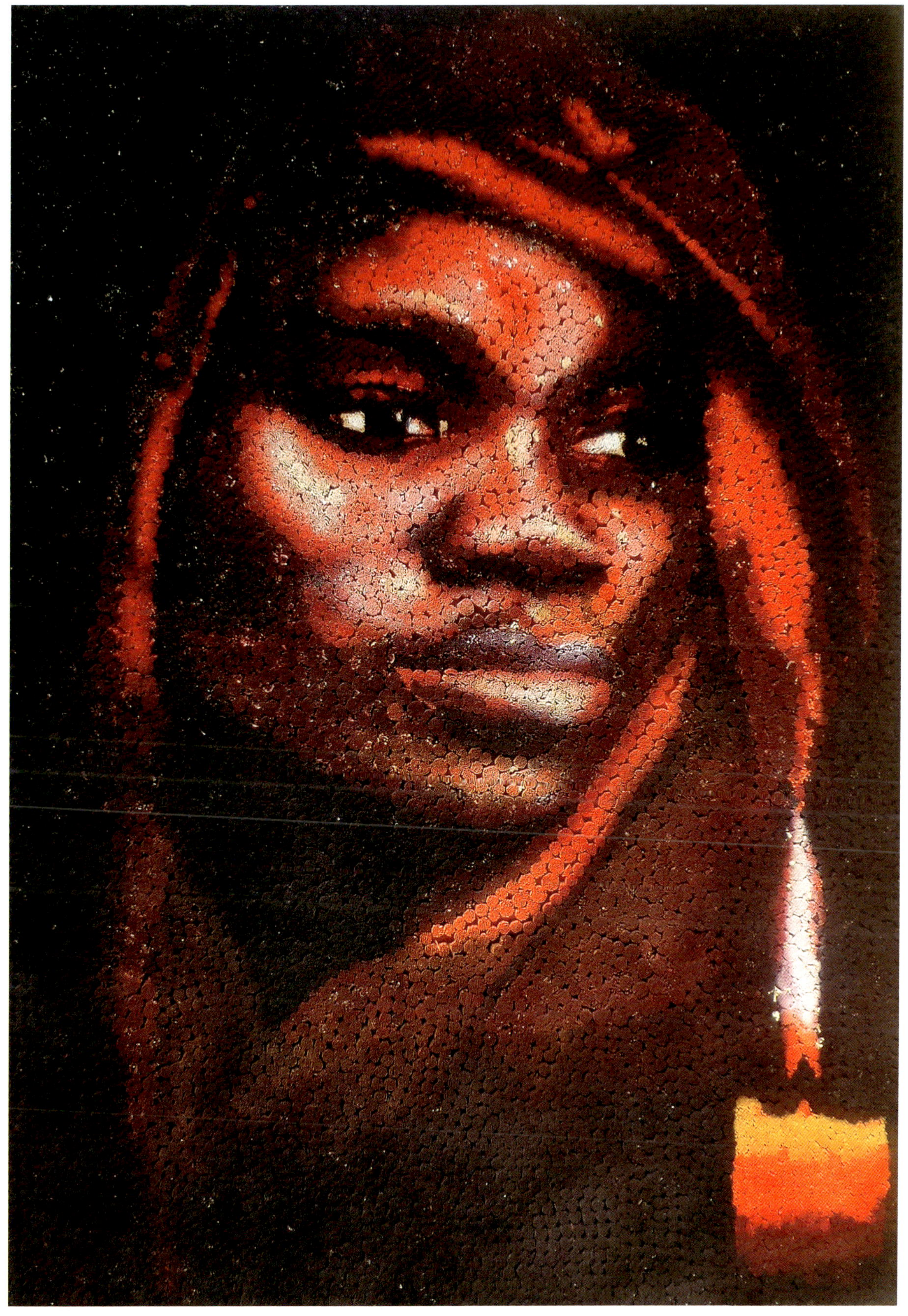

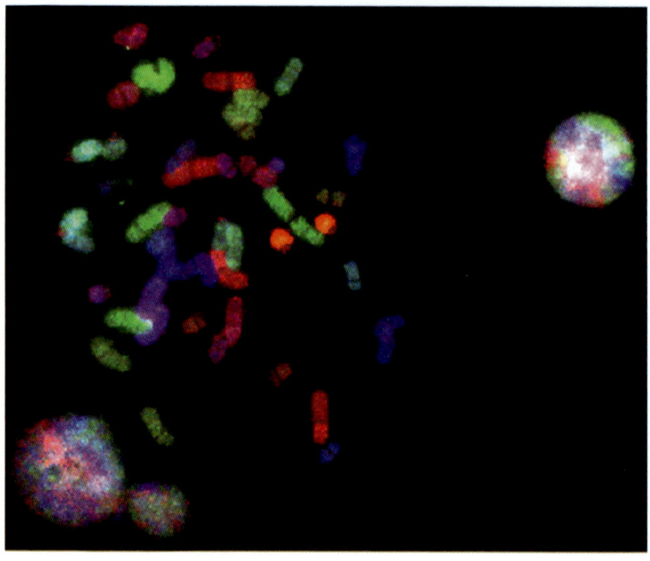

In Posse: Making Female Sperm

Charlotte Jarvis (British), *In Posse: Making Female Sperm*, from the series *Corpus*, 2019, multimedia installation: human cells, HD video. In collaboration with Dr. Susana Chuva de Sousa Lopes and Kapelica Gallery/Kersnikova Institute with support from MU Gallery Eindhoven. Photographs and HD video by Charlotte Jarvis, Miha Godec, and Eleni Papazoglu. Courtesy of the artist.

ABOVE: Initial experiments used to identify artist's chromosomes for subsequent genetic engineering.

OPPOSITE: Video stills.

What would it mean if we could create female sperm? Could changes in reproductive biotechnologies affect interpretations of gender? Artist Charlotte Jarvis is collaborating with scientist Susana Chuva de Sousa Lopes and Kapelica Gallery/Kersnikova Institute to make semen from her ("female") stem cells. To do this they are using induced pluripotant stem cells derived from Jarvis' blood, altering their chromosomes, and differentiating them into the sperm-producing cells found in male testicles.

Jarvis writes that "throughout history, semen has been revered as a magical substance—a totem of literal and symbolic potency. Patriarchal societies have described semen as 'life force,' 'a drop of the brain,' and 'that which sows the seeds of virtue in the female soul.' *In Posse* aims to rewrite this cultural narrative by using art and science to disrupt the hierarchy." The project is presented as part of a contemporary reenactment of the ancient Greek festival of Thesmophoria—a women-only fertility ceremony in honor of the goddesses Demeter and Persephone.

The artist has used the possibility of creating female sperm from her own cells as a starting point for reimagining Thesmophoria—for populating a history without patriarchy and a future in which the gender/genital power balance is redressed. On Jarvis' female sperm altar, we find an early phase of her work surrounded by evidence of the rituals of the Thesmophoria festival. She invites us to pay homage to the mixture of science and art that informs our own beliefs and influences our biotechnological futures.

The experimental sperm, along with a film of a creative reenactment of the Thesmophoria festival, provokes conversations about the way that biotechnology constructs, augments, and complicates sex and gender. *In Posse: Making Female Sperm* extends Jarvis' ongoing investigations of stem cell technology, personalized medicine, transplantation, and augmentation to ask what a human body is. Can we define it? Should we try?

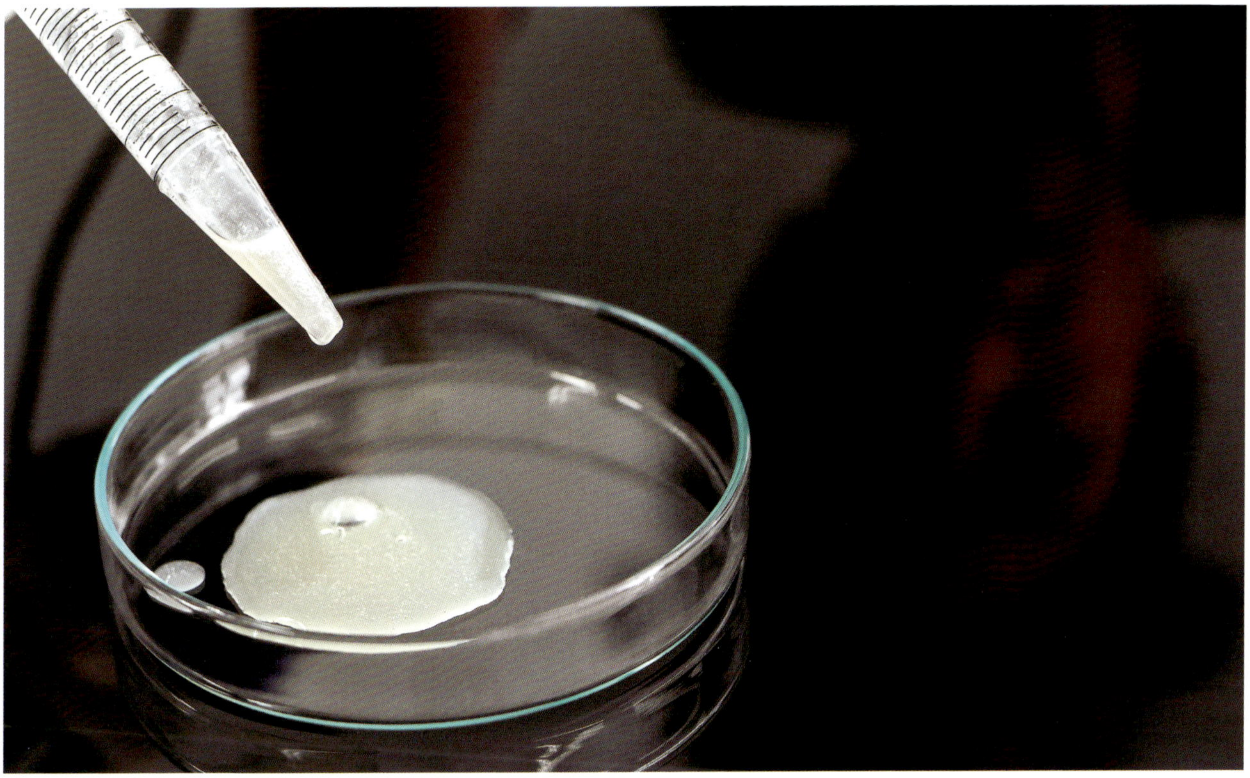

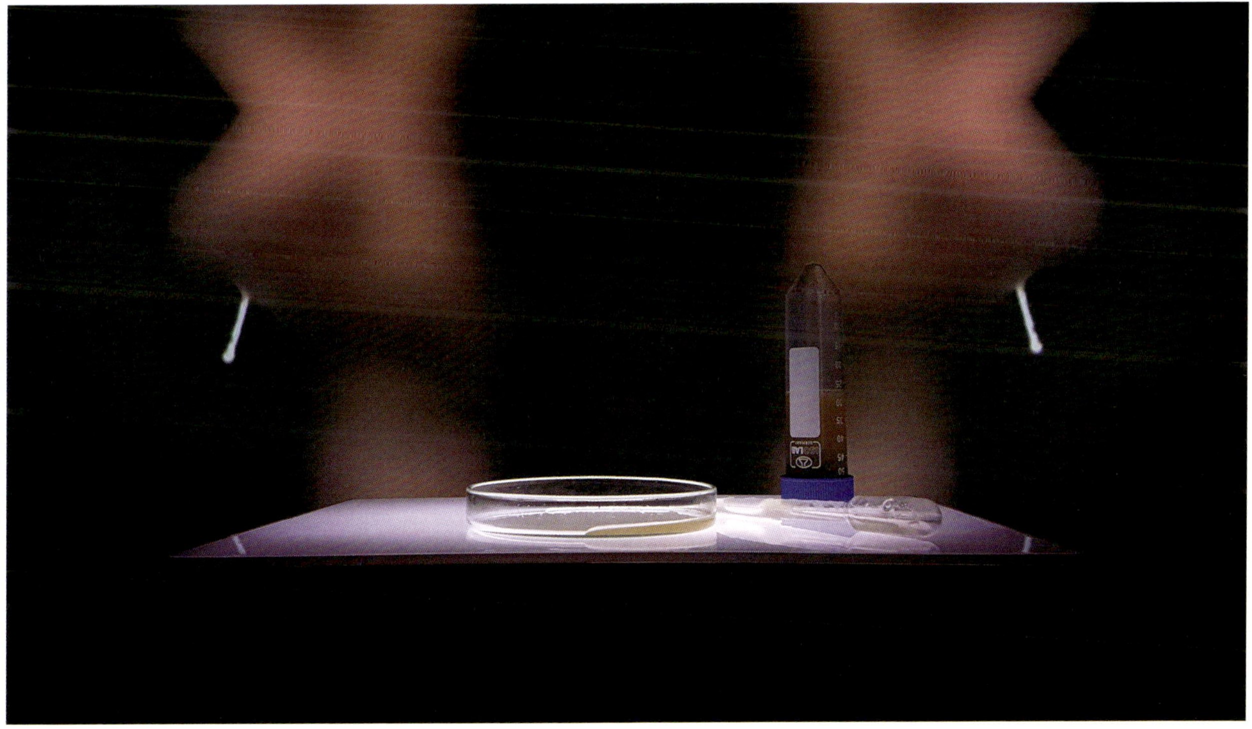

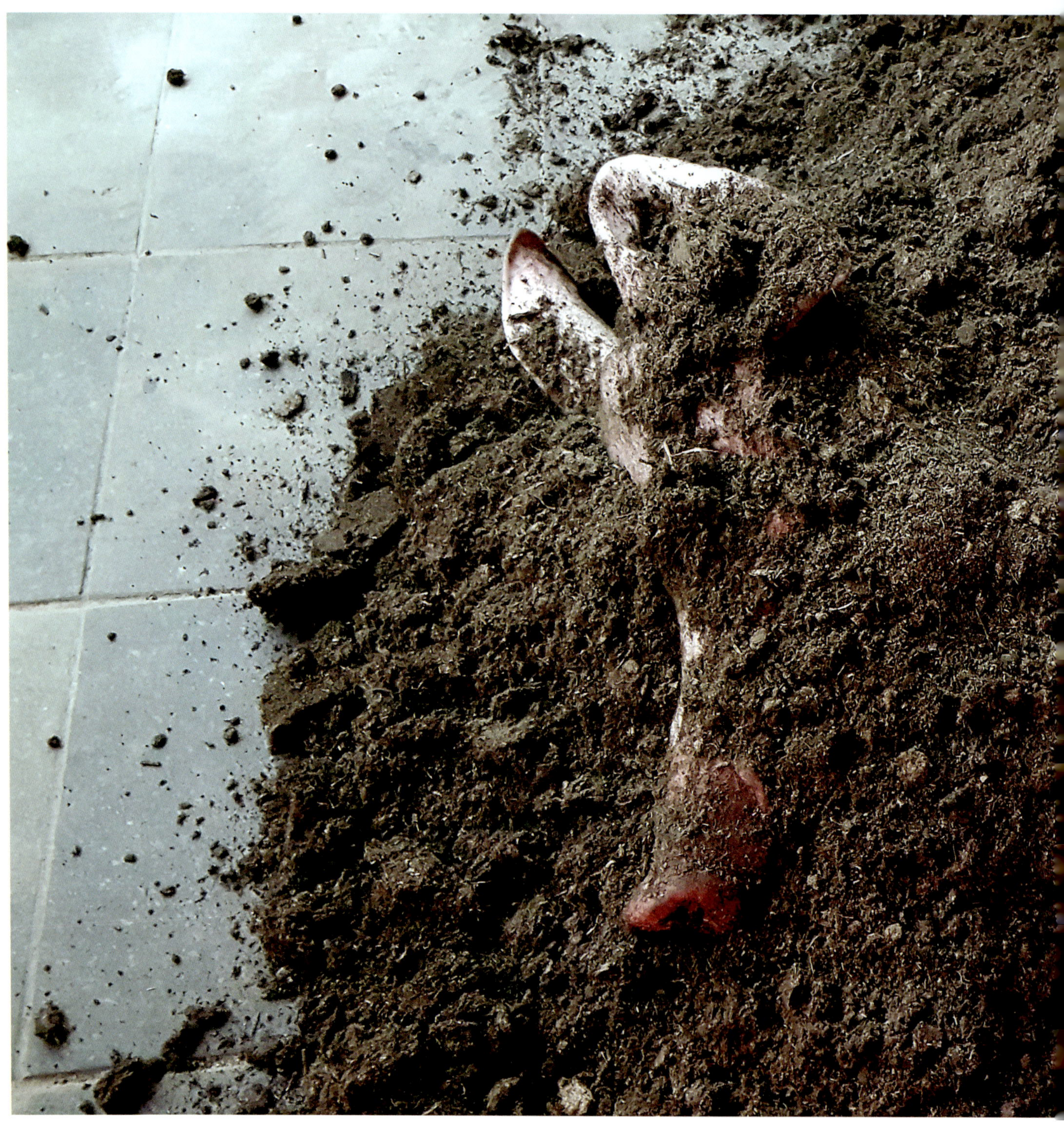

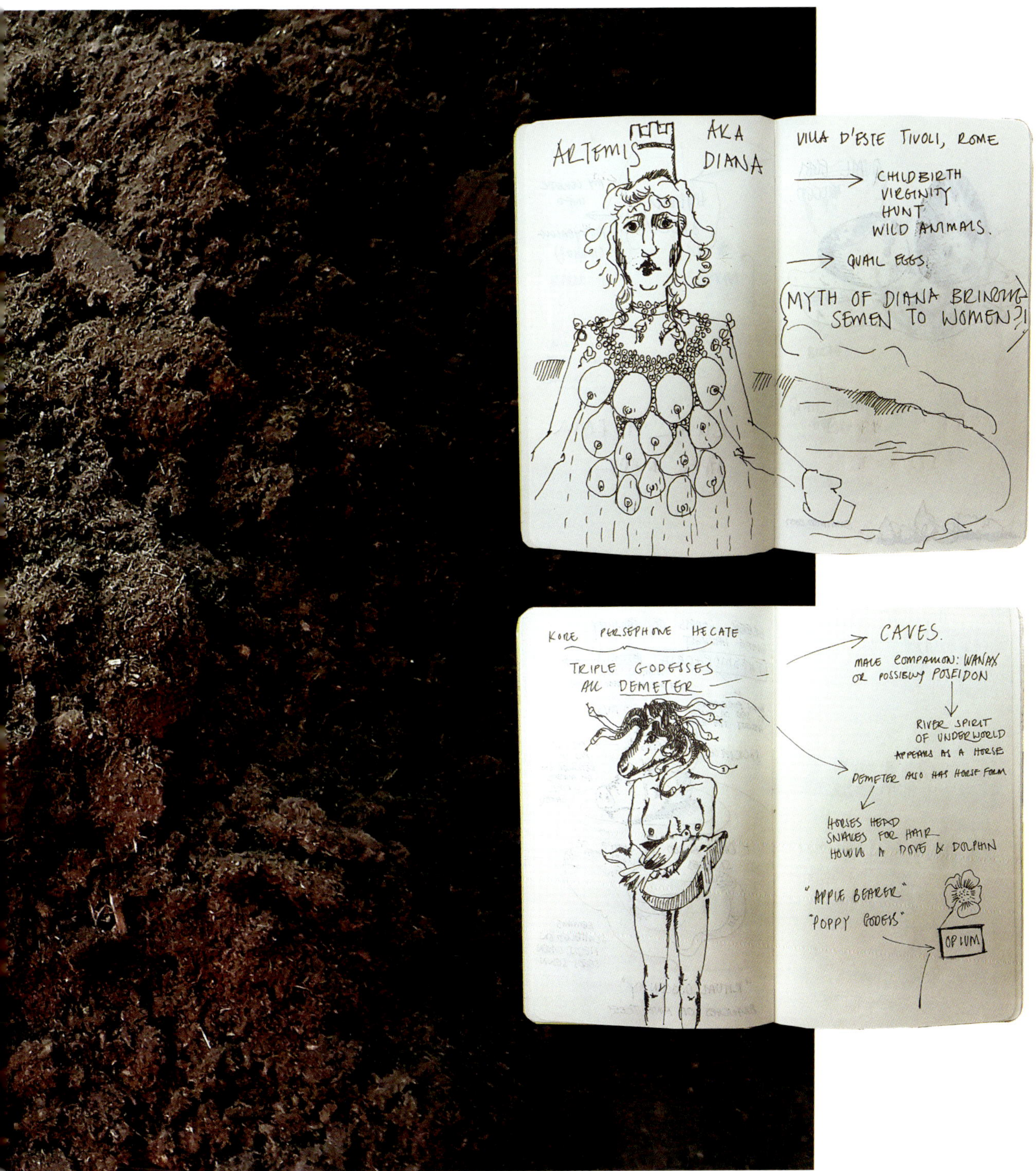

Charlotte Jarvis (British), *In Posse: Making Female Sperm*, from the series *Corpus*, 2019, pig head and soil used in reenactment of Thesmophoria festival, Venice Biennale, 2019. RIGHT: Artist's notebooks. Courtesy of the artist.

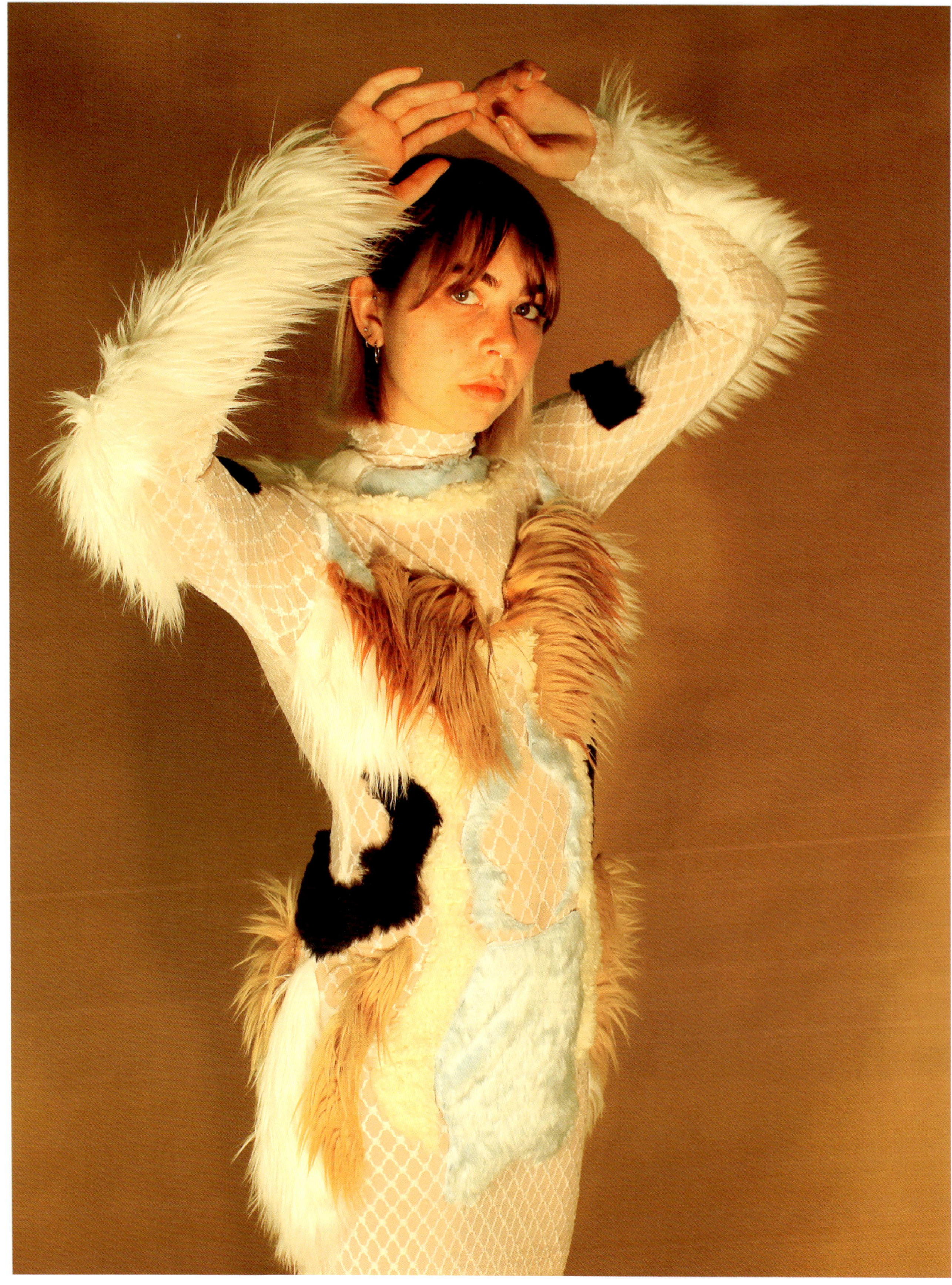

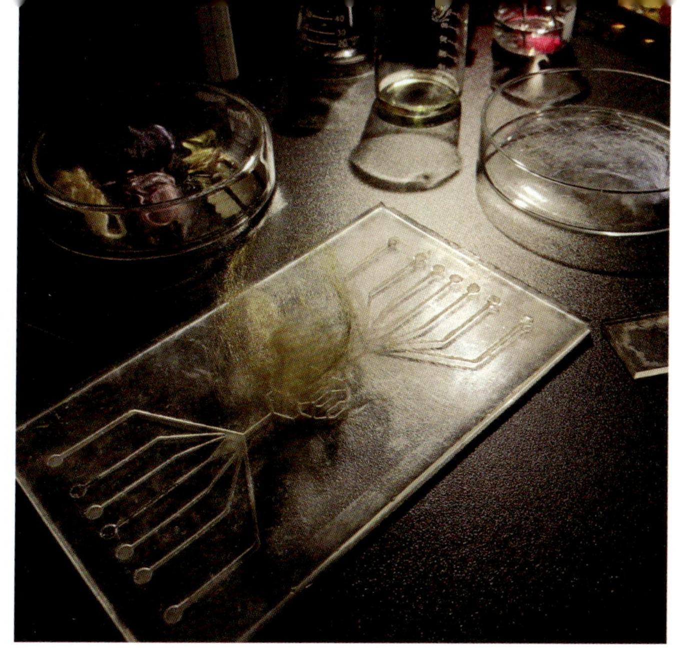

DIANA EUSEBIO

ERIN KIRCHNER

GRACE KWON

RACHEL RUSK

SYDNEY SIEH-TAKATA

Kerasynth

This artwork technically and critically engages the idea of animal-free wool through kerasynth, a synthetically grown, biological material that can replace all keratin-based animal fibers. The team of students from the Maryland Institute College of Art (MICA) participated in the 2018 Biodesign Challenge team under the guidance of Ryan Hoover, creating this work of technical fact and future-oriented critical design fiction. The team has conducted experiments in using tissue engineering to grow wool hair follicle germ (HFG) cells on microfluidic devices designed to provide the cells with nutrients and to remove waste. The subsequent wool fibers could then be harvested and further processed or remain attached to the device.

The artists paid special attention to the use of animals and issues of waste in this project. They note that by using animal-derived growth medium their project cannot be vegan, and no such alternative exists at this time. Kerasynth's creators also considered the social and political dimensions of the future they imagined—not as a utopia of perfect technologies and better people, but a world of new technologies with people very much like those we know today.

Given this imagined future, the team proposes ways for making tissue engineering a more accessible technology through community-based educational models in schools and vocational training programs. To demonstrate these ideas, the team created a speculative spin-off company called DermaWool, which would attempt to provide "material" solutions for consumer needs and animal welfare, including the production of kerasynth-based products.

The project uses the tradition of critical design to propose a future for this fiber through information about the artists' actual research and initial development project, presented through graphics and film, along with garments made of today's materials that help viewers imagine what kerasynth fibers might be able to do in the future. This hybrid artwork is both speculative and technical, demonstrating the potential of microfluidic casting and creative uses for the fiber in futuristic garments, while raising questions about the limitations of tissue culture, which still requires bovine calf serum to keep the growing cells alive.

OPPOSITE: Diana Eusebio, Erin Kirchner, Grace Kwon, Rachel Rusk, Sydney Sieh-Takata (American), *Kerasynth*, 2018, synthetic fiber garment prototype.

ABOVE: Microfluidic substrate, fused polydimethylsiloxane (PDMS), 11.25 x 5 x .2 in. (26.5 x 12.7 x .5 cm). Courtesy of the Kerasynth, Baltimore.

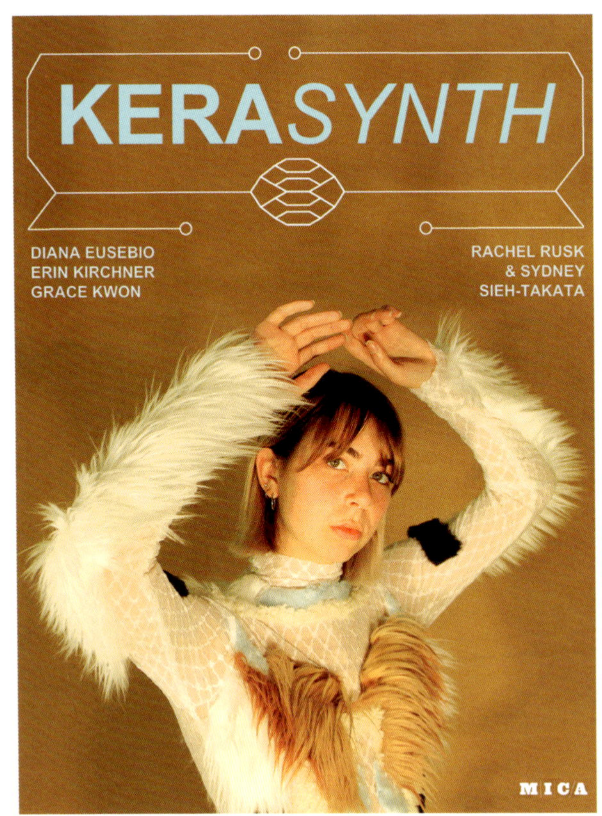

KERASYNTH
DIANA EUSEBIO
ERIN KIRCHNER
GRACE KWON
RACHEL RUSK
& SYDNEY
SIEH-TAKATA
MICA

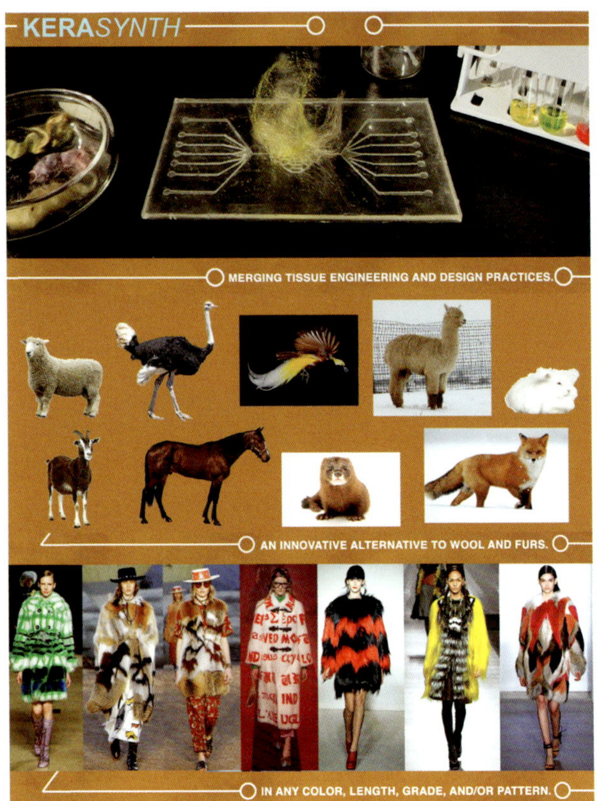

KERASYNTH
MERGING TISSUE ENGINEERING AND DESIGN PRACTICES.
AN INNOVATIVE ALTERNATIVE TO WOOL AND FURS.
IN ANY COLOR, LENGTH, GRADE, AND/OR PATTERN.

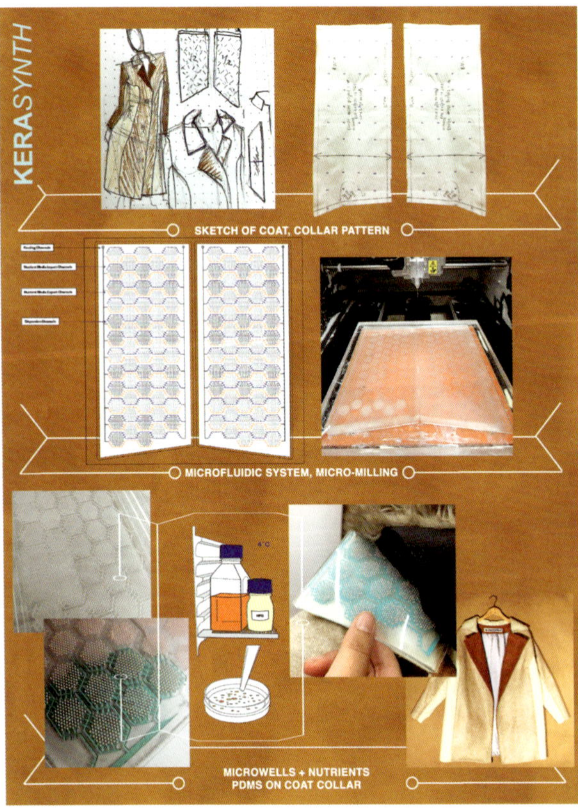

KERASYNTH
SKETCH OF COAT, COLLAR PATTERN
MICROFLUIDIC SYSTEM, MICRO-MILLING
MICROWELLS + NUTRIENTS
PDMS ON COAT COLLAR

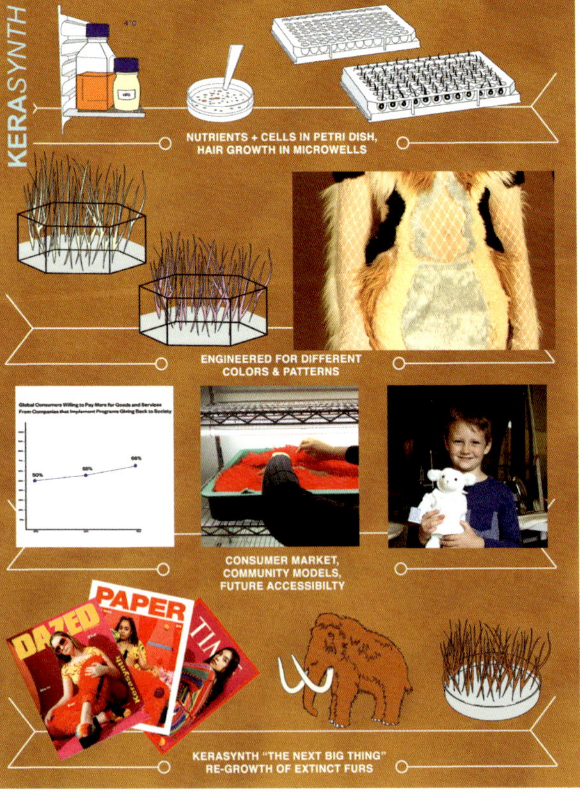

KERASYNTH
NUTRIENTS + CELLS IN PETRI DISH,
HAIR GROWTH IN MICROWELLS
ENGINEERED FOR DIFFERENT
COLORS & PATTERNS
CONSUMER MARKET,
COMMUNITY MODELS,
FUTURE ACCESSIBILTY
KERASYNTH "THE NEXT BIG THING"
RE-GROWTH OF EXTINCT FURS

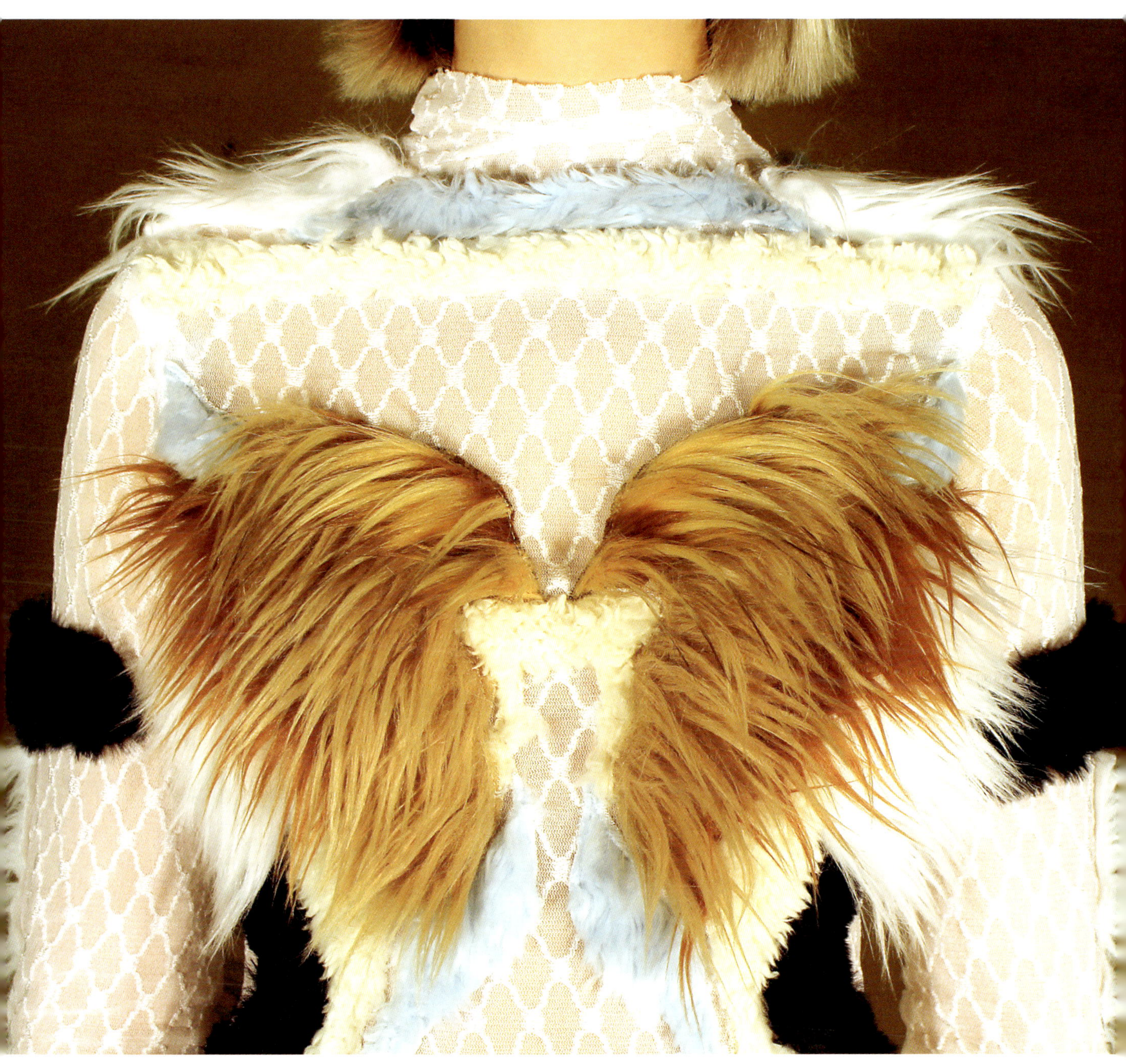

OPPOSITE: Diana Eusebio, Erin Kirchner, Grace Kwon, Rachel Rusk, Sydney Sieh-Takata (American), *Kerasynth*, 2018, process of creating microfluidic substrate and Kerasynth lifecycle diagram. ABOVE: synthetic fiber garment prototype (detail). Courtesy of the Kerasynth, Baltimore.

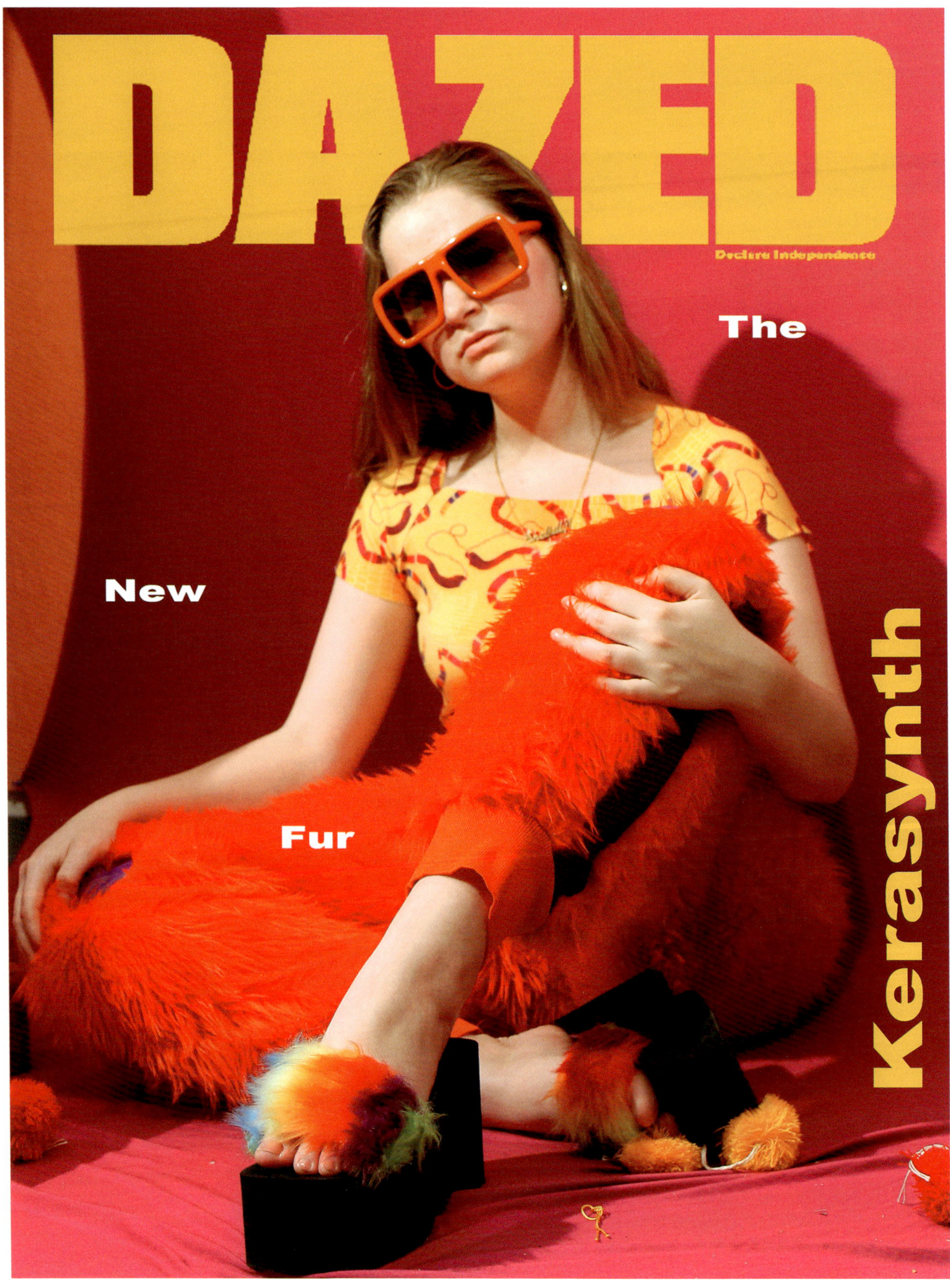

DAZED
Declare Independence
The
New
Fur
Kerasynth

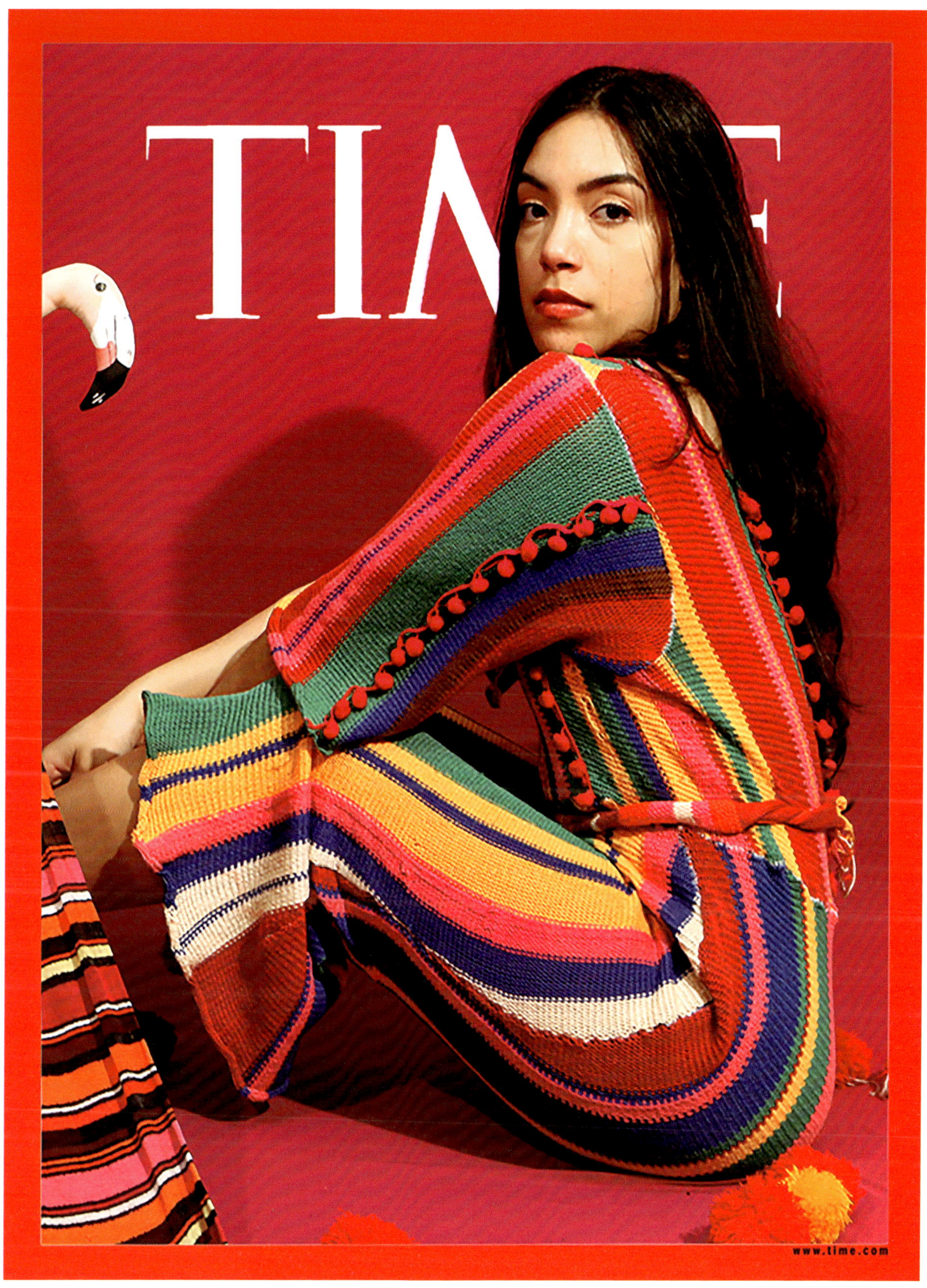

TIME
www.time.com

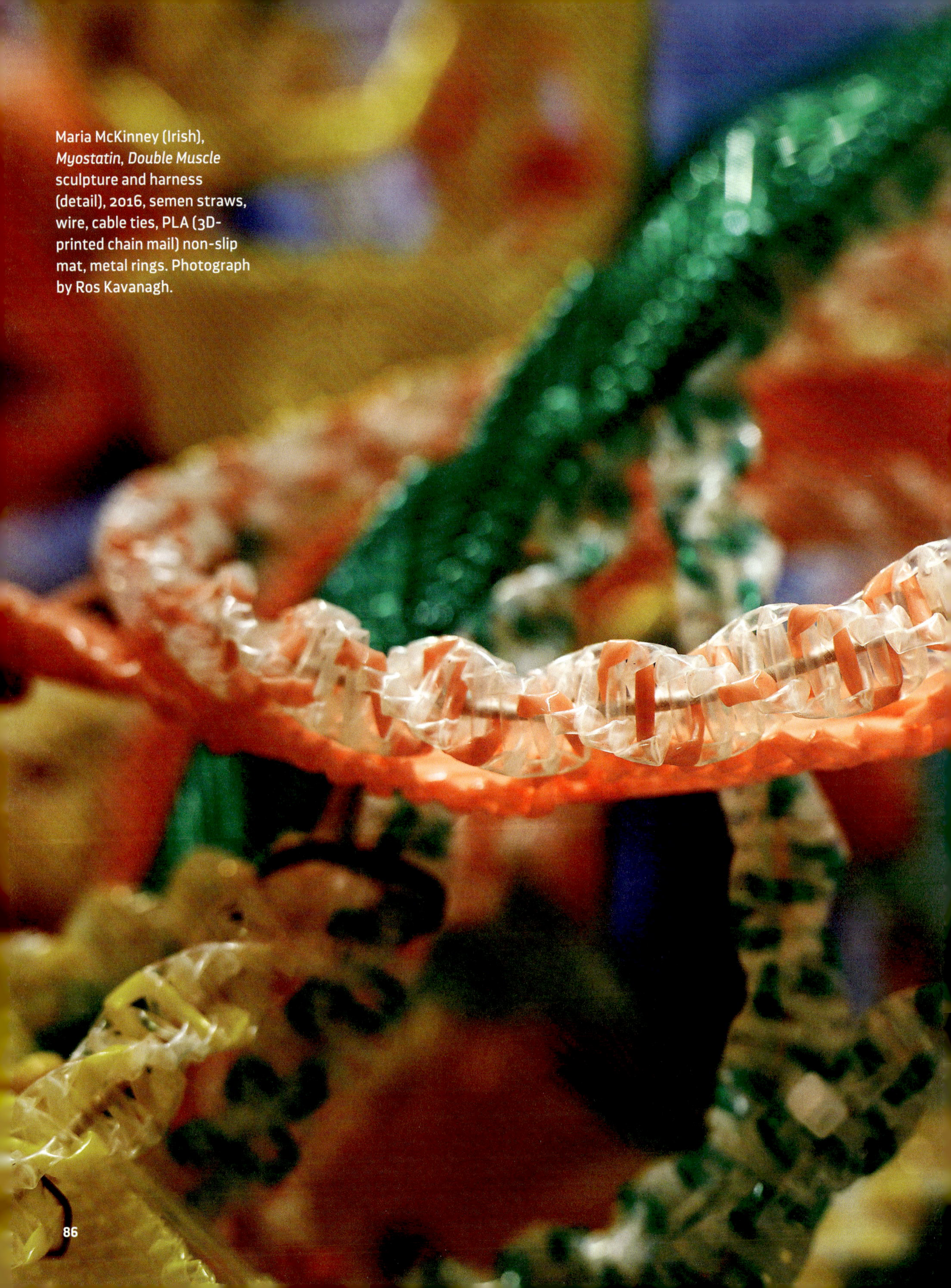

Maria McKinney (Irish), *Myostatin, Double Muscle* sculpture and harness (detail), 2016, semen straws, wire, cable ties, PLA (3D-printed chain mail) non-slip mat, metal rings. Photograph by Ros Kavanagh.

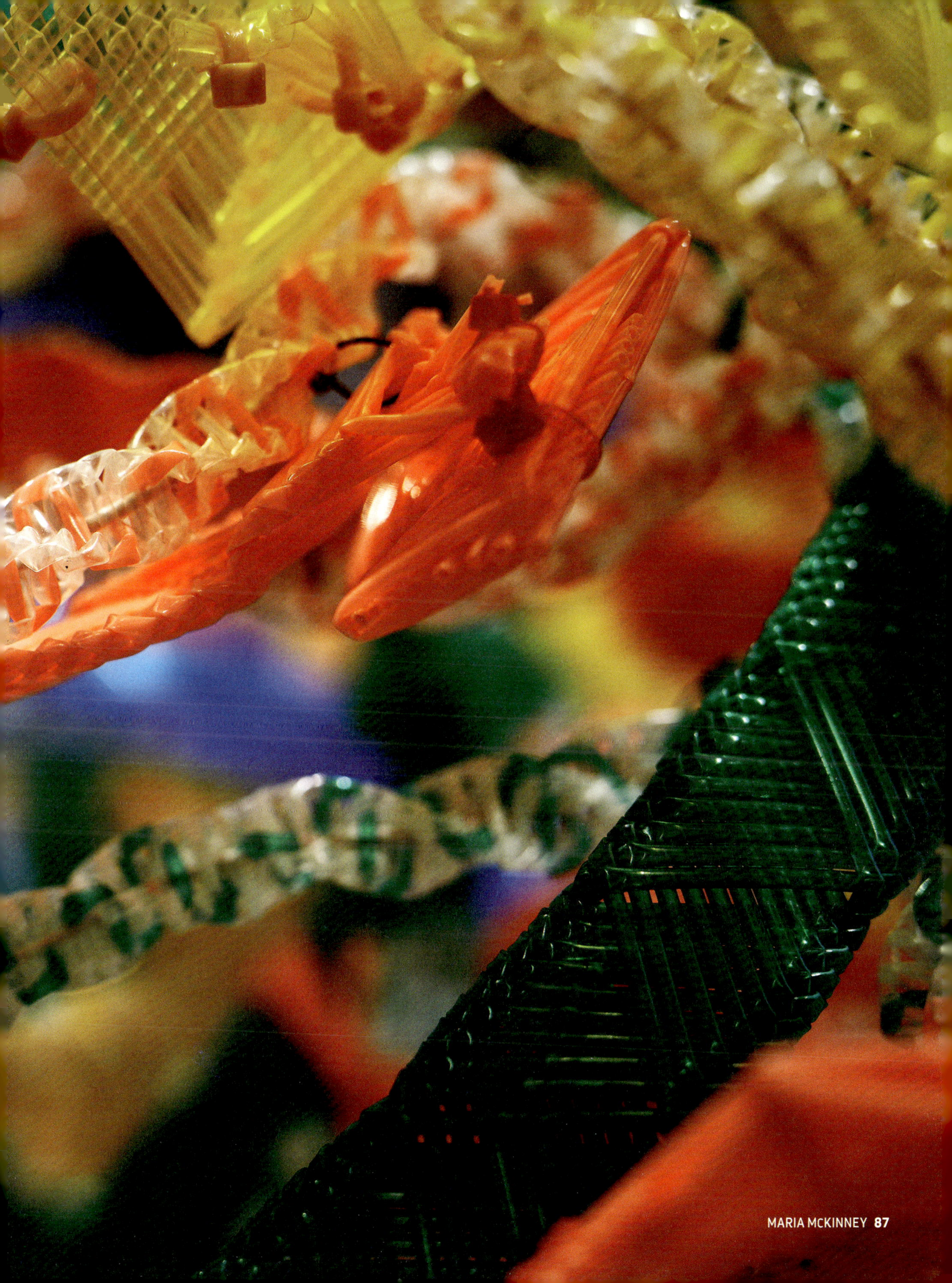

MARIA MCKINNEY 87

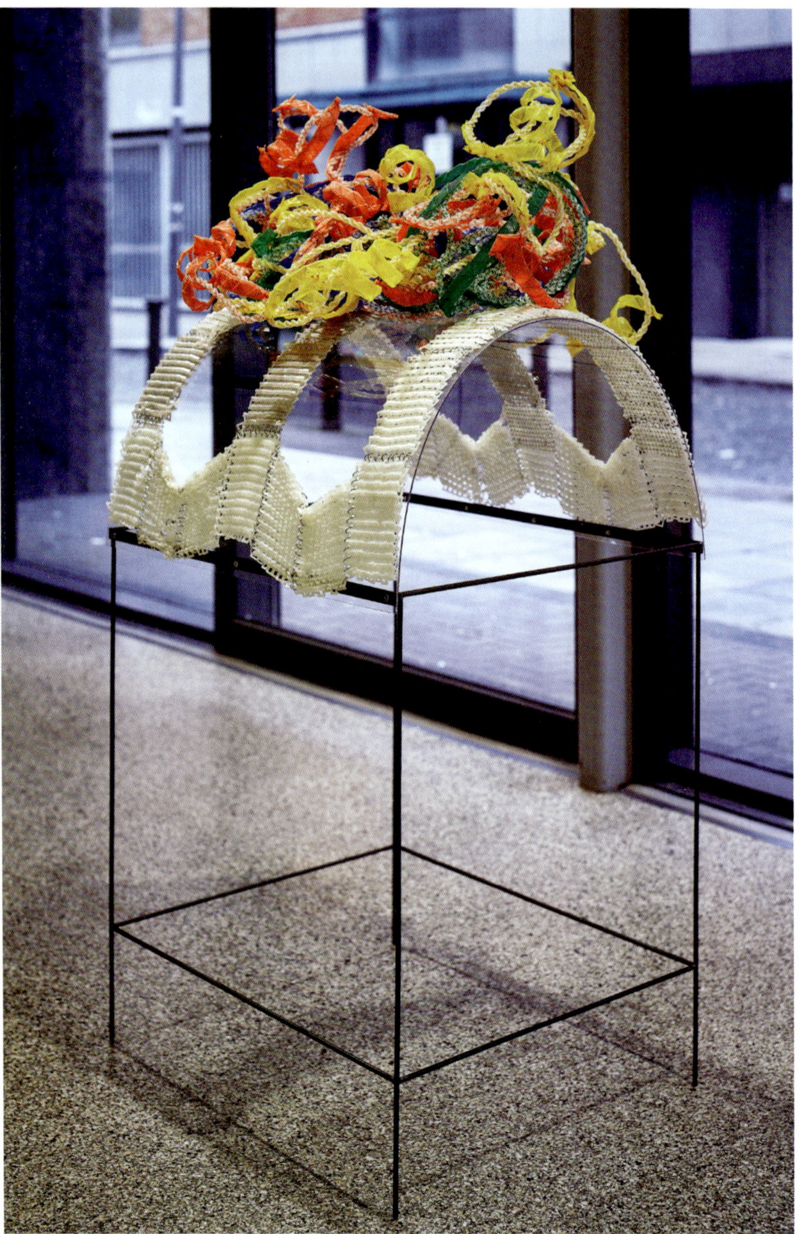

Maria McKinney (Irish), *Myostatin, Double Muscle* sculpture and harness, 2016, semen straws, wire, cable ties, PLA (3D-printed chain mail) non-slip mat, metal rings. Photograph by Ros Kavanagh.

Double Muscle

This Belgian Blue bull is wearing a specially fitted, brightly colored semen straw sculpture. The sculpture is displayed with the film *Double Muscle*, part of the *Sire* series. It is based on the myostatin gene, which is responsible for muscle growth regulation. Through 150 years of line breeding, Belgian farmers managed to manipulate this gene to achieve the "double muscle" Belgian Blue breed. Seeing the bull wearing McKinney's sculpture brings the energy of narrative and the specificity of use to interpretations of the sculpture. This contrasts with the presence of the sculpture itself. Propped on its wire stand, the semen straw sculpture brings the materiality of animal breeding practice into the gallery.

These works visualize genetic changes by pairing images of animals, whose bodies are themselves agri-*cultural* products, with woven sculptures to evoke the history of fertility handicrafts and gesture at the history of these interventions. McKinney explains: "The body of work *Sire* is proposed as a rephrasing of what was once intangible. Now we not only understand these formerly mysterious processes of propagation, but also manipulate them to our own ends."

Sire (pages 90–91)

The photographs comprising the series, *Sire* show cattle wearing specially designed sculptures made of semen straws, a device used since the 1960s to collect and store bovine sperm for artificial insemination. Visitors are offered the opportunity to think in specific terms about the ways humans have shaped nature. In these portraits, informed by pagan rituals and contemporary biotechnology, Ireland-based artist McKinney reflects on our relationships with animals through agriculture

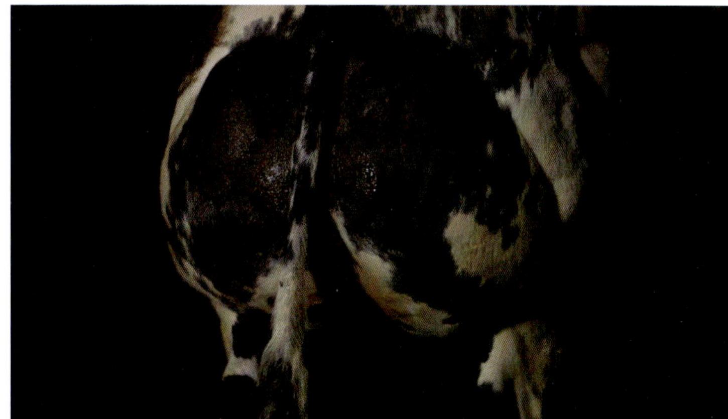

over time. In pre-Christian Europe, where people annually performed customs in relation to the reaping and sowing of the harvest, part of this practice involved making a corn dolly—a symbol meant to enable fertility through the intricate handcraft of binding straw with the final sheaf of that year's crop. This practice was the basis for the semen straw weaving that makes up McKinney's sculptures.

In contemporary society, genomics has given humans the ability to scientifically influence how nature behaves in future generations of animal and plant species. The emergence of bioinformatics has allowed scientists to direct breeding strategies with the objective of achieving more physically healthy and commercially productive animals. Through McKinney's sculptures, she visualizes the intangible genetic interventions and genetic structures now coded into the bodies of these animals.

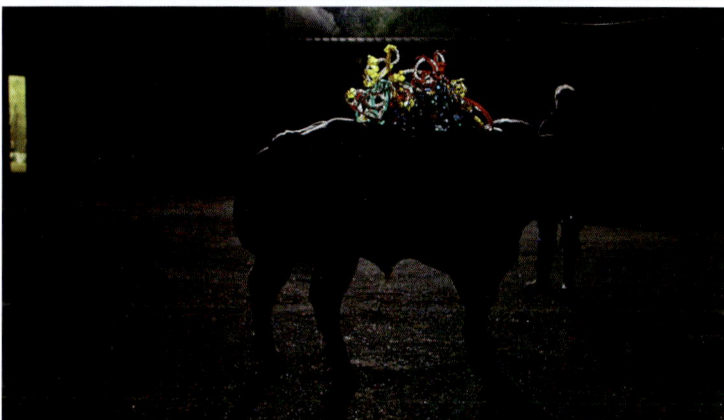

To create *Longevity/Apoptosome, Black Water Lad (HE2067)* and *Reproduction/Chromasome, Templemichael Zebo (FR2279)*, McKinney collaborated with Dovea Genetics, a farm with ninety bulls standing at stud producing semen in a controlled environment. Her scientific collaborators were quantitative geneticist Donagh Berry (The Agriculture and Food Development Authority of the Republic of Ireland), and genome biologist David MacHugh and Head of Veterinary Clinical Studies Michael Doherty (both University College Dublin). The work was realized in consultation with a veterinarian through close work with the animals' handlers to ensure they were not distressed while making the work.

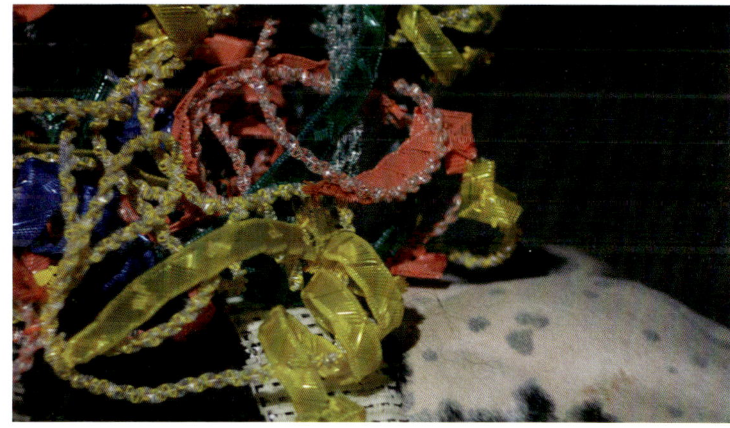

Maria McKinney (Irish), stills from *Double Muscle*, 2016, HD video, silent, 11:09. Courtesy of the artist. *Double Muscle* was made possible with support from Culture Ireland / Cultúr Éireann.

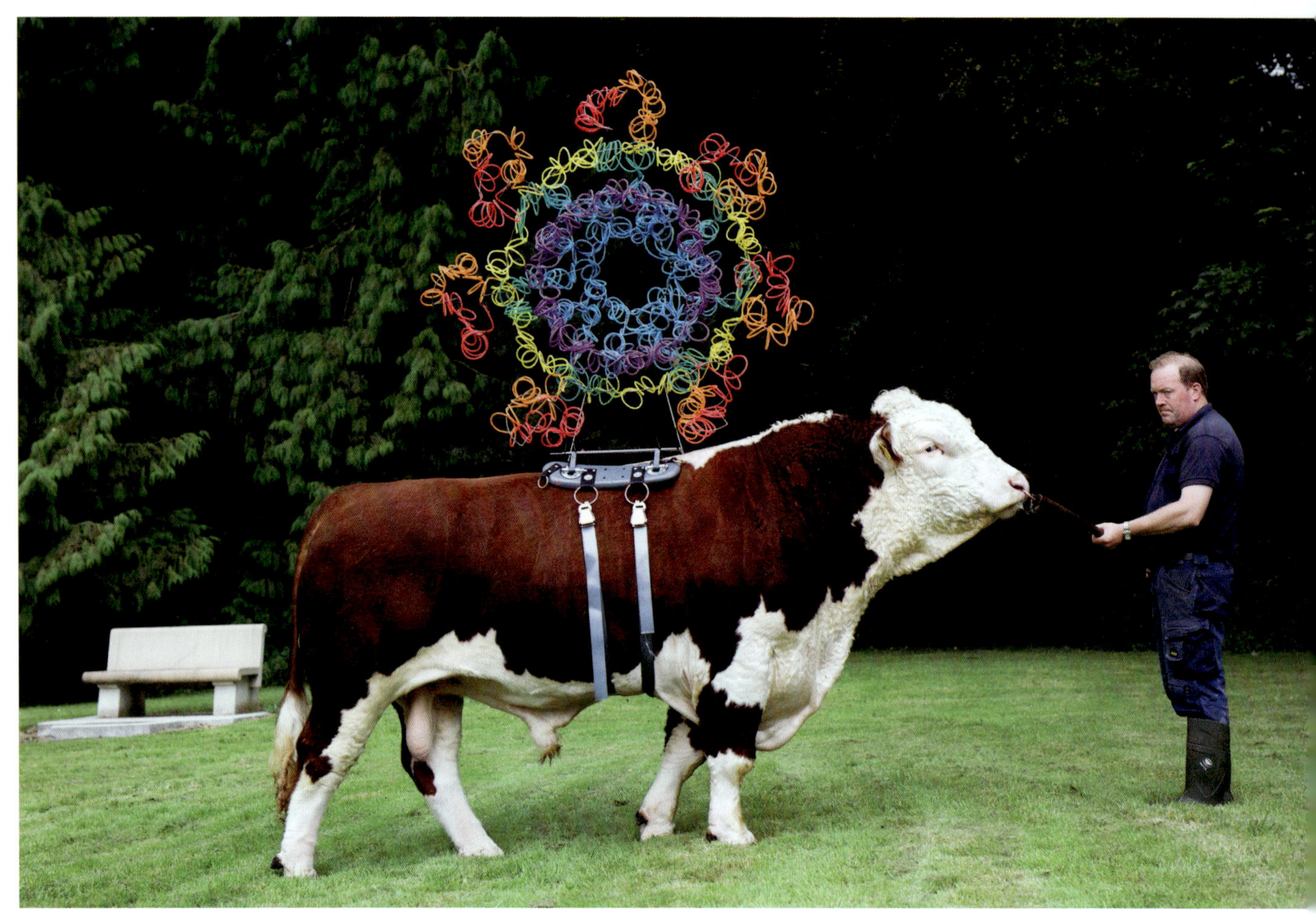

Maria McKinney (Irish), *Longevity/Apoptosome, Black Water Lad (HE2067)*, from the series, *Sire*, 2016, archival pigment print, 49 x 88 in. (125 x 225 cm). *Sire* was made possible with support from Culture Ireland / Cultúr Éireann.

In *Longevity/Apoptosome, Black Water Lad (HE2067)*, the structure of the sculpture is based on an apoptosome—a large protein molecule involved in programmed cell death within an organism in response to internal or external stimuli. For example, as a human fetus is developing in the womb, it changes from a ball of cells into a fully formed organism. At one point, a paddle-like extremity that will eventually become a hand requires the cells between the soon-to-be fingers to die in order to allow the organism to fully develop. The apoptosome is released to target these cells and tell them to expire.

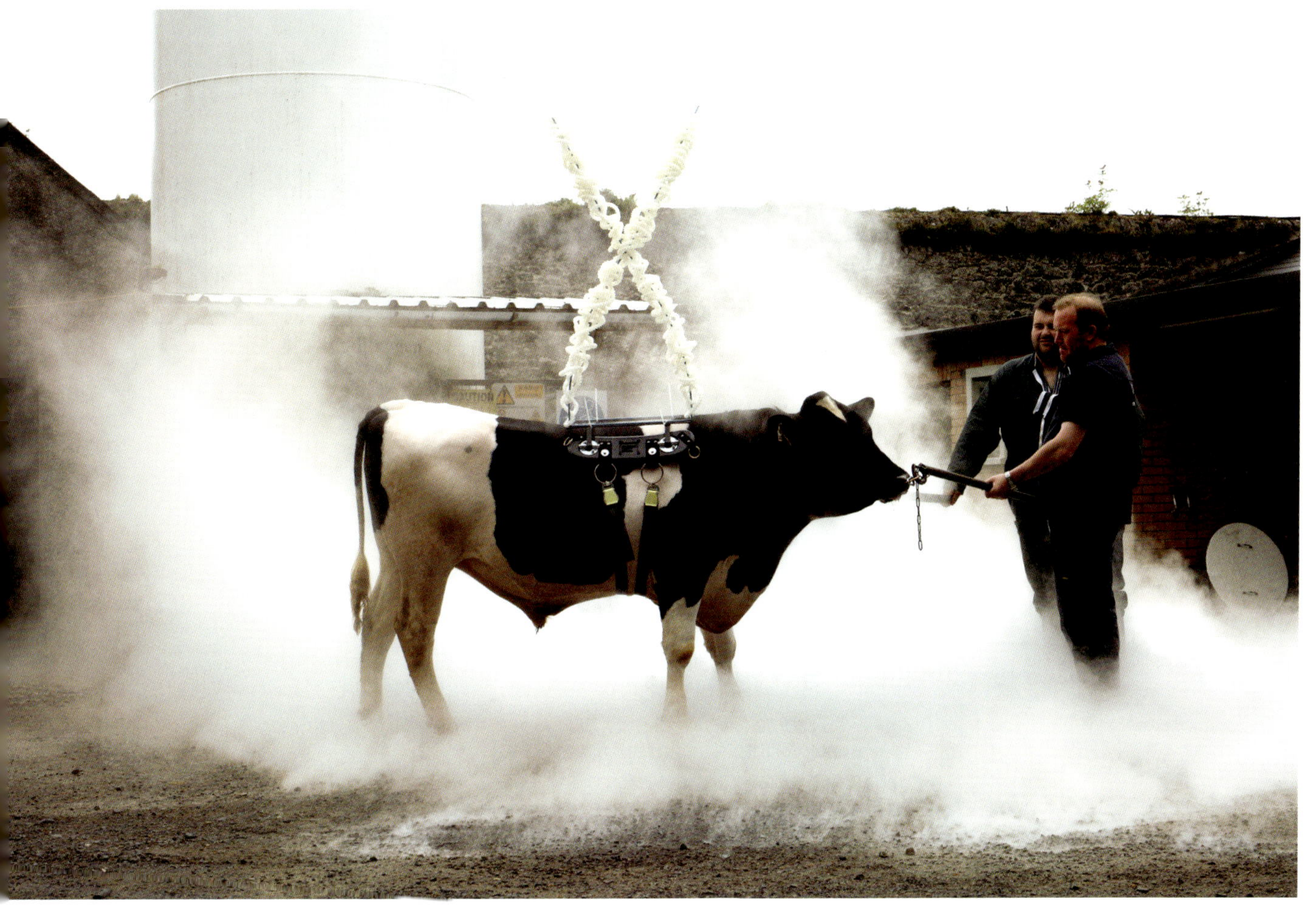

Reproduction/Chromosome, Templemichael Zebo (FR2279) makes reference to the X chromosome, one of the two sex-determining chromosomes in mammals (X for female and Y for male). Embedded within the spiraling DNA strand in this sculpture are tiny blue/red and green/yellow pairs of beads through which McKinney intended to show scientists looking at specific points of interest within the genome, rather than the entire genome sequence, to make changes to improve livestock commercially. The mist seen in this image is rapidly-evaporating liquid nitrogen that is used to preserve the collected semen. The straws are kept frozen right up until a moment before insemination. This is possible by transporting the straws in small mobile vats, which the AI technician regularly tops off with liquid nitrogen.

Maria McKinney (Irish),
*Reproduction/Chromosome,
Templemichael Zebo (FR2279)*,
from the series, *Sire*, 2016,
archival pigment print,
49 x 88 in. (125 x 225 cm).
Courtesy of the artist.

Terra Et Venti

Joel Ong's *Terra Et Venti* is a speculative research project that explores the role that synthetic biology may play in planetary-scale geoengineering and weather modification practices in the future. This artwork builds on the tradition of treating the genetic sequences as a medium for artistic expression through a multi-modal installation.

Pseudomonas syringae, a plant pathogen, is involved in atmospheric biological ice nucleation and the formation of clouds. The bacteria, which are ubiquitous in the soil, on plants, and in the air, travel freely on planetary circulation systems and are literally rainmakers. The bacteria expresses a protein on its surface that encourages an orderly arrangement of water molecules. That in turn acts as a nucleation site, stimulating the formation of ice at temperatures far higher than those normally required. Scientists have studied microorganisms found in precipitation since the 1960s. Research presented to the American Society for Microbiology suggested that the bacteria may have evolved to use the water cycle to facilitate their own dispersal.[1] These bacteria have even been found in hailstones, suggesting further association with the earth's hydrological cycle. *P. syringae* also has commercial applications as part of the mixture added to snow machines.

In *Terra Et Venti*, the ice-nucleation activity of the bacteria is simulated with parametric speakers tracing lines across the space as a digital version of a cloud is created in real time. The computational system presented in the gallery generates text for insertion into the genome of a specific bacteria. In addition, along with Natalie Plociennik, Ong created renderings of the biological processes of the *P. syringae.* Ong's research was supported through a residency in microbiology at the interstitial ecologies of soil and wind at the Coalesce Centre for Biological Art.

1. Palmer, Jason. *BBC News.* "Bacteria-rich hailstones add to 'bioprecipitation' idea." Aired May 25, 2011, on BBC.

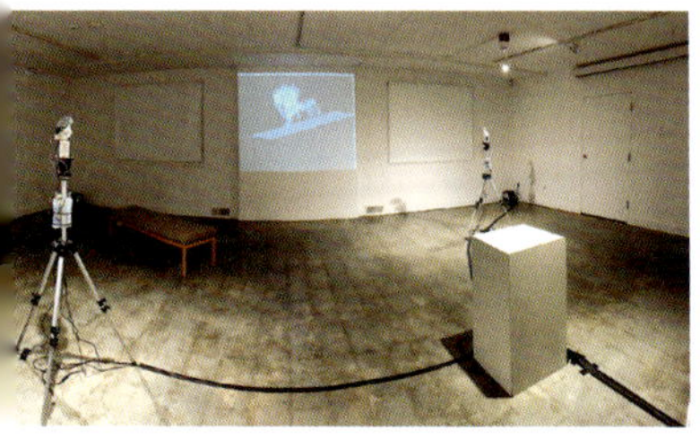

ABOVE: *Terra Et Venti*, installation view.

OPPOSITE: Joel Ong (Singaporean, lives in Toronto), *Terra Et Venti*, artist rendering of *Pseudomonas syringae* ice-nucleation process, 2019, digital prints, 24 x 36 in. (61 x 91 cm). Computer visualization by Natalie Plociennik. Courtesy of the artist.

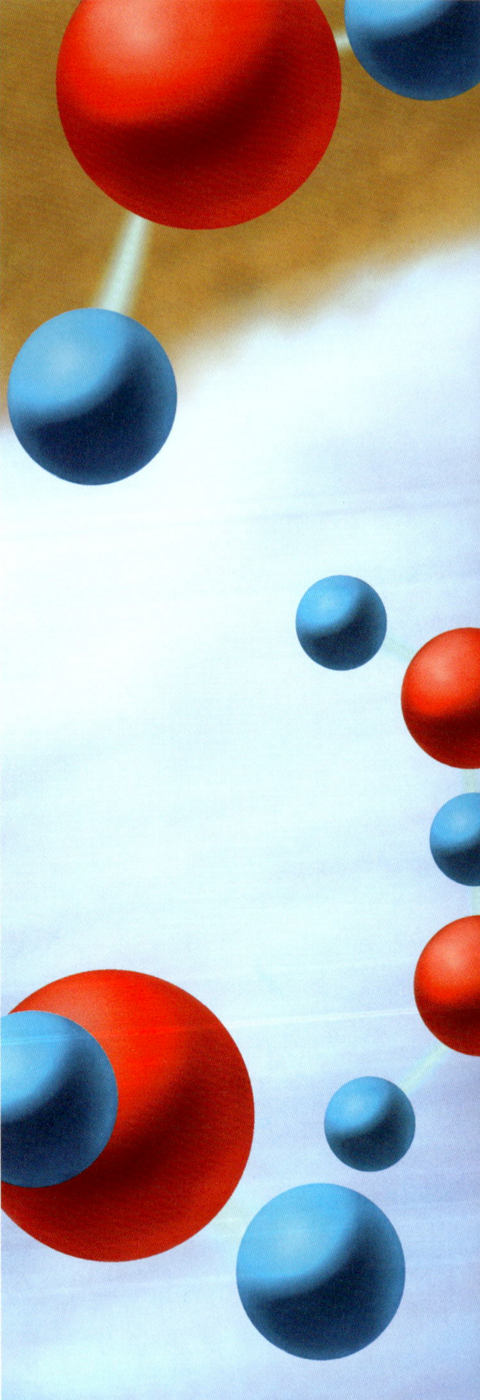

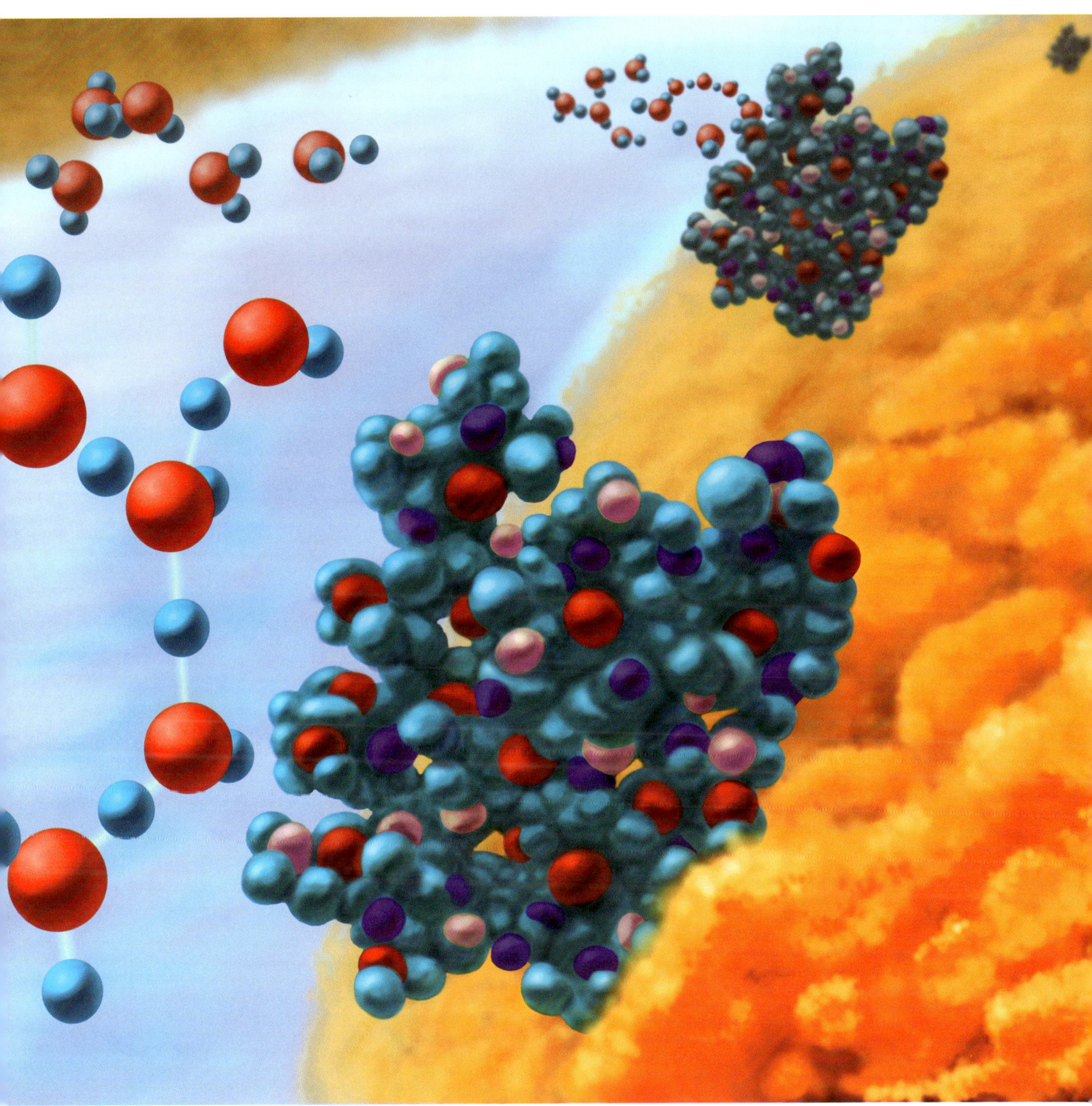

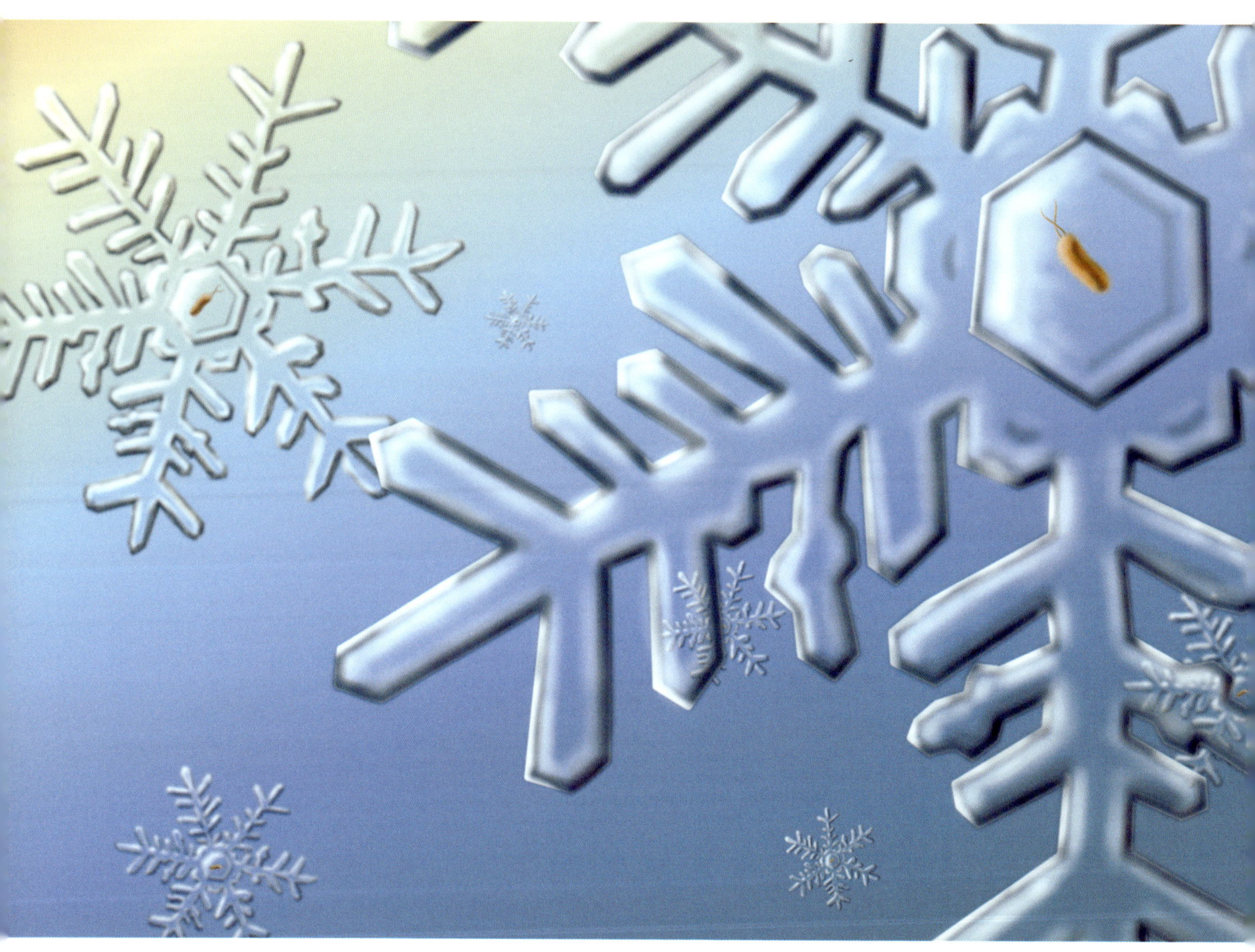

Joel Ong (Singaporean, lives in Toronto), *Terra Et Venti*, artist rendering of *Pseudomonas syringae* ice-nucleation process, 2019, digital prints, 24 x 36 in. (61 x 91 cm). Computer visualization by Natalie Plociennik. Courtesy of the artist.

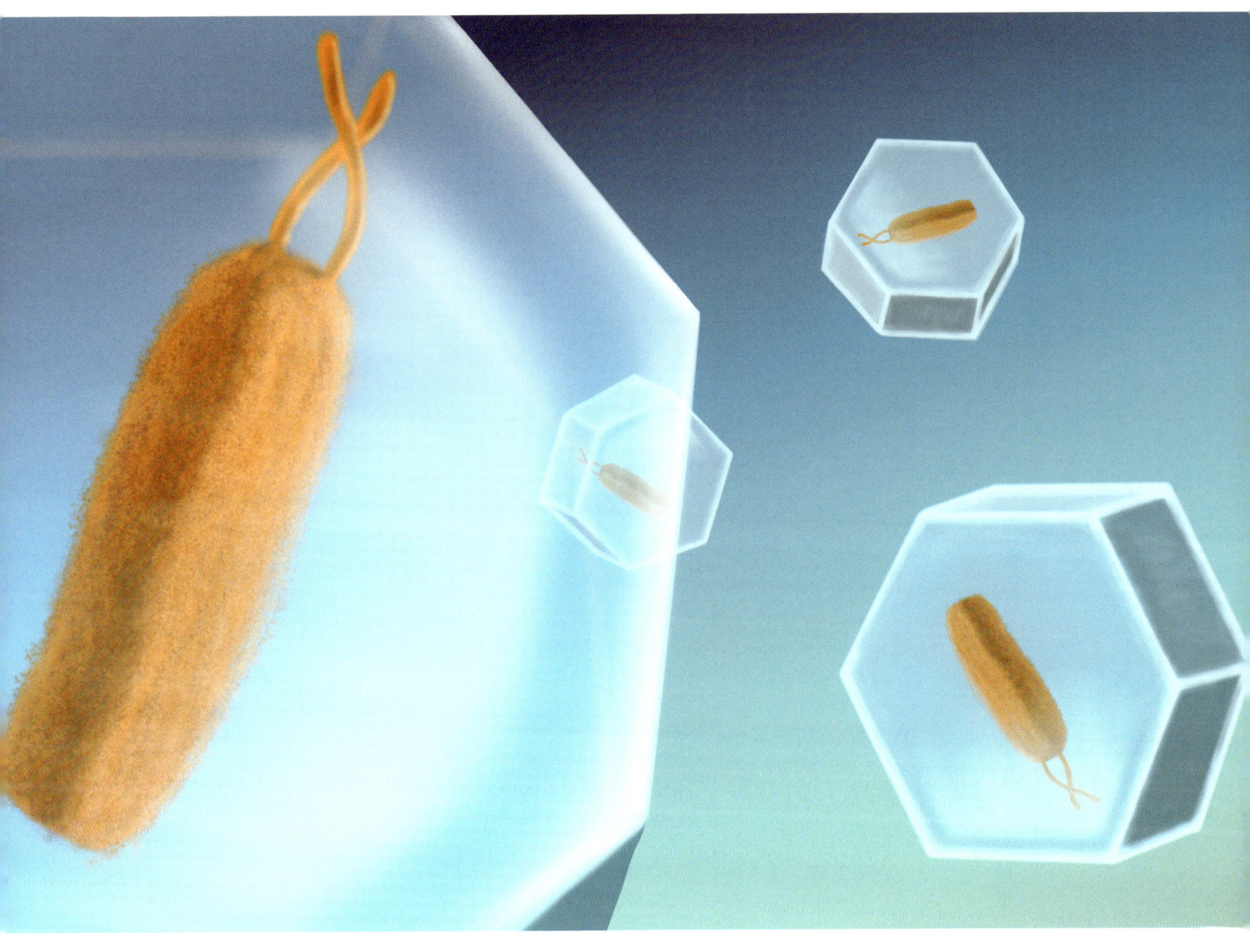

RICHARD PELL

The Mermaid De-Extinction Project

The mythological mermaid as we know it today is the result of an evolutionary process of conflicting and contradictory cultural forces. In this artwork, Pell presents a brief survey of mermaid sightings that have occurred within the rational view of science during the last three hundred years, based on the research of Vaughn Scribner, who is in the final stages of publishing a human history of mermaid sightings.

Anchoring the survey are the physical bodies of two kinds of mermaids. One is believed to be the mermaid specimen that was exhibited in Pittsburgh in 1832, the other is an anonymous submission purporting to house the partial DNA sequence of a mermaid. Attempts to evaluate the veracity of the mermaid genome have thus far remained elusive, as costs associated with synthesizing the actual DNA molecules of the sequence currently run into the hundreds of millions of dollars.

The Mermaid De-Extinction Project presumes to bring the Feejee mermaids of the nineteenth century into the twenty-first. However, rather than visually creating a mermaid, this project is aimed at creating DNA that genetically resembles a mermaid. The DNA sequence is stored on a small computer that is suspended in a glass vessel filled with fluid, akin to a mermaid habitat.

The title of the work invokes the research on de-extinction that purports to bring animals like the passenger pigeon and woolly mammoth back from extinction through gene sequence recreation. Opponents of de-extinction work have argued that species do not exist without their environments and ecological niches, including accompanying microorganisms that enable their biological processes and that, even if it were technically possible, the resources expended in these efforts would be better spent attempting to save today's endangered species. This critical artwork raises questions about what our society values as a biotechnology investment and the ways that our cultures and beliefs are enacted through genetic manipulation.

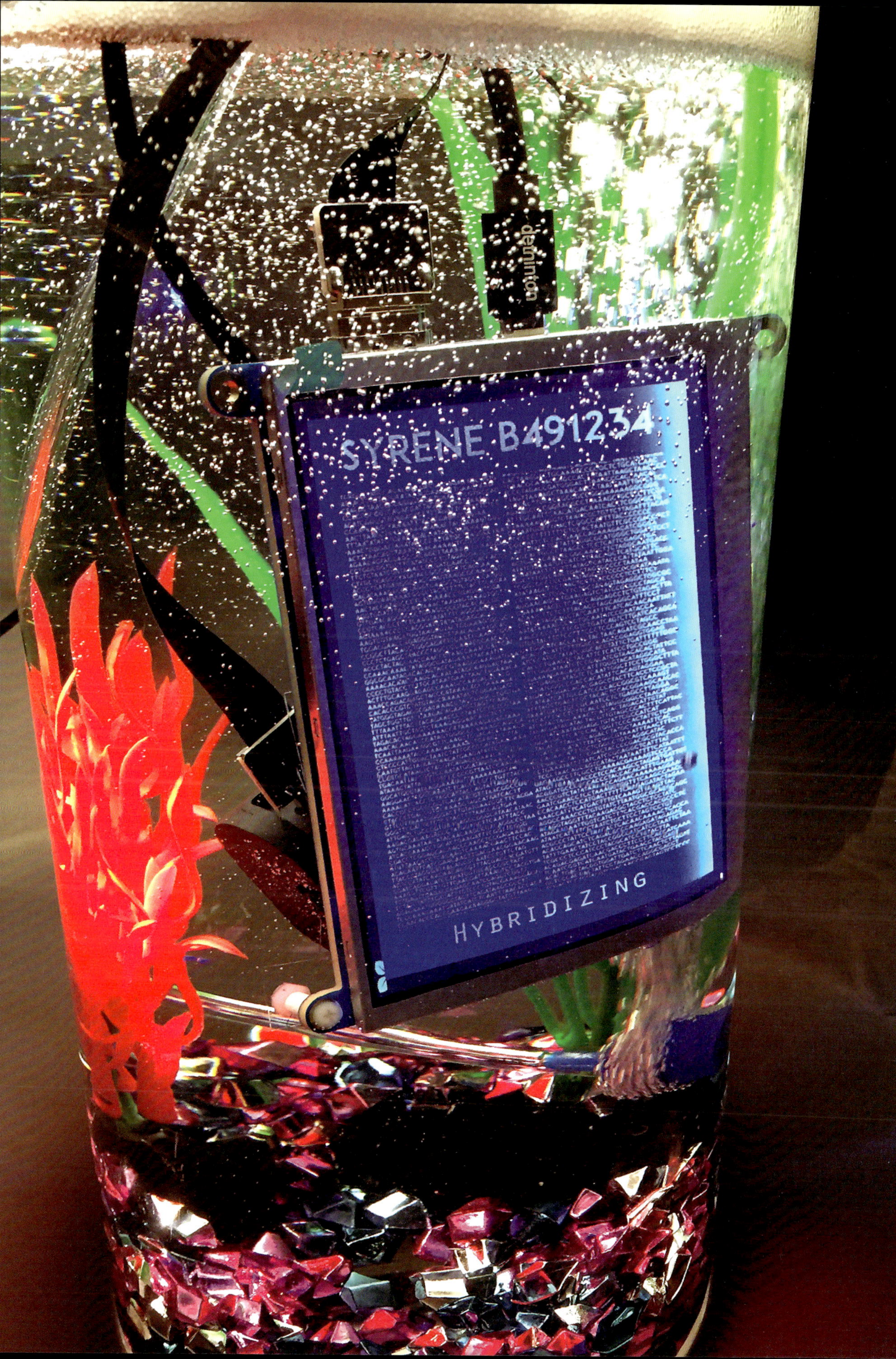

definition
SYRENE B491234
HYBRIDIZING

During the summer of 2018, I presented the concept of the Mermaid De-Extinction Project, including the accompanying essay, at two conferences: Google's SciFOO and the University of Minnesota's Genome Engineering. I was hoping to find researchers willing to comment on the record regarding the plausibility of creating a mermaid or mermaid-like creature from the ground up using genomic engineering. Reception was lukewarm.

However, several days after my presentation at Google X Headquarters, I received an email that I nearly disregarded as spam, but for one detail that caught my eye. The email included the subject line "Anthemoessa." It was just a conspicuous-looking word that looked kind of Greek. The body of the email contained one line of Greek and a link. While treating it as somewhat radioactive spam that had somehow bypassed my spam filter, I nonetheless copied and pasted the subject line into Google, thinking I might find other people receiving the same spam.

```
From: anthemoessa
  <anthemoessa@protonmail.
  com>
Subject: Για την προσοχή
  σας
Date: July 2, 2018 at
  4:24:14 PM EDT
To: "info@postnatural.org"
  <info@postnatural.org>
Reply-To: anthemoessa
  <anthemoessa@protonmail.
  com>
Λάβετε υπόψη: αυτός ο
  σύνδεσμος θα λειτουργεί
  μόνο μία φορά. Θα
  εκπνεύσει αυτή την ώρα
  αύριο.
```

It turns out Anthemoessa is one of several islands in Greek mythology that is cited as the origin of

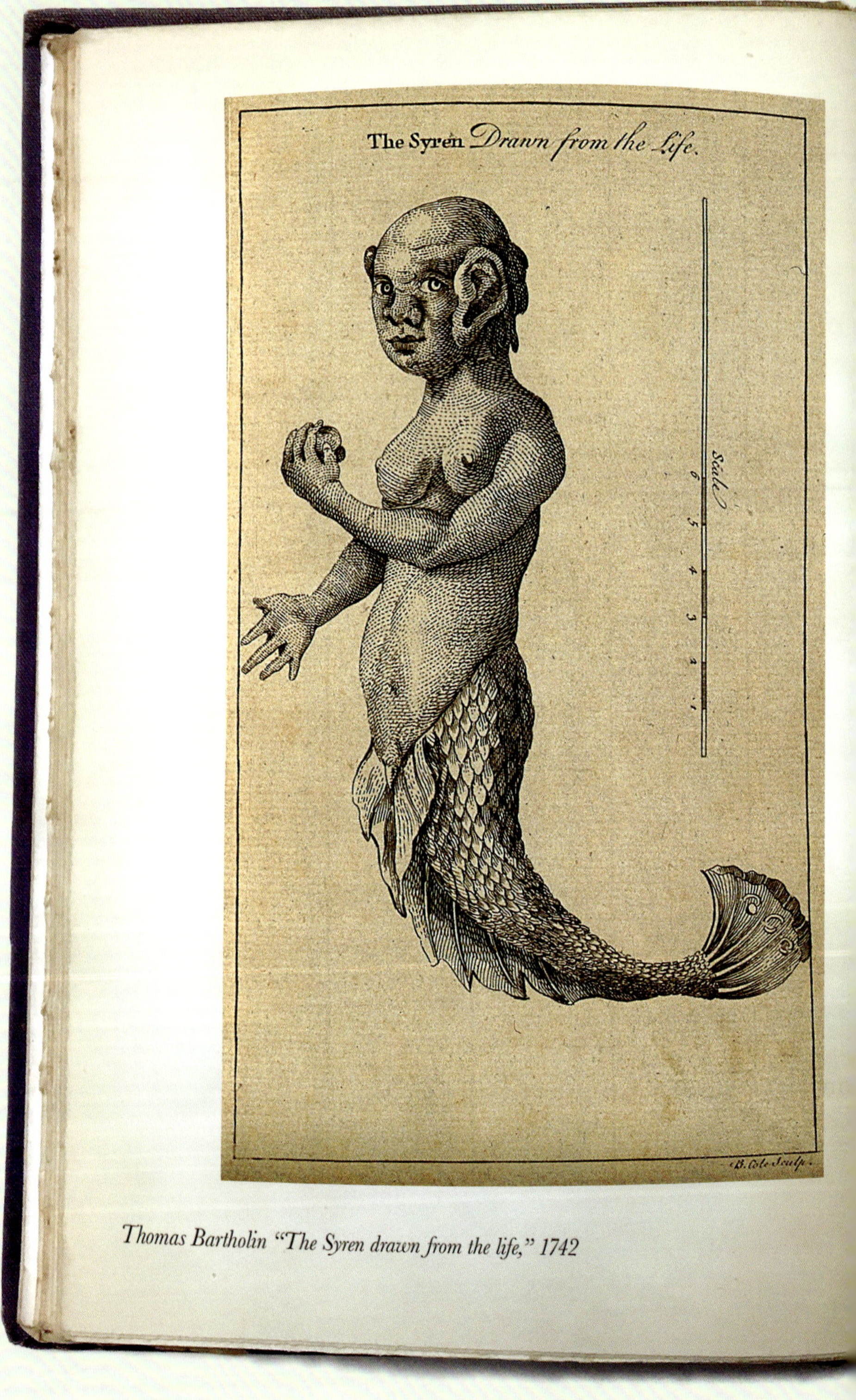

Thomas Bartholin "The Syren drawn from the life," 1742

ON MERMAID DE-EXTINCTION

RICHARD PELL

Breeding mermaids

Stories of intelligent human-fish hybrids that occupy the seas have existed in the deep mythological mind of humans from cultures across the globe. These beings often occupy the far reaches of the water, calling sailors to venture further out in stormy weather. Through the male sailors' gaze, mermaids provided seductive reasons to explore the edge of the map, as well as a cautionary tale for those who might be so inclined. It often ended badly for them.

In science, there is a similar tension between the driving force of the pursuit of knowledge and the dangers of falling in love with one's own hypotheses. Despite best attempts at creating a rational process for generating repeatable and falsifiable results, scientific curiosity is often propelled and humbled by grand and fallible human desires.

The mermaid myth itself is a hybrid of many mythological narratives, fusing together Greek Homerian sirens

mermaids. Okay, now you've got my attention. I copied and pasted the Greek line from the body of the mail into Google Translate and got this chestnut: "Note: this link will only work once. It will expire this time tomorrow."

At this point, I felt like I was being personally challenged to click on the shadiest-looking link I've ever received in an unsolicited email. The kind of link that humiliates you, then implicates you in an unspeakable crime before wiping out your life savings. A life-ruining link.

It looked like this: `https://send.firefox.com/download/6d-20cf8b53/#C5qiYtf _ 9nzMt-jUx9P6GvA`

Would you click on that? Well I did.

Here's what I got back:


```
SYR10518 Syrene bartol MT
TTTTTCTCCACTAAAAAAGGAAGGAATCGAACCTCCTAAAGCTG-
GTTTCAAGCCAACCCCACAACCTCCATGACTTTTTCAAGAGA-
TACTAGAAAAACCATTTCATGACTTTGTCAAAGTTAAGTTACAGGC-
CAAACCCTGTGTATCTTAATGGCGCACGCAGCACAGGTAGGTTTA-
CAAGACGCTACCTCTCCTATCATAGAAGAATTGGTCATCTTTCACGAC-
CACGCCCTCATAATCATTTTCCTAATCTGCTTCCTAGTCCTGTACGC-
CCTATTCCTAACACTCACAACAAAACTCACCAACACCAGCATCTCAGAC-
GCCCAAGAGATAGAGACTATTTGAACTATCCTACCGGCCATCATCCTA-
ATTCTAATCGCCCTCCCATCCCTACGCATCCTCTACTTAACAGAC-
GAGATCAACGACCCTTCCTTCACCATCAAATCAATCGGTCATCAATGA-
TACTGAACCTACGAGTACACTGACTACGGTGGATTGATCTTCAACTCT-
TACATGCTCCCACCAGTATTCCTAGAACCAGGCGACCTTCGACTCCTC-
GACGTCGACAACCGAGTAGTCCTCCCAGTCGAAGCTCCCGTTCGCATA-
ATAATCACATCCCAAGACGTCTTACACTCATGAACTGTACCCTCACTAG-
GCCTGAAAACGGACGCAATCCCCGGACGCCTAAACCAAACCACAT-
TCACTGCCACGCGACCAGGAGTGTACTATGGCCAATGCTCAGAAATCT-
GTGGAGCTAACCACAGCTTTATGCCTATCGTCCTAGAACTAATC-
CCCCTAAAAATCTTCGAAATAGGGCCCGTATTCACTTTATAACTTC-
CCCCACCCCCACAACCCATGCTAGAATGGCACATCCCTCACAACTAG-
GATTCCAAGACGCGGCCTCCCCTGTAATAGAAGAACTTCTTCATTTC-
CACGACCACGCTCTTATGATTGTTCTTCTTATCAGCACACTAGT-
GCTTTATATCATCGTAGCAATAGTCTCTACTAAACTTACTAATATG-
TATATCCTTGATTCTCAAGAAATCGAGATCGTTTGGACTGTCCTCCCAG-
CAGTTATCCTTATTCTCATCGCTCTCCCTTCCCTCCGAATTCTCTATCT-
TATGGACGAAATTAACGACCCCCACCTTACTATTAAAGCAATAGGCCAC-
CAATGATATTGAAGCTATGAATATACCGACTACGAAGATTTAGGCTTT-
GACTCTTACATAGTCCCCACTCAAGATTTAGTGCCAGGCCAATTC-
CCGTCTTCTAGAGACAGATCATCGAATAGTTGTCCCTGTAGAATC-
CCCAATCCGAGTTCTCGTCTCAGCTGAAGACGTCCTTCACTCCTGAGC-
CGTTCCTTCTTTAGGTGTAAAGATAGACGCAGTTCCAGGACGATTAAAC-
CAAACAGCCTTTATTGCCTCTCGACCTGGAGTATTCTACGGACAAT-
GTTCTGAGATCTGCGGGGCTAACCATAGCTTCATACCTATCGTTGTT-
GAAGCGGTACCCCTAGAACACTTCGAGAAATGATCCACTATGATACTT-
GAAGATGCCTCACTAAGAAGCTAAATCGGGAATAGCGTTAGCCTTTTA-
AGCTAAAGATTGGTGGCCCCAACCACCCCTAGTGACATGCCCCAACT-
CAACCCCGCCCCTGATTTGCTATTTTAGTATTCTCGTGACTG-
GTTTTCCTAACTGTTATTCCCCAAAAGTCCTTGGCCACACTTTCA-
CAAATGAGCCTACCTCACAAGCACTGAAAAAGCTAAGCCCGAACCCT-
GAAACTGACCATGACACTAAGCTTCTTCGACCAATTTATGAGCCCCA-
CATACCTAGGTATCCCACTTATCGCCGTAGCATTAACCCTCCCATGAAT-
TCTTTTCCCTACCCCCTCTGCCCGATGATTAAACAACCGCCTAATTAC-
CCTGCAAGGGTGGTTCATCAACCGATTTACCCAGCAACTTCTTTTAC-
CGCTAAATCTAGGCGGTCACAAGTGAGCAGCTCTACTAACTTCCCTCAT-
ACTATTTCTTATTACCCTAAATATACTTGGCCTACTTCCATATACAT-
TCACCCCGACCACACAGCTCTCCCTAAATATGGGCCTCGCAGTCCCACT-
GTGGCTTGCTACAGTAATTATCGGCATACGAAACCAACCTACGGCCGC-
CCTCGGCCATTTATTGCCTGAAGGAACCCCCGTTCCACTGATCCCAG-
TACTGATCATTATCGAAACAATTAGCCTTTTTATCCGCCCCGCCCTTGG-
CGTACGACTTACAGCCAATCTCACAGCAGGCCACCAACTAATTGCTA-
CAGCAGCCTTTGTTCTTCTACCTATAATACCTACAGTAGCAATCCTA-
ACTTCTATTGTCCTCTTTCTACTCACCCTTCTCGAAATCGCCGTAGC-
CATGATTCAAGCCTACGTTTTTGTCTTACTCCTAAGCCTCTATTTA-
CAAGAAAACGTTTAATGGCACACCAAGCACACGCATACCACATGGTT-
GACCCAAGCCCCTGACCTCTGACCGGCGCAATTGCCGCCCTTTTACTTA-
```

(human-bird) and Sumerian goat-fish gods along with myriad pagan and Christian characters. The form which mermaids take often reflects the assumptions, desires, and fears of a particular time and place. When it serves the storyteller, they are voluptuous femmes fatales of the sea, and other times hideous creatures bearing only a passing resemblance to humans.

Mermaids seem to know things that we don't, often literally appearing at the outer edge of the map. They are most likely to be seen when our human capacity to act on the world outpaces our understanding of it. Their legendarily sweet songs beckoned sailors to sail further out to sea, ultimately entrapping them in a paradoxical embrace that ended in tragedy. Mermaids are at home precisely where we are the most out of our element.

Stories of mermaids provide not only a colorful metaphor for the inherent risks of scientific exploration, they have also been the subject of scientific inquiry. During the eighteenth century, mermaid belief was trending, with a growing consensus around the credulity of mermaid sightings. In the essay "Such Monsters Do Exist in Nature: Mermaids, Tritons, and the Science of Wonder in Eighteenth-Century Europe," historian Dr. Vaughn Scribner points out ". . . well-respected philosophers such as Carl Linnaeus, Cotton Mather, Benoit de Maillett, Peter Collinson, Erik Pontoppidan, Jacques-Fabien Gautier, François Valentijn, and Louis Renard transformed mermaids and tritons from creatures of lore into specimens worthy of in-depth scientific investigation."

The practice of science is a human invention, and mermaids have an intrinsic role to play. They are evidence of our humanness. Not a bug, but a feature.

CATCAGGCACTGCAGTCTGATTCCATTTCCACTCGCTCACACTTCTTACCTTAGGTAACATTCTCTTACTTCTAACCATATACCAATGATGGCGGGATATCATCCGAGAAGGTACCTTTCAAGGACACCACACGCCCCCAGTCCAAAAAGGGCTACGATATGGCATAATCTTATTTATTACCTCCGAGGTATTCTT
CACTATCTTACTGGGATTTTACTTCACTTTCCTACAAGGTATAGAATACTACGAAGCCCCATTTACAATCGCTGACGGCGTATACGGCTCTACTTTCTTTGTCGCTACAGGATTCCATGGCCTACACGTAATTATTGGCTCTACCTTTCTGGCCGTTTGCCTTCTACGACAAGTTCAATACCACTTTACATCTGAA
TACTAGCCACTATTTCTTTCTGATTACCACAAATCTCCCCAGACGCAGAGAAGTTATCCCCCTACGAATGTGGATTTGACCCCTTAGGGTCCGCCCGCCTGCCCTTCTCCTTACGCTTCTTTCTAATCGCGATCTTATTCCTCCTATTTGATCTAGAAATCGCCCTCCTTTTGCCCCTACCTTGAGGGGATCAACTC
GGCTTATAGGACTCGCGTTTCACCGCACCCACCTTCTCTCAGCCCTTCTATGCCTAGAAGGAATAATACTCTCTCTATTCATCGCCCTCTCCCTCTGAGCCCTCCAAATGGAAGCGACTGGCTACTCAGTGGCCCCGATACTTCTCCTAGCGTTCTCAGCCTGTGAAGCCAGCGCAGGGTTAGCCCTACTAGTAGCA
TATTTAGCAACTGACCCCCTATCAACACCCCTGCTAGTATTAACCTGCTGACTACTTCCCCTTATAATTCTTGCTAGCCAAAGCCACCTCTCTCCTGAACCCTTAAATCGCCAGCGAGCCTACATCTCCCTCCTGGTCTCCCTTCAAACGTTTCTAGTATTAGCATTCGGGGCCACTGAAATTATCATATTTTACGT
TAAACTGTGATGAGCTGCCTGCCTTTTAGCCTTCCTTGTAAAAATACCCCTATACGGTGTTCACCTTTGACTCCCAAAAGCCCACGTAGAAGCTCCAATCGCCGGATCCATAATCCTAGCGGCTGTTCTCCTCAAGCTGGGAGGATACGGCATAATACGTATAATAGTTATACTAGACCCGTTAACCAAAGAACTGG
CCAATACTAGCTACGAACGCACCCACAGCCGAACCATACTACTTGCCCGAGGAATACAAATAATTCTCCCCTTAATAACCACTTGGTGATTTGTAGCTAGTTTAGCAAATCTGGCCCTCCCCCCTCTCCCCAACCTAATAGGAGAACTAATAATCATCACTTCTATATTTAACTGGTCGTATTGAACCCTTATTCT
CATTAGATTGTGATTCTAAAAATAGAGGTTAAAATCCTCTTATCCAC-
CAGTTAAATTCTGTGGTTCACTCGTGCTTCTAAAGGATAATAGCTCATC-
TATGCACCCGACTACACTCATCTTAAGCTCATCCCTTTTAATA-
CCCCCAACACAAAAACTGGGCCCTTACTCACGTAAAAACTGCTAT-
CAAGGAACCGAAACTATCGTGACTAACTGACAATGAATAAACACCA-
TATTTTTACCCCTATTGCCCTGTACGTAACCTGATCTATTCTAGAATTC-
TACCTCCTCCTCTTCCTAATCGCCATAATTATTTTAGTAACCGCCAA-
CATTTCTCCTCATTGGATGATGACACGGACGAGCTGACGCTAACA-
TATCCTAAGTATAGCCTGGTTCGCAACAAACCTAAACTCCTGAGAAAT-
TATAGGCCTCATTCTAGCCGCCACCGGCAAATCAGCGCAATTTG-
GCCCTACTACACTCCAGCACCATGGTCGTGGCGGGCATCTTCCTATTA-
GCTTATGCCTAGGAGCCCTAACTACCCTCTTCACCGCTACCTGCGCCCT-
CAACTAGGGCTTATAATAGTCACCATCGGACTTAATCAACCA-
TATACTTTTCCTATGCTCAGGCTCAATTATTCATAGTTTAAACGAT-
CATCCTCTTGCCTCACAATCGGAAGCCTTGCACTAACTGGCACCCCAT-
CACCTCCCACCTCAACGCCTGAGCCCTTACTCTTACCTTACTAGC-
CATAGGACACCCCGCTTTACGGCAACAGCCCCTGTTAATGAAAATAAC-
CGGGGCTTCTAATTACCTCAAACTTCCTACCCACCAACACCCCCG-
TATCTCGGGCCTTCTCATTGCATTAGAACTTGCGTCACTAACTAACAAA-
ACTGGGATTCTTCCCGCCATCATCCACCGATTGACCCCAAAGCTA-
GATTTGAGAAAGTAGGTCCGAAGGAATTATTTCAACTCACCTGCCTA-
ACCTCACCCTATTTTTCCTTTCAACAACTCTAGCTGTTCTATTAACAT-
CAACACCACAAAAAGTGTTAATAGGAGTACCCACGCGCACGCAATTA-
CCCACGCAATACAGAAAACTCCTTAAACTCGTCCACTGCTACCCATGAG-
CGTATATACCACCACATACCCTAAGACCGAACGATCCCCTCAAGACTC-
CATCCCCCCAAGTAAATCAAAAATAGTACTAAAGACAAGAAAGATC-
CAACCCCAAAGCAGCAAAGTAAGGTGCAGGGTTAGATGCAACAGCTA-
CATAATTCCTGCTCGGACTCTAACCGAAACTAATGACTTGAAAAAC-
CCACCCTCTCCTAAAAATCGCTAATGACGCACTAGTCGACCTCCCAG-
CCTATGTTTAGCTACCCAAATTCTTACCGGGGCTCTTCCTAGCCATGCAC-
[illegible]
CACCTCCCTTACACCGAGAAGACATCCGTGCAAATCGGGTCACCCT-
ACCCCAATAAAACTTAGAATTAAGTCAACAACCATTTTTCCACCT-
CAAGGGGAAGCTGAAAGAGAATTGAAATAACCCATTTAAGCCTA-
CACACCTGAGCAAAGAGAACTTTAGTTTAGGCCCCGAAACTAGAC-
CAAAAGAGTGGGACGAGCCCCGAGTAGAGGTGATAAACCTATCGAG-
GCTTTCTTAGGACCTTAAGGTAAAACTAATATTGTCCCAAAGAAACCAG-
TAACAGGCGGCTAAGGATCATAGTTCCAAGGTAACCTGTTACAGTGG-
CAAACCTCTTATCCTGATAAGAAATCCCACCCCCCTAACCGTACTAAG-
GAGTACAACTCTCTCCCAGCACATGTGTAAGTCGGACCGGACCCCCCAC-
CACCAAGAAAAACTACACCAACAAATCGTTACCCCCACACAGGAGTG-
CCTCGCCTGTTTACCAAAAACATCGCCTCTTGCAAATCAAACATAGAG-
GCGAAGGTAGCGCAATCACTTGTCTTTTAAATGAAGACCTGTATGAAT-
GATCTGCCCGTGCAGAAGCGGACATAAGCACATAAGACGAGAAGAC-
TAACAAGTAAAAACGCAGTAGACCCCTAGCCCATATGTCTTTGGTTGGG-
CCCCACCAGCCGAGAGCTACAGCTCTAAGCACCAGAATATCTGAC-
TAACAGCGCAATCCTCTCCCAGAGTCCCTATCGACGAGGGGGTTTAC-
GTTCGTTTGTTCAACGATTAAAGTCCTACGTGATCTGAGTTCAGACCG-
GAAAGGACCGGAAAGAAGGGGCCCATGCTTGAGGCACGCCCCAC-
CAAGATTGCCTAAAAGAACGGCGCGCTAAGGTGGCAGAGCCCGGTA-
TAGCTATGATTACCCTAATTACCCACGTTATTAATCCACTAGCATA-
GAAAAGTCCTTGGGTACATGCAACTCCGAAAAGGGCCCAACATCGTCG-
TAAAGAAACGGTTCGACCTTCCACCTCTTCACCCTTTCTATTTCTCGC-
ACCTATTCCTTACCCTGTTACAGATCTTAACCTCGGAGTACTATTTG-
GCATCAAACTCCAAATACGCTTTAATTGGCGAACTCCGGGCAGTGGCA-
ATTATCATCACGGGAGGATTTACTCTTCAAACCTTCAACGTAGC-
CATATGATACATTTCTACCCTCGCGGAGACAAACCGTGCACCCTTT-
TAGAATATGCTGGAGGGCCCTTTGCCCTATTTTTCCTAGCCGAATAT-
CATCCCACATCCCTGCTTTCCCTGAACTAACTGCCCTAAACCTAATAAC-
CCGCGATTTCGGTATGATCAACTCATACATTTAGTTTG-
CACTTCCCATCGCACTAGCAGGCCTCCCCCCTCAGCTTTAGCCCG-
GGTTCAAGTCCCCTCAATTCTAGAGAGAAGGGGCTCGAACCCATCCT-
GTCAGCTAATTAAGCTTTCGGGCCCATACCCCGAATATGTTGGT-
TACTTTCTAGCCTAGGACTAGGCACAGTCCTCACCTTTGCCAGCTC-
TATCCCGATCATAGCGCAACAACACCACCCCCGAGCAATCGAAG-
ATCCTTTTTGCCAGCACCACCAACGCCTGACTAGTCGGGGAGT-
AGCCCTCGCCCTCAAACTTGGACTAGCACCCGTTCACTTCTGACTAC-
GACCTGACAAAAACTCGCACCCTTTGCACTTATAATTCAAGTAGC-
CACTTGTGGGAGGCTGAGGTGGACTTAATCAAACCCAACTACGTAAAAT-
CAATTCGCACCCTCTCTCACACTCCTCAGTCTCTCCCTGTATATCGT-
CATCAATACTCTCGCAACTTCATGAACTAAATCCCCGACCCTTGCCG-
CAGGCTTTATACCAAAATGACTTATTTTGCAAGAACTAACGAAACAG-
CCTTTACTTTTATCTACGACTCTGCTACGCCTTAACCCTCAC-
CAACTTTACCATAATTACCCTACCCCTTTCAATTACTACTATTATAGC-
TAATAAGGGCTTAGGATAGTACTTAGACCAAGAGCCTTCAAAGCTCTA-
CCACATCTTCTGAATGCAACCCAGACACTTTAATTAAGCTAAAG-
CAGCTAAGCGCTCTATCCAGCGAGCATCCATCTACTTTCCCCCGC-
CCTACTTCTTCAGATTTGCAATCTAACGTGTGGTACACCACAGGGCTT-

GCCTTCTACCACGCCAGCCTCGCCCCCACACCTGAATTAGGAGGTTGCTGACCCCCCGCAGGTATTACTACTCTAGACCCCTTTGAGGTACCCCTTCTTAATACTGCAGTCCTTCTAGCATCTGGTGTCACCGTAACATGAGCCCACCACAGCATCATAGAAGGTGAACGAAAACAAACCATTCAAGCTCTTACTCT-
GCTGCTGCCTGATATTGACACTTTGTAGACGTTGTATGGCTCTTCCTATACGTCTCTATTTACTGATGAGGCTCATAATCTTTCTAGTATTAATACGTATAAGTGACTTCCAATCACCCGGTCTTGGTTAAAATCCAAGGAAAGATAATGAATTTAATCACAACAATCATCACTATTACCATCACATTATCCGCAG-
CCATCTGATCCACTGCCGTTCTAGCCCTTCTTACTCTTGGCTTAATCTATGAATGAACCCAAGGAGGCTTAGAATGAGCCGAGTACGGAGTTAGTCCAAAACAAGACCCTTGATTTCGGCTCAAAAGACCATGGTTTAAGTCCATGACCGCCTTATGACACCAGTACACTTCAGCTTTACCTCAGCCTTTATTTTAG-
CAGACCGCCTCCAAAGCTTAAACCTCCTCCAATGTTAAAGATCCTCATCCCCACACTCATGCTTTTTCCAACGATCTGACTCAGCCCCGCGAAATGATTATGAACTACATCAATCGCCCAAAGTTTAATTATTGCCCTAGCAAGTTTATCCTGACTTAAATGATCGTCAGAAACCGGATGATCCTCCTCCAACCTC-
CTCCCCACCCTTATTATTATCACCCGATGAGGAAATCAAACTGAACGCCTCAATGCCGGTACCTACTTCTTATTTTATACCCTAGCTGGCTCCCTACCCCTCCTCGTGGCCCTGCTTCTTATACAAAACGACAACGGAACCCTATCTATGTTTACCCCTGCAGTATACGCAACCCCTACACCTTCTAACGTGAGGAGA-
GGCCTTGTGAGGTATCATTATAACAGGATCTATTTGCCTACGTCAAACAGACCTGAAATCACTAATCGCATACTCTTCAGTCGGCCACATAGGATTAGTCGCAGGGGGTATTTTAATTCAAACACCTTGAGGATTTACTGGTGCAATTATTGTCATAATCGCACACGGCCTTGCCTCCTCAGCGCTATTCTGCTTAG-
ATTACAGCAAGCTACTCCCTTTATCTGTTCTTAATAACTCAACGGGGACCCCTACCTTCCCATATTATTGCTCTTGAACCCACCCACACCCGAGAACACCTACTTATTATTCTGCACCTCATCCCAATTGTCCTTCTAATCCTAAAGCCTGAGCTCATGTGAGGCTGATGTTTCTGTAGATATAGTTTAACCAAGA-

Carl Linnaeus, Dissertation on Siren lacertina. 1766

> ...e non vi[rgines]... & alia infolitæ figuræ...
> jas & ...ora ejectam pro miraculo habebant.
> leis finubus exarata fronte, talem ho[minem]
> fuafuro. Homines primis tempori[bus]
> gantes in itinerariis fuis multa nobis
> a, inque hic SIRENES, a Græcis m[a]
> uas fedentes, virginibus fimiles,
> us & facie humana, binis brachiis
> ongiore, inferiori parte in pifcem
> ...in Hodæporico Indiæ Orien[talis]
> philolog. p. 520. Hift[or]. Barthol.

The emergence of mermaid science

With the advent of global commerce and scientific exploration, stories of mermaids came into contact not just with sailors, but with rationality itself. When the father of taxonomy, Carl Linnaeus, published his massive catalog of all the world's living things, *Systema Naturae* (1735), he included mermaids (*Syrene barthol*). In 1766, he co- published a treatise on mermaids and lobbied heavily for the Danish Royal Academy to fund an expedition to confirm their existence suggesting, "It could result in one of the biggest discoveries that the Academy could possibly achieve" (Carl Linneaus and Abraham Osterdam 1766; Linnaeus correspondence 1749). He assigned them the binomial title, *Syrene barthol*, named for Danish physician Thomas Bartholini who claimed to have performed an autopsy on a mermaid (Bartholin 1742). Benjamin Franklin reported on a mermaid sighting in his *Gentlemen's Quarterly* journal and Boston physician Cotton Mather was convinced of their existence by newly credible sightings (Franklin 1736, Mather

CGAGAGAAATCTGTTGATAACAGAGACTGCTAATCTTCTGCCCCCT-
CATTGGTCTTAGGAACCAAAACTCTTGGTGCAAATCCAAGTAGCAGC-
ATCTTCACACTTCTAATTTATCCTCTTATTACCACCCTCACCCCAAC-
CAAAATAGCCTTCCTAGTGAGCCTGCTCCCCCTTTTTGTCTTCCTAGAC-
CAACCTTTGACATTAACCTTAGCTTTAAATTTGACCACTACTCCAT-
GCATCCTGATATATACACGCCGACCCCAACATAAACCGATTCTTTAAG-
CAACATGTTCCAACTATTTATCGGCTGAGAGGGAGTCGGAATTATAT-
CAGCTGCTATACAAGCTGTAATTTACAACCGAGTAGGAGACATCGGACT-
TCAACAAATATTTGCCTCTTCAAAAGGACTTGACCTCACACTCCCTCT-
GACTTCACCCGTGACTTCCCTCCGCGATAGAGGGTCCTACGCCGGTATCT-
ATTCGACTCCACCCTCTAATAGAAGATAACCAAACAGCCTTAACCGTAT-
CACCCAAAATGACATCAAAAAAATTGTCGCATTCTCTACATCCAGC-
CAACTAGCCTTCCTCCACATCTGCACCCACGCATTCTTTAAAGC-
GAGCAAGACATTCGAAAAATAGGTGGTATACACAACCTCACCCCCTCTA-
TCTTAGCTGGGTTCTTCTCCAAAGACGCTATTATTGAAGCCTTAAA-
CACCTCATTTACTGCCATTTATAGCCTCCGAGTCATCTTTTTTGTCTC-
CCATCCGTAATTAACCCAATCAAGCGACTAGCCTGAGGAAGCATCATTG-
TAATAACCATGCCCACCCACTTAAAATTAGCCGCTCTCCTGGTTAC-
CAATTTAAACTACACCCAACCCTTACACTACATAACTTCTCCAACAT-
AACTTAACTTTAGGACAAACCATCGCCAGCCAAATGGTAGATCACACAT-
ATAGTCACAACAACAAGTAATATCCAACAAGGCATAATTAAAACAT-
TAACCTAAACTGCTCGAAGCGCCCCCCGACTCAATCCCCGTGTTAATTC-
ATATCCCCCTCCATGAGAGTATATCAATGCCACCCCACTTGTATC-
GTTTCATACCACCCACCCCAGAATAGACCTGCCACCAACACCACCCCCAC-
CGGAAAAGGCTCAGCAGCCAAAGCCGCTGAATAAGCAAATACCACAAG-
CCCCGTGACCCACCAAAACCCCACAACCCACACCTGCTGCTACAAC-
CAAGCCCTAAAACCAGCCCTAAAAGAAACAAAGACACAAGATAAGT-
CACCGTTGTTATTCAACTACAAGAACCTAATGGCCAACCTCCGAAAAAC-
CACCTTCTAATATCTCAGTCTGGTGAAACTTTGGCTCACTACTAGG-
TATACCTCCGACATTTCAACAGCTTTCTCCTCTGTTTGCCACATCTGC-
CATCTTTCTTTTTTATCTGTATTTATATACATATCGCCCGAGGACTTTAC-
TACTTTTACTTCTCACTATAATAACTGCCTTTGTAGGCTACGTCCTC-
CAAACCTCCTCTCAGCTGTACCATACGTAGGAGGCGCCCTAGTACAAT-
GATTTTTCGCCTTTCACTTCCTATTCCCCTTCGTCATTGCAGCCGCTAC-
CAGGGATTAACTCTGATGCTGATAAAATCTCATTCCACCCTTACTTCT-
ACATCCTTAGCTCTTTTTGCACCAAATCTCCTAGGGGACCCAGA-
CCGAATGATACTTCCTATTCGCTTACGCAATCCTACGATCCATCCCCAA-
GTTGTCCCCATCCTACACACTTCTAAACAACGAGGACTTACCTTTCGAC-
CACCTGAATCGGAGGCATACCTGTAGAACACCCCTTCATTATTATCGGA-
TAGCCGGCTGGGCCGAAATTAAAGCCCTCCAATGAGCCTGCCCTAG-
AAACCCTCCCTAGTGCTCAGAGAGAGGAGATTTTAACTCCCACCCTTA-
TATGTACAACTGTAAATGTTATAACTTGTAAACCCAATGTTATACTA-
GCTTGTGAGTAGTACATTATATGTATTATCAACATACGGTGATTTTTAAC-
GATAATAACCAACTAAGTTGTTTTAAACTGATTAATTGCTATATCAATA-
CAGTCCGGCTTAATGTAGTAAGAACCGACCAACGATTTATCGGTAGG-
GTGAATTATTCCTGGCATTTGGTTCCTAAGTCAAGGGCTATCCTTA-
GTCAATCTTATTGCCCGTTACCCACCAAGCCGGGCGTTCTCTTATATG-
CAAGTGCAAGCAAAGAAGTCTAACAAGGTCGAACTAGATCTTGAATTC-
ACTTGGATATCAAGTGCATAAGGTCAATTATTTTCTTCACAGATACCTA-
GAAAGATCCTTATGTTCCTGTTAAACCCCTAAACCAGGAAGTCTCAAAT-
CATTTGGCACCGACAGCGCTGTAATGCGTACACTTCCATAAATAAAG-
CAACGCTGTTATCAATGCCATTTCCACGCACAGCCCGCCGCTGACG-
CCTAGAAAGTCCCGCTAGCACAAAGGCTTGGTCCTGACTTACTAT-
GCCCTTAATCCCTGCCCGGGGACGAGGAGCCGGCATCAGGCACGCCCAGG-
GATAAATATTAAGCCATAAGCGAAAGCTTGACTTAGTTAAGGTTAAGAG-
CCTAGTTGATAACTACCGGCGTAAAGAGTGGTTATGGAAAATATTTA-
GAAGACCTACTGCGAAAGCAGCGTTTAACTATGCCTGACCCCACGA-
AACCTTGATAGAAATATACAATTGATATCCGCCAGGAACTACAAGCGC-
GAGGAGCCTGTTCTAGAACCGATAACCCCCGTTCAACCTCACCAC-
CACACCGCCCGTCACTCTCCCCAAGTTCAACCTGTCCTTCTAACTA-
TACCGGAAGGTGCGCTTGGAATAACCAGAGTGTAGCTAAAATAGGAAAG-
GAGCTGACTAGCTAGCCAACATATTTGGTCCAACACCACAACATACAT-
TAGTAGGGGCGACCGAAAAGGAGATAATTGAGCAACAGAAAAAGTACCG-
GAGAAGCAGAGATTAAATCTCGTACCTTTTGCATCATGATTTAGCCAG-
GAGCTACTCCGGGACAGCCTATTGTAGGGCCAACCCGTCTCTGTGG-
CCTAGTTATAGCTGGTTGCTTAGGAAATGAATAGAAGTTCAGCCCCCCG-
GAGAGTTAGTCAAAGGAGGTACAGCTCCTTTGAACAAGGACACAACCT-
GCCTAAGAGCAGCCACCTGCACAGAAAGGGTTAAAGCTCAGACAGATA-
CCGTTCCATGCCCCCATGGAAGAGATTATGCTAGAATGAGTAATAAGA-
CGACAAATAACGAACCCAAACCAAGAGGGAACTGTAGGCCAGAACAAA-
CCCCAAGGGAAAGACCCAAAGGAAGAGAAGGAACTCGGCAAACACAAG-
GTCCGCCTGCCCTGTGACTATGGGTTTAACGGCCGCGGTATTTTGACCGT-
GGCATCACGAGGGCTTAGCTGTCTCCTCTTCCAAGTCAATGAAATT-
CCTATGGAGCTTTAGACACCAGGCAGATCACGTCAAGCAACCTTGAAT-
GCGACCGCGGGGGGAAAATTAAGCCCCACTGTGGACTGGGGGGCACTG-
CAAATATGATCCGGCGAACGCATTCAACGGACCGAGTTACCCTAGGGA-
GACCTCGATGTTGGATCAGGACATCGTAATGGTGCAGCCGCTATTAAGG-
GAGTAATCCAGGTCAGTTTCTATCTATGAAGTGATGTTTCCTAGTAC-
CCCCACCTGATGAAGGCAACTAAAACAGACAAGGGGGCACAC-
ATTTGCGAGAGGCCTAAGCCCTCTTTCTCAGAGGTTCAAACCCTCTCCT-
CATTGTACCCGTTCTGTTAGCAGTTGCTTTCCTCACCCTACTTGAAC-
GCCCCTACGGACTACTACAACCCATCGCAGACGGCCTAAAACTATTTAT-
TACACCCATACTTGCCCTTACACTTGCACTCACTCTATGAGCCCCCAT-
TACTTGCACTATCCAGCCTGGCCGTGTATTCTATTTTAGGGTCAGGATGG-
CAAACTATTTCCTACGAAGTTAGCCTAGGCTTGATCTTACTCAGCGTA-
CCAAGAAAGCATCTGACTACTCGTGCCGGCCTGACCACTTGCCGC-
GACCTCACAGAAGGAGAGTCAGAATTAGTCTCCGGATTCAATG-
GCTAATATCCTTCTAATAAATACGCTCTCAGCCGTCCTATTTTTAGGCG-
GAAAGCCGCCCTCCTCTCCGTTGTATTTTTATGAGTACGAGCTTCCTAC-
GAAAAGCTTCCTACCCCTGACTCTGGCCCTTGTACTATGACATTTAG-
GAATTGTGCCTGAATGCTTAAGGACCACCTTGATAGCGTGGCTAATAGG-
CAAGAGATCAAAACTCTTGGTGCTTCCACTACACCACTTTCTAGTAAG-
TAAAATCCTTCCCTTACTAATGAACCCCTACGTACTCACCATCT-
CCACTGACTACTTGCATGAATAGGCCTAGAAATCAATACCCTAGCCAT-
CAACAACCAAGTATTTTTTGACACAAGCAACCGCCGCAGCAATA-
GAGAAATTCACCAGCTATCACACCCACTAGCAACTACAACAGTAATATT-
CAGAAGTCCTTCAGGGACTTGAACTCACTACAGGATTAATCCTGTC-
CCCAACCATCAATTCTTCCCTACTTGTCACAATCGGCCTTCTATCAA-
TCTAGCATATCTTCCAATTGCCCATCTAGGATGAATAGTACTAATTCTA-
CATGACATCTTCAGCCTTCCTCACATTAAAAACCAACAACTCTTTAAC-
CATTAACCGCTCTTGTATTATTGTCCCTTGGAGGTCTCCCCCCTCTCT-
GGACTCCCACTATCTGCCACACTAGCTGCTATAACAGCCCTCCTAAG-
TATTTATCCCAACACCCTAACTGCTACTGCCCCATGACGCCT-
CCTAGGACTACTACCCCTCACACCAGCTGTGACTGCGATATTAGCTTTG-
AACGGGGGTGAAATCCCCCAGCCCTTGTAAGACTTGCAGGACTTTATC-
CCTTTCTAGGTGGGAAGGCCTCGATCCTACAAACTCTTAGTTAA-
CCCCGGGGGGGGGAGCGAGGCGGGGAAAGCCCCGGCAGGCTATTAG-
GATAAGGAGAGGAGTCAAACCTCTGTTTATGGAGCTACAATCCACCGCT-
TAAGCTCTCAGCCACCCATCCTGAGAAAGGGAGGAATTGAACCCCTAT-
GTGCTGGTTTCAAGCCAACCGCATAACCACTCTGCCACTTTCTTCTA

Fig. 1

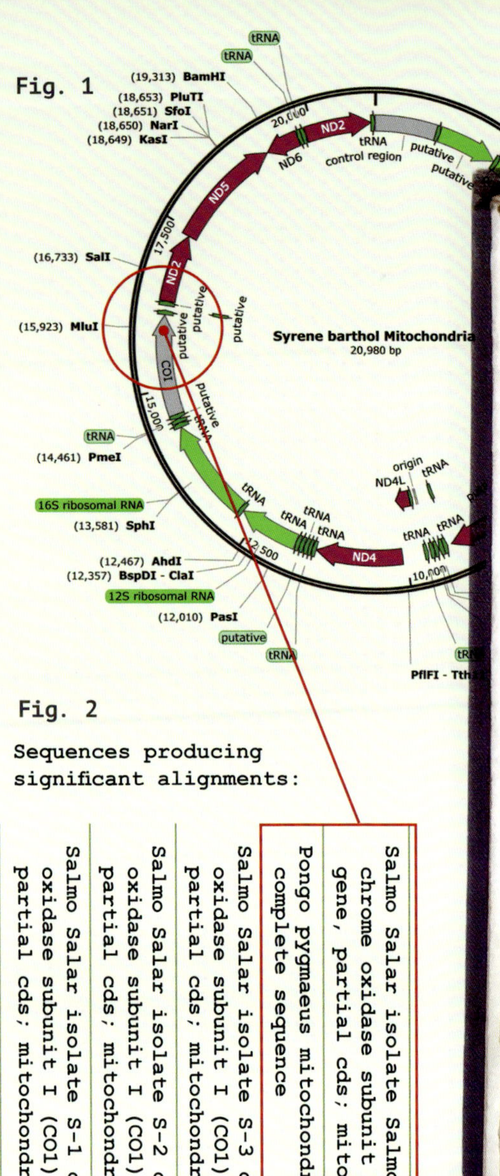

Fig. 2

Sequences producing
significant alignments:

Salmo Salar isolate Salmon1 cytochrome oxidase subunit I (CO1) gene, partial cds; mitochondrial

Pongo pygmaeus mitochondrial DNA, complete sequence

Salmo Salar isolate S-3 cytochrome oxidase subunit I (CO1) gene, partial cds; mitochondrial

Salmo Salar isolate S-2 cytochrome oxidase subunit I (CO1) gene, partial cds; mitochondrial

Salmo Salar isolate S-1 cytochrome oxidase subunit I (CO1) gene, partial cds; mitochondrial

I was at least expecting a .exe file that I would avoid perturbing from the relative safety of my Mac, or at best a photo of something that I could never unsee. Instead I got a text file with nothing but thousands of lines of ATGCs, the letters of DNA. No explanation. No header or metadata.

1911). Against this backdrop, it is understandable that for some, the bodies of desiccated carcasses appearing to be half-primate, half-fish could genuinely be evidence of merpeople.

Physical specimens of mermaid began appearing in the nineteenth century, some even making their way into natural history collections, including the Harvard Peabody Museum in the US (*PM #97-39-70/72853*). They arrived in Europe during a time when global trade was bringing wonders from the far reaches of the globe to the West. While specimens of the newly discovered duck-billed platypus were initially greeted with suspicion due to the lack of precedence in the scientific literature, the mermaid specimens benefited from a century of consensus-building sightings (Bondeson 2014).

The most famous mermaid specimen was first acquired by Captain Eades in the South Pacific and brought to London in 1822 (Bondeson 2014). "The Feejee Mermaid" was received with requisite fascination and skepticism, with prominent voices both confirming and dismissing it. It toured the United States where it traveled extensively and changed hands several times before arriving at its ultimate destination, P.T. Barnum's American Museum, where it debuted in 1842 (Bondeson 2014). Close examination of the Feejee Mermaid ultimately revealed it to be a well-executed taxidermy chimera, of the upper torso and head of a juvenile orangutan and the lower half of a salmon.

The expanded mermaid sighting

These mermaids are object lessons in our attempt to determine what is real. The fact that the specimens were manufactured by people is no small detail. They exist as a

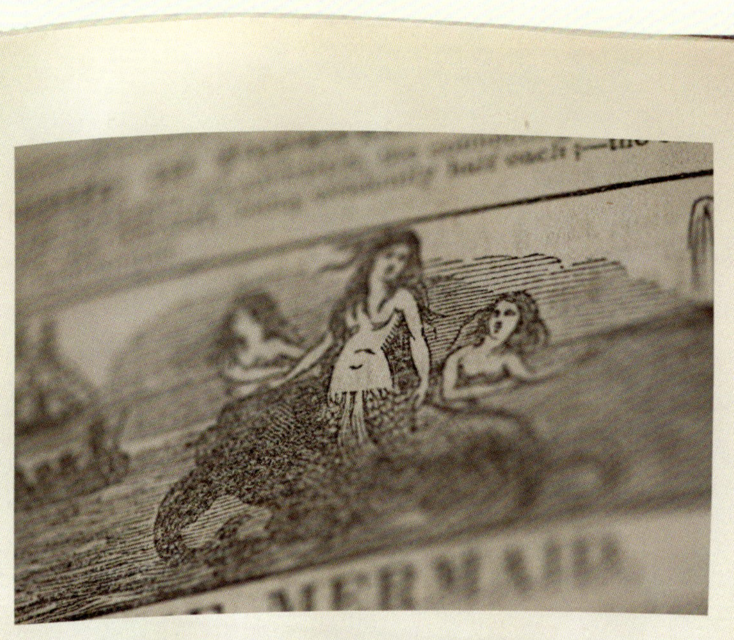

Advertisement for Kimball's Museum Boston, 1856

hoax only within the limited economy of carnival barkers and Coney Island sideshows. In the broader cultural landscape they are well-crafted false positives, beckoning rational minds to cross the perimeter of scientific rigor. By design, they simultaneously inspire and humble us.

Let us suspend for a moment our assumptions about what a mermaid looks like and focus rather on what they do. With respect to the science of the eighteenth century, mermaids seduced rational minds into believing that they could finally suspend their disbelief and enjoy living in a world with a bit more wonder in it. If we look for evidence of this "expanded mermaid," we begin seeing mermaids that have ventured well beyond the confines of our terrestrial oceans.

Despite attempts to maintain rigor through standardized measurements, repeatable studies, and peer review, scientists still confront the objects of their own desires. Sometimes they succumb. This could be a rare data point that confirms a

I forwarded it on to a biologist friend who quickly pointed out that it was way too small to be a whole organism. Almost too small to be anything. Smaller than the smallest bacteria genome. A virus maybe? Did someone send me an actual virus on my computer? She suggested that I try and find a program for viewing genomic data and see if there were any recognizable genetic elements: start and stop codons; things that could be genes.

I downloaded some free software (SnapGene Viewer) and it created a circular depiction of the genes it contained, showing arrows pointing in either direction and, in some cases, what looked like names. I sent a screengrab to a friend, Dr. Jose Padial, a herpetologist with the American Museum of Natural History with a strong background in taxonomy. He said it was interesting because it had a gene he recognized from mitochondrial DNA. So, not a virus or a bacteria, but rather this smaller piece of DNA that exists in plant and animal cells that is not a part of the larger chromosomes that are in the nucleus of the cell. In Mr. Twilly's biology class in high school, he always called the mitochondria the "powerhouse" of the cell and would kind of pump his fist in the air. I guess that's why I remember this. (Fig. 1)

Dr. Padial pointed out a gene labeled "CO1" that is sometimes used in identifying species. It's a gene that every species has, but is a little different in each. It's useful because if you have a database of all the CO1 genes for a bunch of different species you can then use it to quickly narrow down what the species is from only looking at that one gene.

He said a quick way to test out this theory would be to copy and paste the DNA sequence of that specific gene into a genetic search engine like BLAST and see what came back. After reading my way down a deep Wikipedia rabbit hole I managed to do this.

The search engine returned a long list of Latin species names associated with various scores. Most of the names on the list, including the first, were in the genus *Salmo*, while the second name on the list was in the genus *Pongo*. (Fig. 2)

Again, I am not a scientist. And the last science class I had was with the aforementioned Mr. Twilly. But I am very curious and unafraid to ask questions and wander down rabbit holes that may or may not go anywhere. I copied the Latin names of the top two species matches, *Salmo salar* and *Pongo pygmeaus*, into the usual search engine. It returned the Wikipedia pages for two very different species: salmon (yes, the fish) and orangutan (yes, the great ape).

This one gene is most closely associated with two completely different species that also happen to be the two species most commonly used in the manufacture of taxidermy mermaids in the nineteenth century. Lovely. I brought this news to a lecture I gave in November 2018 to a group in Brooklyn called Biotech Without Borders. Basically told them this same story, shared the file, and then opened things up for discussion.

The audience split loosely into two groups. A smaller group was concerned with assessing the biological origins of the DNA. They wanted to verify or falsify it by synthesizing the DNA and trying to see if it would "run" in cell culture. The other, larger group assumed the DNA files to be biologically meaningless and want-

Radio telescope data annotated by Jerry R. Ehman, 1977

particularly beloved theory, or an outlier that is so miraculous that it suspends the normal capacity for skepticism. Isn't this what mermaids do?

On August 15, 1977, a researcher named Jerry R. Ehman working for the Search for Extra-Terrestrial Intelligence (SETI) was reviewing data at the Big Ear radio telescope at The Ohio State University and came across a reading so unusual that it held the possibility of being an intelligent signal from beyond the solar system. He excitedly scrawled "WOW!" in red pen on the computer printout. If outer space is the final frontier, then this is a mermaid sighting.

Conclusion

The Mermaid De-Extinction Project argues that these "expanded mermaid sightings" provide something essential: A tool for exploring the epistemology of science. They are objects of study that have the power to penetrate the hard shell of certitude. Or, more simply, they remind us what we actually wanted to begin with.

Today we are faced with an unprecedented degree of uncertainty in every domain. We find ourselves in the process of sailing confidently beyond the perimeter of scientific evidence, beyond knowability, deep into uncharted waters. It's at these times that the "siren call" of the mermaid can be heard most clearly.

Bibliography

Bartholin, Thomas. "Of the Mermaids, &c. From the Miscellanea Naturae Curiosorum, Dec. 1, 1671." In Acta Germanica: or, the literary Memoirs of Germany, &c. Vol. 1.120. London: G. Smith, 1742.

Bondeson, Jan. "The Feejee Mermaid and Other Essays in Natural and Unnatural History." Cornell University Press, 2014.

Carl Linnaeus to Kungliga Svenska Vetenskapsakademien, 29 August 1749. "The Linnaean Correspondence." http://linnaeus.c18.net/Letter/L1041.

Linnaeus, Carl, and Abraham Osterdam. Siren lacertina, dissertatione academica orbi erudito data. Uppsala, 1766.

Mather, Cotton. Diary of Cotton Mather, 1681-1708. Volume 7. Boston: The Massachusetts Historical Society, 1911.

Pennsylvania Gazette, 6 May 1736.

Peabody Museum of Archaeology & Ethnology, PM #97-39-70/72853.

Scribner, Vaughn. "Such Monsters Do Exist in Nature: Mermaids, Tritons, and the Science of Wonder in Eighteenth-Century Europe."

ed to look for signatures of simple human manipulation.

Consensus across all groups was that they would need more data. Is there more? A single piece of mitochondrial DNA can't even make a single cell. Regardless of its origin, it is biologically useless without the chromosomes of a much larger genome.

So, I should email them back? Yeah.

"Dear Anthemoessa, Thank you for the weird DNA. I'd be very interested in receiving more, if there is any. Thank you."

About a millisecond later I received a response. Another email with the exact same text in Greek: "Note: this link will only work once. It will expire this time tomorrow." And another creepy link.

I clicked.

Another text file. This time however, there's no DNA, just a long document written in English. It's a kind of contract from "Siren Genomics." I ike a software license agreement that was written by Dr. Bronner. It seems to indicate that in order to receive any more data, I'll need to agree to the terms of the contract. Most of it I can't really even follow the logic of. There's a lot about ownership and responsibility, but also consequence and retribution. It's hard to tell exactly what I'd be agreeing to. It ends with a doozy: "By replying to this email you will be agreeing to the terms of this contract." And so there it remains, at the time of this writing, unaddressed in my inbox.

1. Parkinson, J. 1640. *Theatrum Botanicum: The Theater of Plants or An Herball of Large Extent,* 1110–12. London: Tho. Cotes.

Ciara Redmond (Australian, lives in Tokyo), *We Make Our Own Luck Here*, 2018, white clover (*Trifolium repens*). Courtesy of the artist, with support from Waseda University.

We Make Our Own Luck Here

What if every clover had four leaves? *We Make Our Own Luck Here* investigates the relationship between biotechnology and culture using four-leaf clovers, a symbol for good luck. Using traditional selective breeding methods (mating two plants with desirable traits and harvesting the seeds), the artist created white clover (*Trifolium repens*) plants with high numbers of four-leaf clovers.

The four-leaf clover is a variety of the three-leaf clover. Usually, around one in five thousand clovers has this mutation. It is not known if the factors leading to four leaves in clovers are environmental, genetic, or a combination of these and other factors. The four-leaf clover has become associated with good luck because its natural occurrence is rare. The earliest mention of "Fower-leafed" grass occurs in the dramatically named 1640 text *Theatrum Botanicum*[1] and their continuing cultural importance is born out in their symbolic use by today's SpaceX company, which uses a four-leaf clover emblem on embroidered patches associated with each launch.

By exploring and modifying the genetics of a plant to create a "lucky" specimen, Redmond proposes that we play with the ideas of fate and destiny, whether they be genetic or supernatural. Are lucky four-leaf clovers still lucky if we use science to make them common? Scientists use biotechnology to transform our societies but we can quickly take these innovations for granted. Can biotechnology bring us joy? Or should we be critical of how humanity might frivolously use its power? Could there ever be a genetic alteration conducted by humans that is not a cultural product?

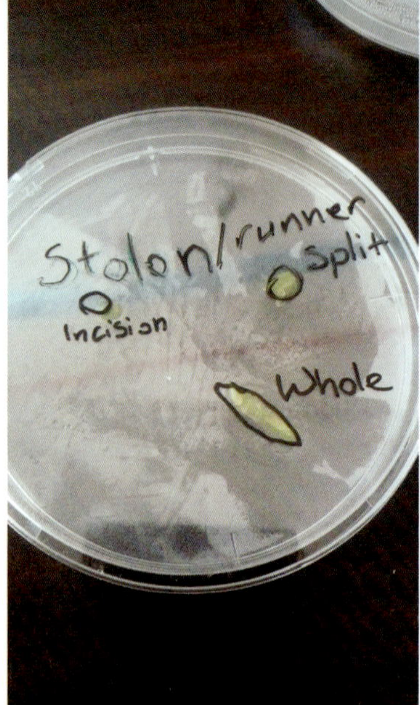

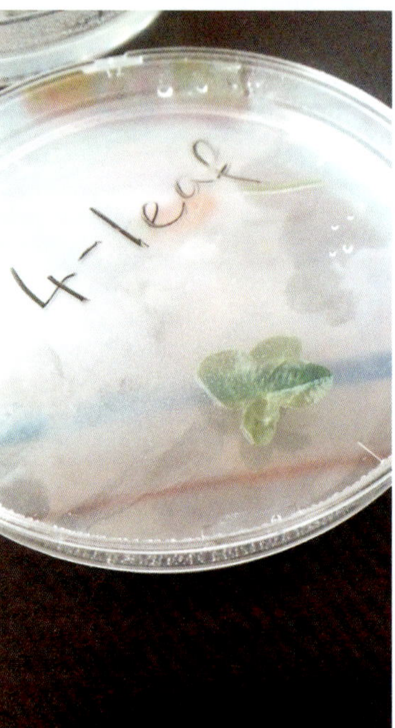

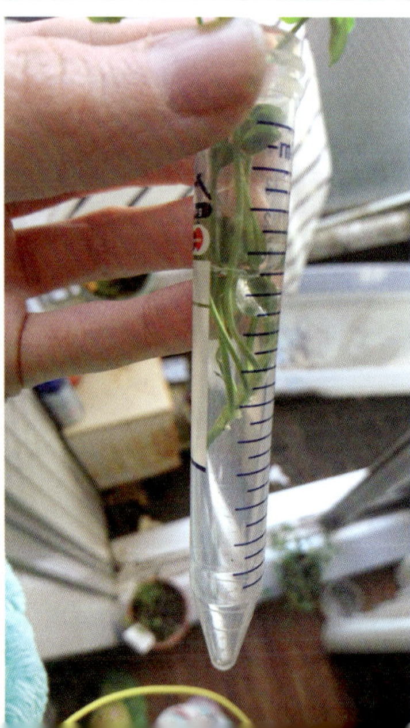

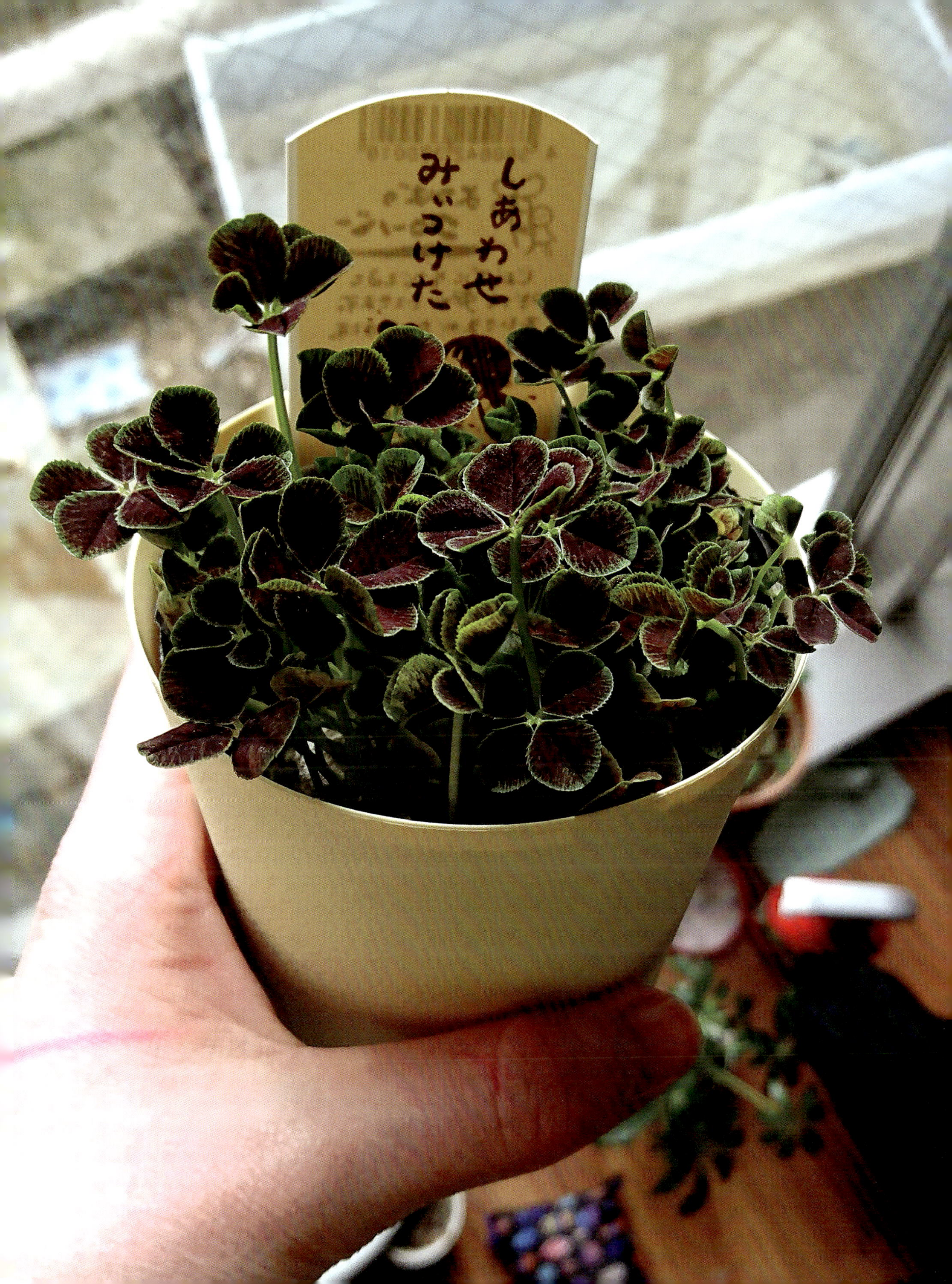
しあわせ
みぃつけた

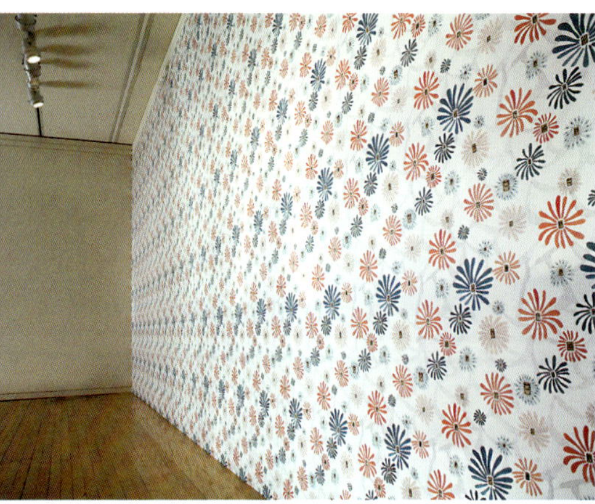

ABOVE and pages 110–11: Kirsten Stolle (American), *Miracle Grow,* 2019, custom-designed wallpaper, 24 in. (61 cm) roll. Courtesy of the artist.

Chemical Bouquet II

In *Chemical Bouquet II,* Stolle examines the overuse of pesticides and the introduction of GMOs through the lens of ornately framed, nineteenth-century floral still life paintings. "Still life" is a translation of the sixteenth-century Dutch term *stilleven.* Sometimes used as painterly technical challenges or to display an individual's skills, the *stilleven* was associated with careful study. During the golden age of Dutch painting, still life paintings increasingly focused on symbolism as the concept of *vanitas* became highly developed. Stolle's resonances with symbolist traditions and attention to detail take on a new cast in this work.

Stolle's Victorian flower bouquets overflow with familiar botanical plants that have been subverted and populated with odd and unsettling imagery associated with chemically intensive farming practices. In Stolle's still life collages, beautiful flowers have been replaced with bloated cow udders, syringes, medicinal and botanical plants from the eighteenth through the twentieth centuries (corn, soy, rapeseed, cotton), Agent Orange barrels, and aspirin pills and bottles—all components associated with Monsanto Company products. The artist collected collage material from vintage botanical lithographs, pharmaceutical catalogs, and agricultural (USDA) manuals.

Stolle's work contrasts with many critiques of Monsanto and other industrial agrichemical corporations because it makes its point through the details of the artwork. *Chemical Bouquet II* participates in an artistic protest tradition that asks viewers to look closer, mimetically enacting the careful observations the artist is asking us to make about the interaction between corporations and their life science products.

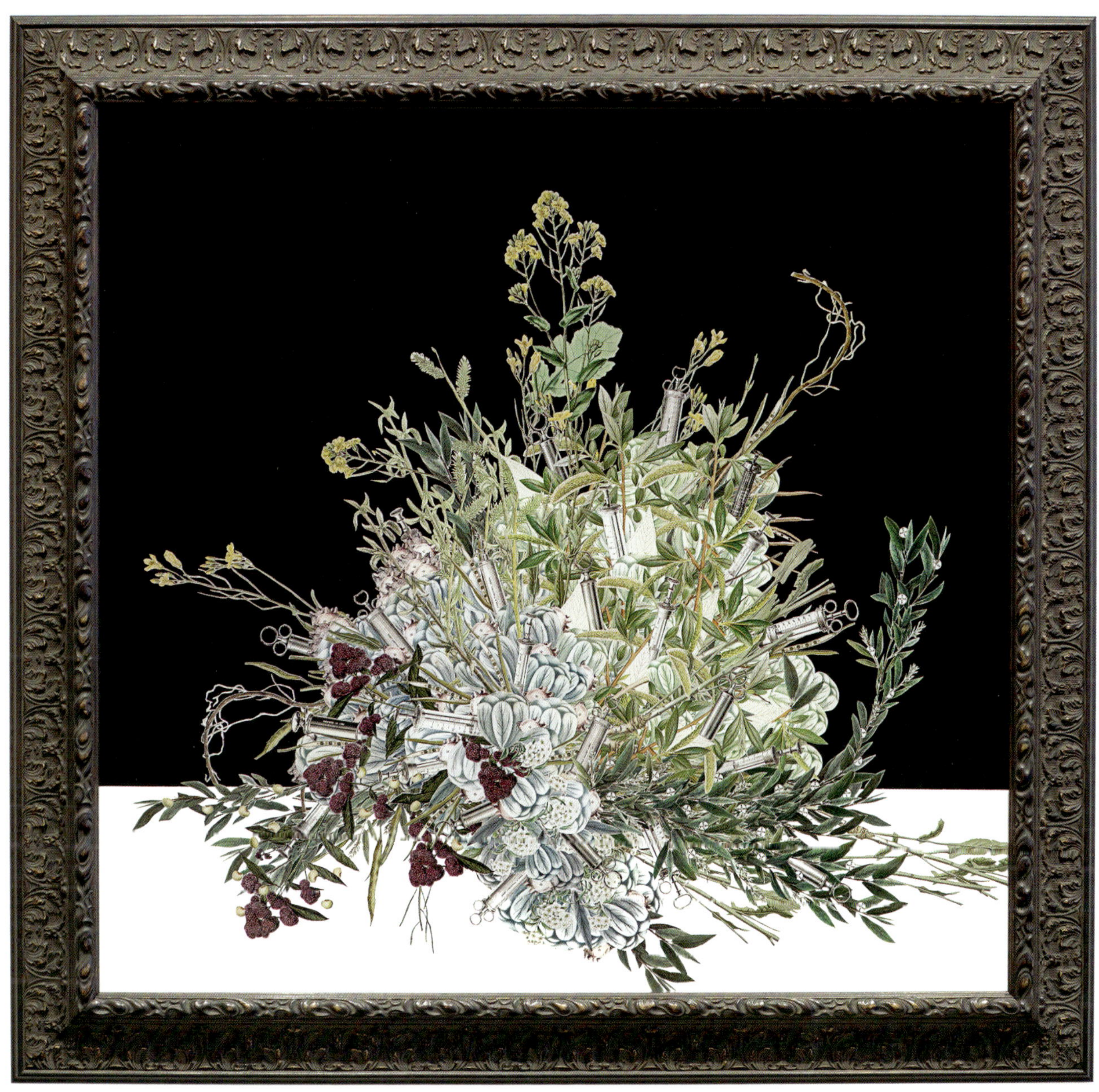

Kirsten Stolle (American), *Chemical Bouquet II*, 2016, collage on paper, 34.25 x 36.75 in. (99.7 x 93.3 cm). Courtesy of the artist and Tracey Morgan Gallery, Asheville.

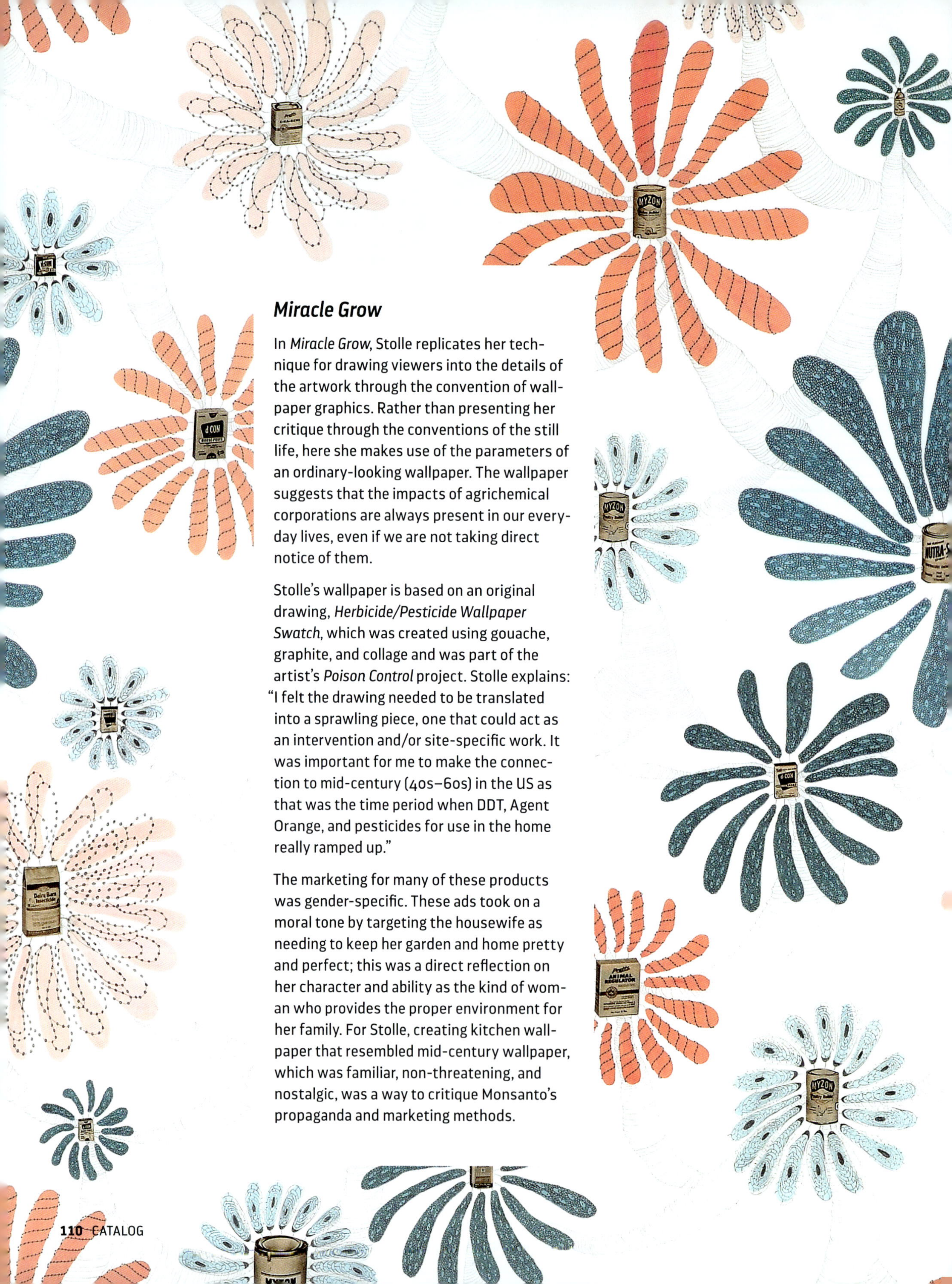

Miracle Grow

In *Miracle Grow*, Stolle replicates her technique for drawing viewers into the details of the artwork through the convention of wallpaper graphics. Rather than presenting her critique through the conventions of the still life, here she makes use of the parameters of an ordinary-looking wallpaper. The wallpaper suggests that the impacts of agrichemical corporations are always present in our everyday lives, even if we are not taking direct notice of them.

Stolle's wallpaper is based on an original drawing, *Herbicide/Pesticide Wallpaper Swatch*, which was created using gouache, graphite, and collage and was part of the artist's *Poison Control* project. Stolle explains: "I felt the drawing needed to be translated into a sprawling piece, one that could act as an intervention and/or site-specific work. It was important for me to make the connection to mid-century (40s–60s) in the US as that was the time period when DDT, Agent Orange, and pesticides for use in the home really ramped up."

The marketing for many of these products was gender-specific. These ads took on a moral tone by targeting the housewife as needing to keep her garden and home pretty and perfect; this was a direct reflection on her character and ability as the kind of woman who provides the proper environment for her family. For Stolle, creating kitchen wallpaper that resembled mid-century wallpaper, which was familiar, non-threatening, and nostalgic, was a way to critique Monsanto's propaganda and marketing methods.

EMILIA TIKKA

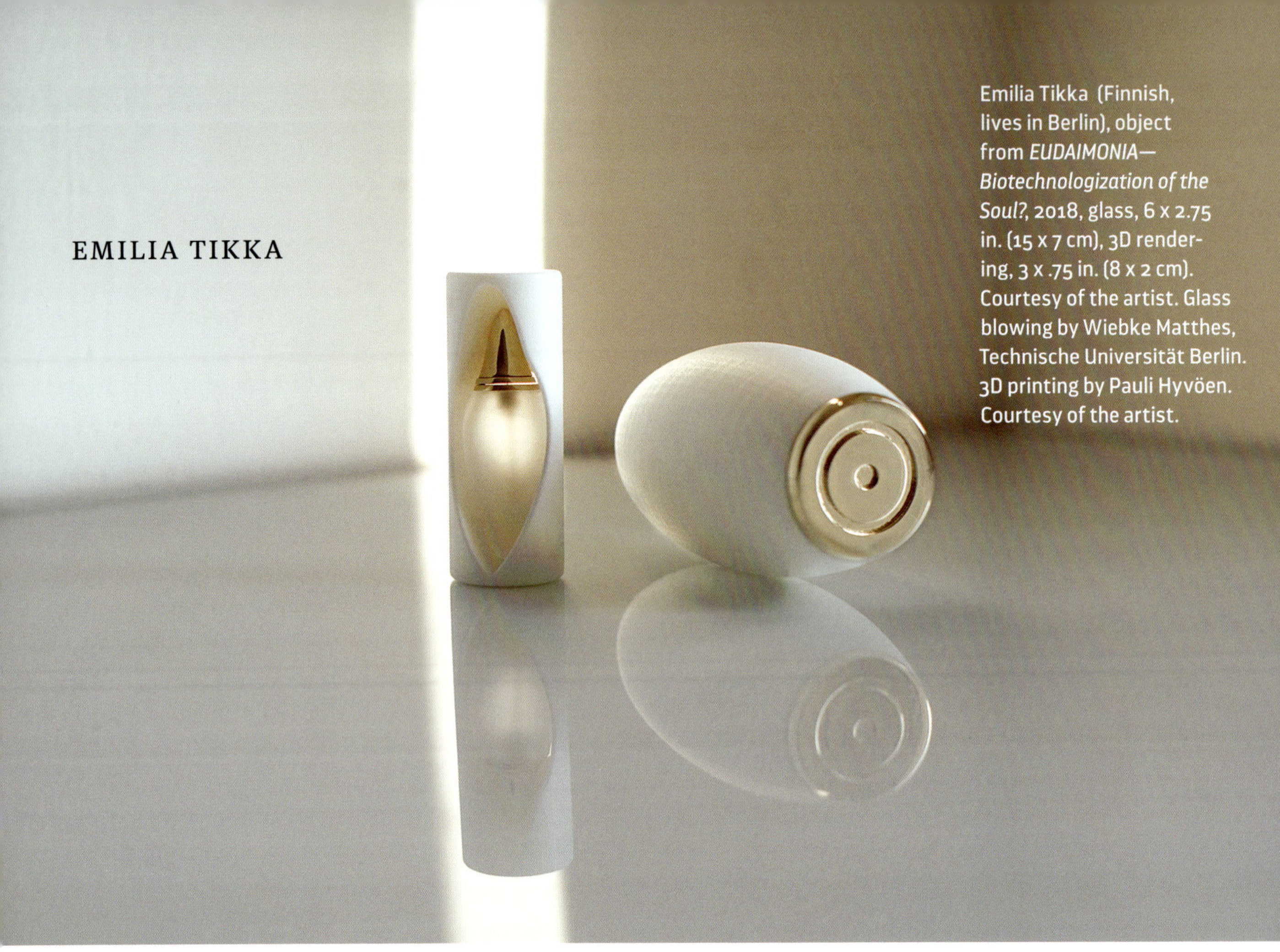

Emilia Tikka (Finnish, lives in Berlin), object from *EUDAIMONIA— Biotechnologization of the Soul?*, 2018, glass, 6 x 2.75 in. (15 x 7 cm), 3D rendering, 3 x .75 in. (8 x 2 cm). Courtesy of the artist. Glass blowing by Wiebke Matthes, Technische Universität Berlin. 3D printing by Pauli Hyvöen. Courtesy of the artist.

OPPOSITE: Emilia Tikka (Finnish, lives in Berlin), stills from *EUDAIMONIA— Biotechnologization of the Soul?*, 2018, film, 11:13.

Written and directed by Emilia Tikka; Eduardo Mattos, director of photography; Arata Mori, editor; Cristian Cassara, music; Shannon Bower, sound; Sammi Mann Yang, hair and makeup. Cast: Stefan Becker, "Daniel;" Tania Carlin, "Nina;" Lucas Englander, "Aaron;" with Dilsad Budak, Ida Luise Frizi Kromm, and Lewin Bochow. Location collaborators: Charité Hospital Berlin and artist Alexander Iskin.

EUDAIMONIA—Biotechnologization of the Soul?

What would a biotechnologization of the soul mean? Emilia Tikka's *EUDAIMONIA* is a philosophical-speculative future scenario in which the human psyche and character has become a matter of molecular biology and can be altered with a personalized genome-editing device. In the imagined future of this artwork, scientists claim to have found that specific genes fundamentally determine human behavior. Explicit features of character, and psychological qualities such as empathy and creativity, are traced to even a single allele of a gene.

These claims open up the question of whether the "optimization" of the human psyche would become an issue of genome editing and biotechnology. Tikka's work raises questions about possible impacts of the novel genome-editing technology CRISPR through a critical, near-future scenario. The artwork is realized as a fictional genome-editing device. This injector-object is designed as a desirable consumer product. The model object is paired with a short film that makes use of the technology through narratives about people who might use this future product. The film suggests the possible societal impacts of the technology. The narrative unfolds in segments that create a dark poetic story of three individuals seeking help from a mysterious technology in their quest to find happiness in the contemporary Western capitalistic world. The near-future scenario thematizes the phantasmatic drive towards happiness as the ultimate goal of human existence.

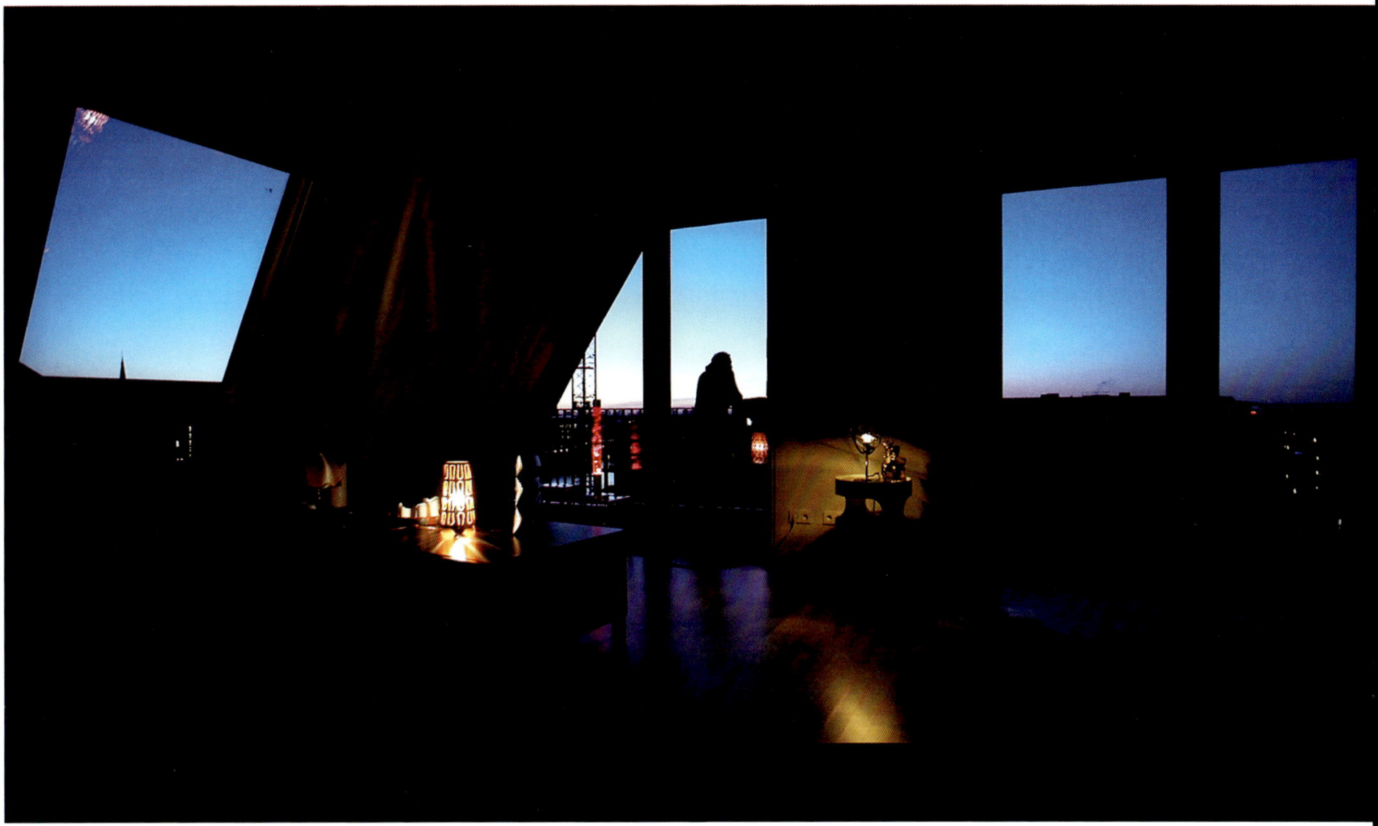

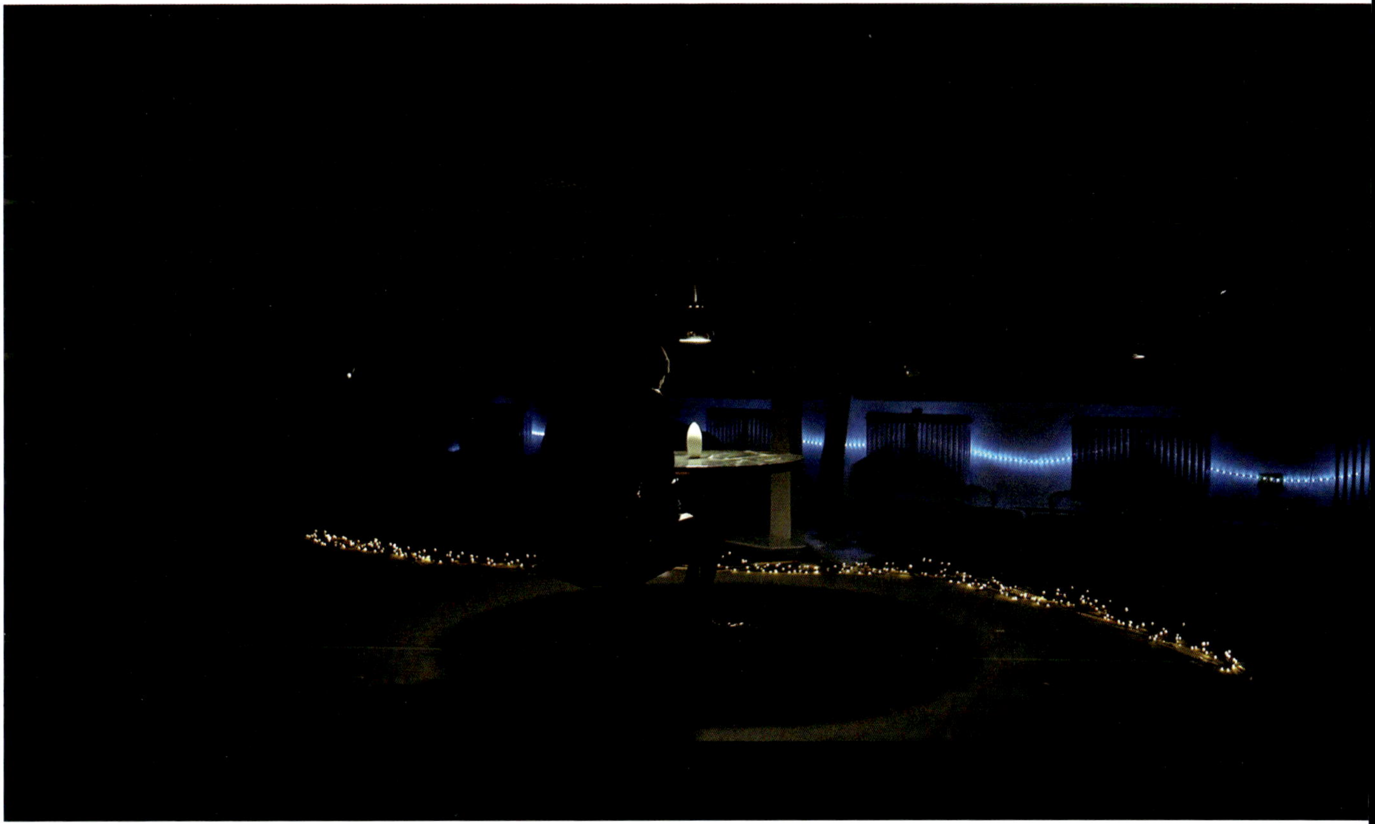

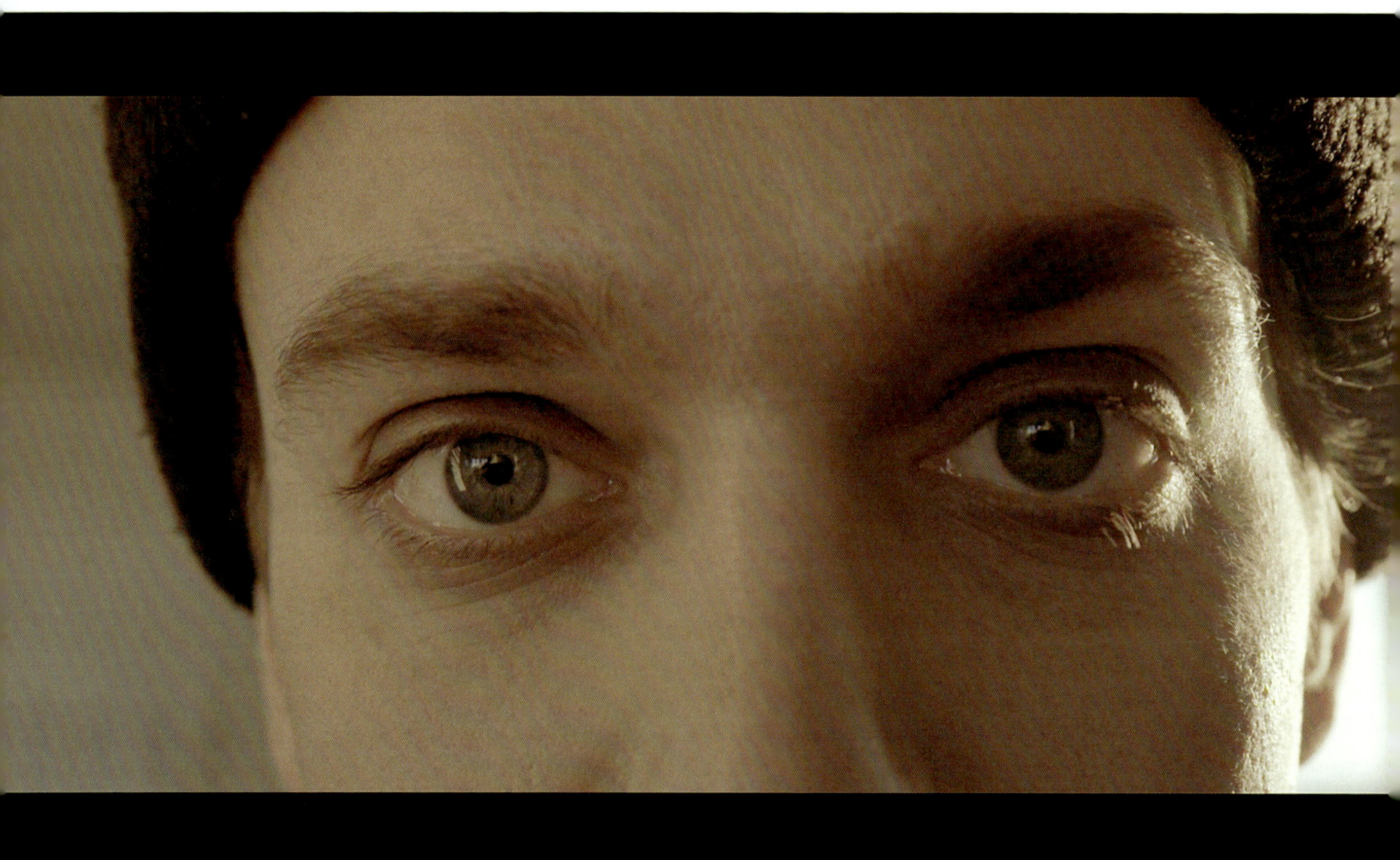

Emilia Tikka (Finnish,
lives in Berlin), stills
from *EUDAIMONIA—
Biotechnologization of the
Soul?*, 2018, film, 11:13.

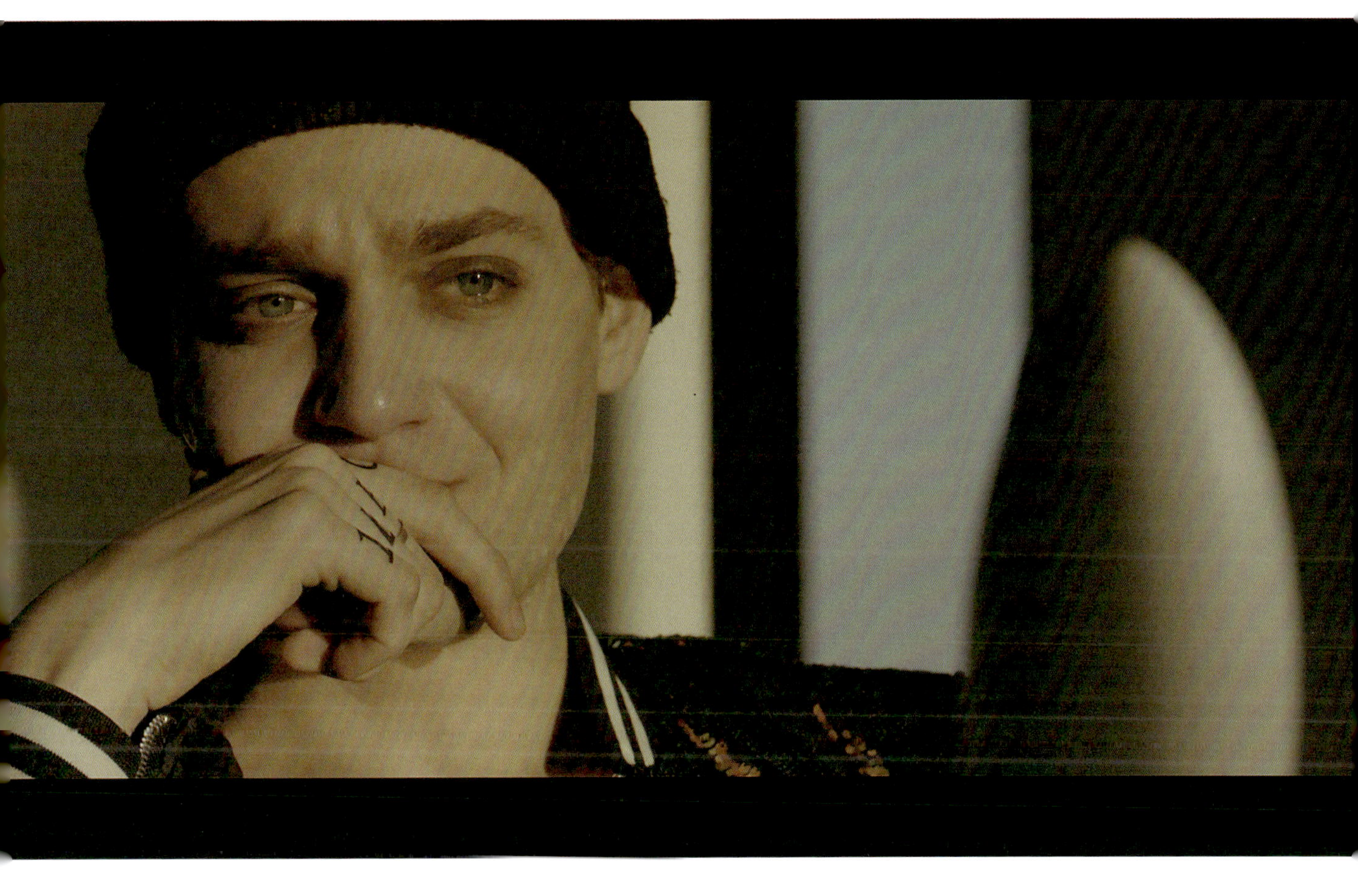

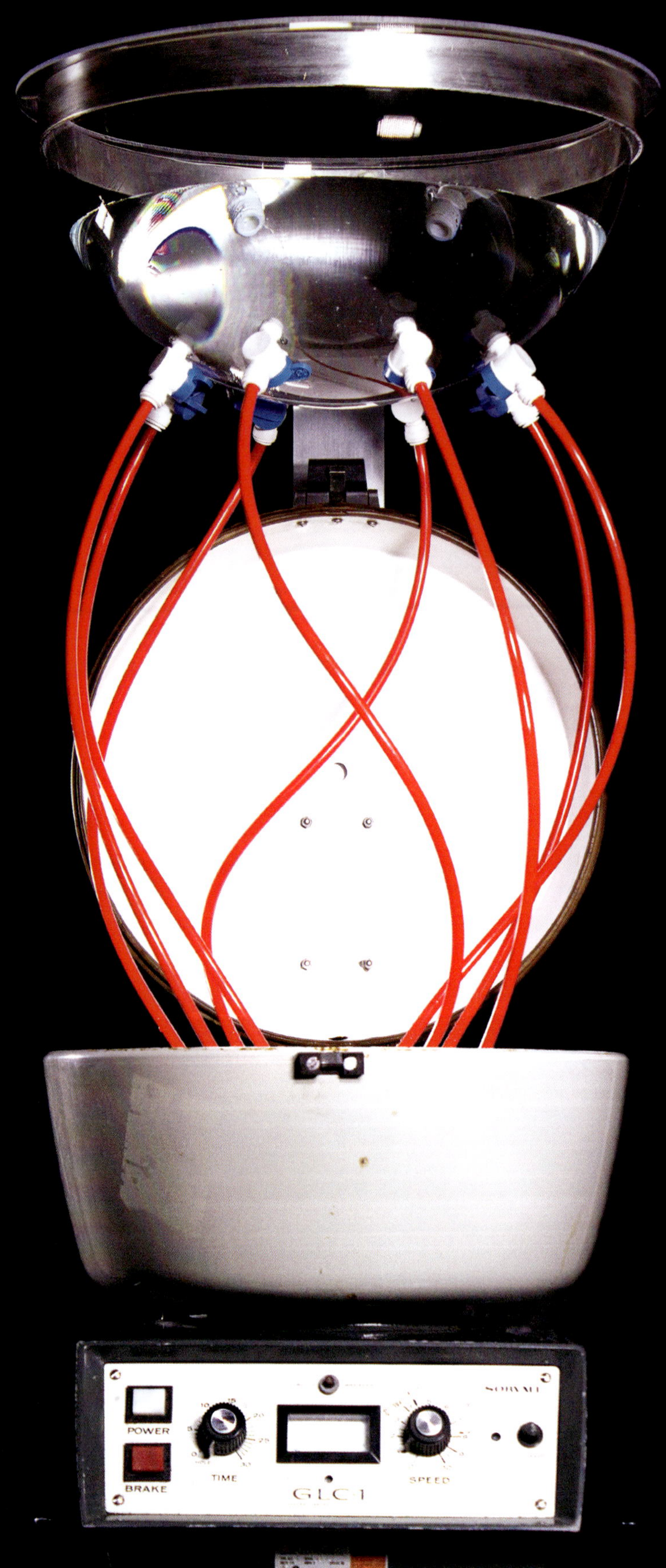

PAUL VANOUSE

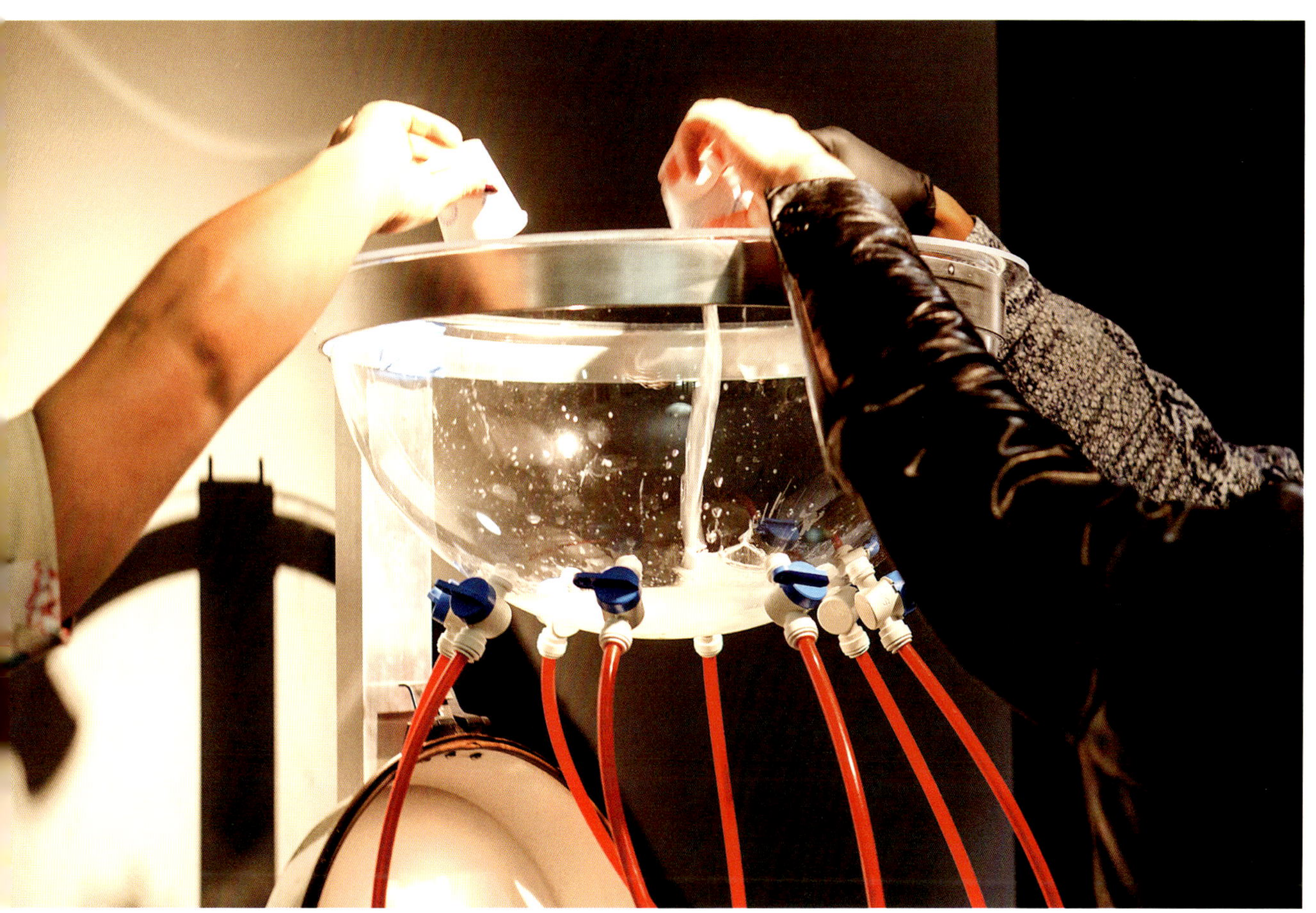

PHOTOGRAPH BY KEN HUANG

America Project

America Project is a biological art installation centered around DNA gel electrophoresis, also known as DNA fingerprinting, a process Vanouse has appropriated to produce recognizable images. The piece builds on his early work *Latent Figure Protocol*, which drew attention to the differences between the metaphorical fingerprint and the image produced by gel electrophoresis. In that work, lengths of DNA were cut using known enzymes and arrayed to create a specific image. Vanouse worked to draw attention to the details of the technology—and particularly to the lack of standardization in the use of enzymes—given the widespread use of DNA fingerprinting in court cases.

America Project consists of a spittoon where participants may offer a DNA sample by swishing saline in their mouths. This sample is then run as a single-gel electrophoresis tray. Vanouse has created specialized software that inverts the typical process, so that the artist can cut the DNA in specific locations to create a pattern. The fact that it is possible to use the mixture of DNA in the spittoon to create a predetermined image (for example, a flag or a crown) demonstrates that humans have much more shared DNA than differentiating sequences. The work emphasizes that we all share more than 99 percent of our DNA and subverts a biotechnology usually employed to differentiate between individuals to show how we are collectively much more biologically similar than different. The artwork was the winner of Distinction in the Hybrid Art category of the 2017 Prix Ars Electronica, the premiere cyberarts festival and competition in the world.

Paul Vanouse (American), *America Project*, 2016, spittoon and video projection. Courtesy of the artist. Scientific collaborator: Solon Morse.

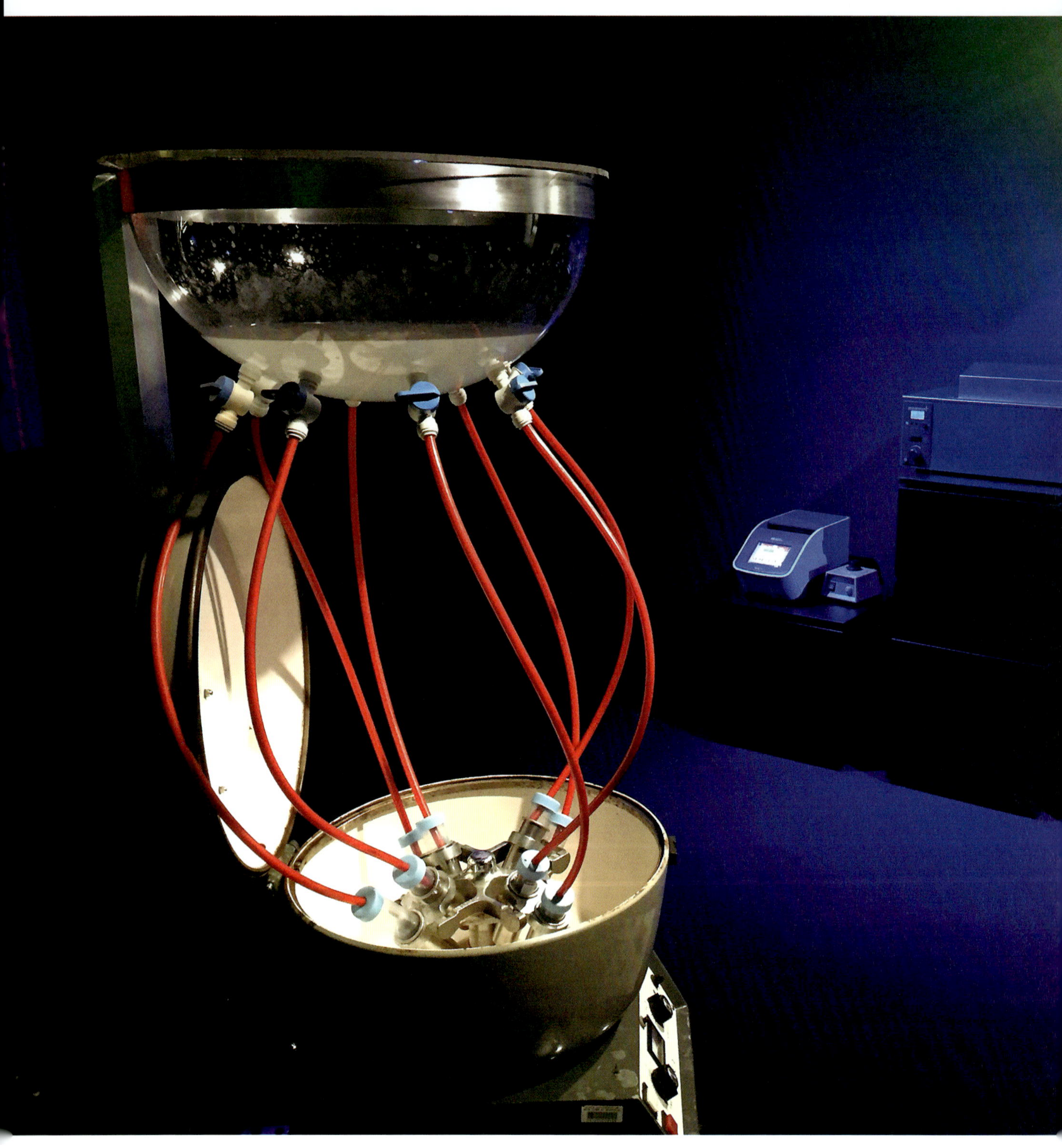

Paul Vanouse (American), *America Project*, 2016, spittoon and video projection.
Courtesy of the artist. Scientific collaborator: Solon Morse.

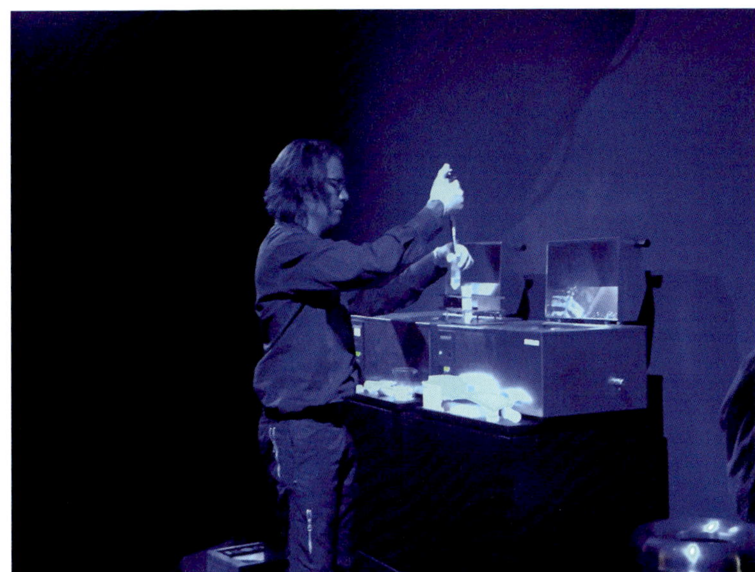

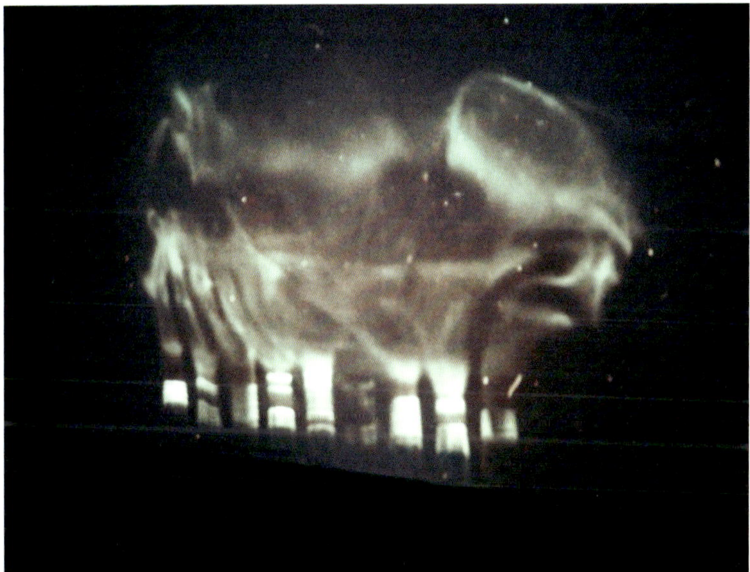

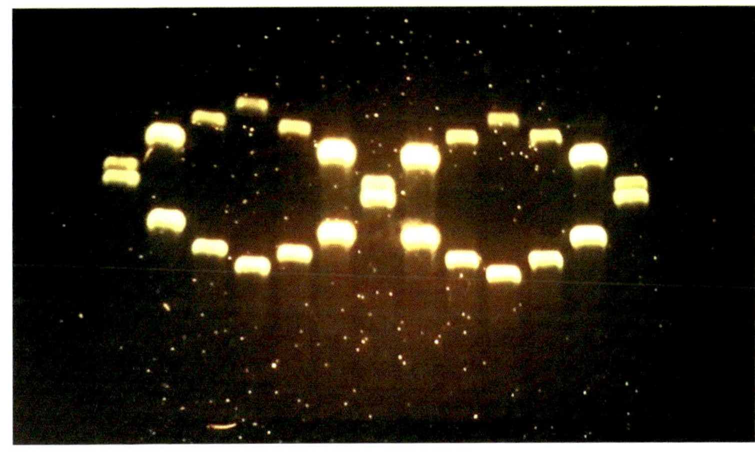

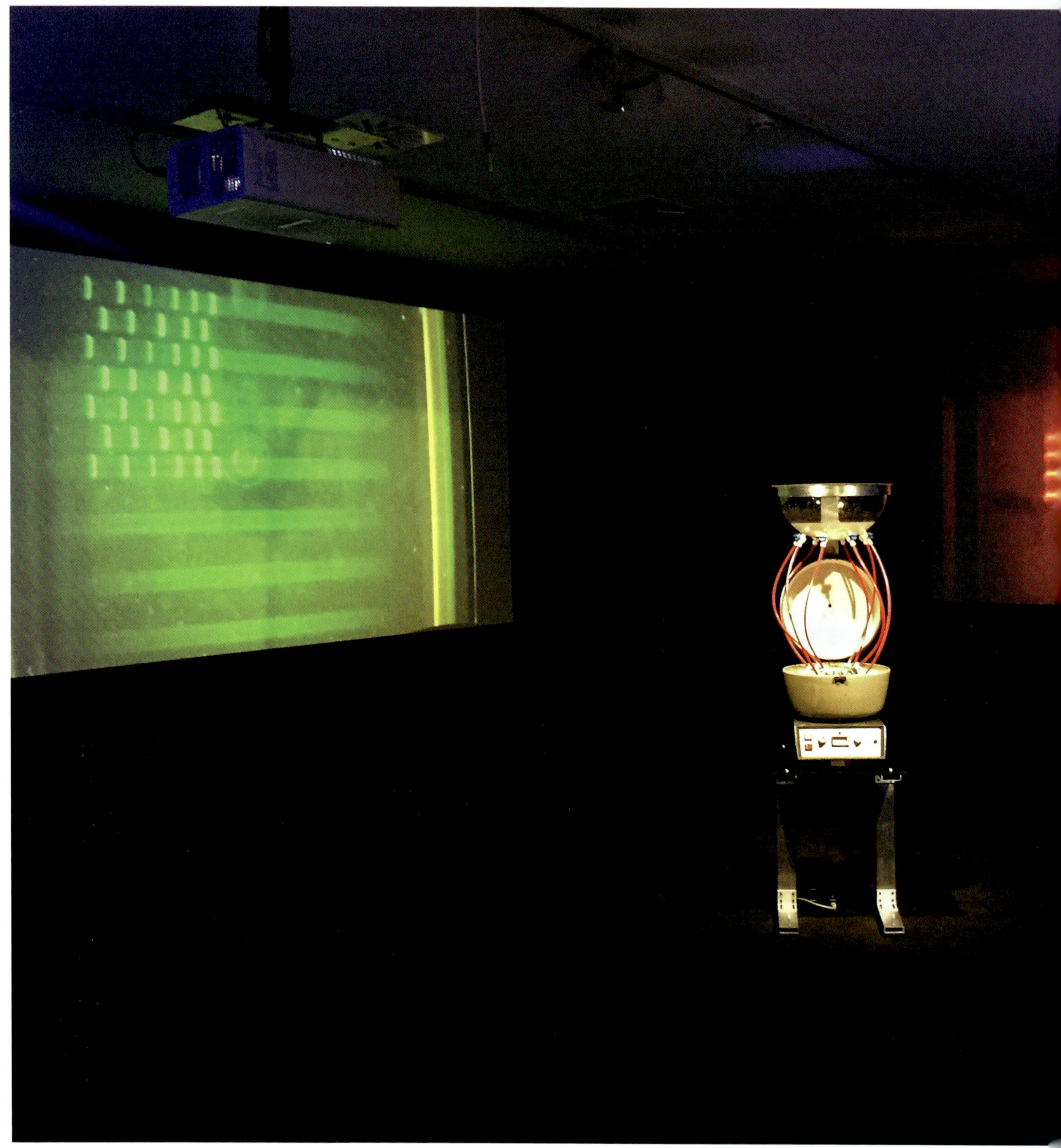

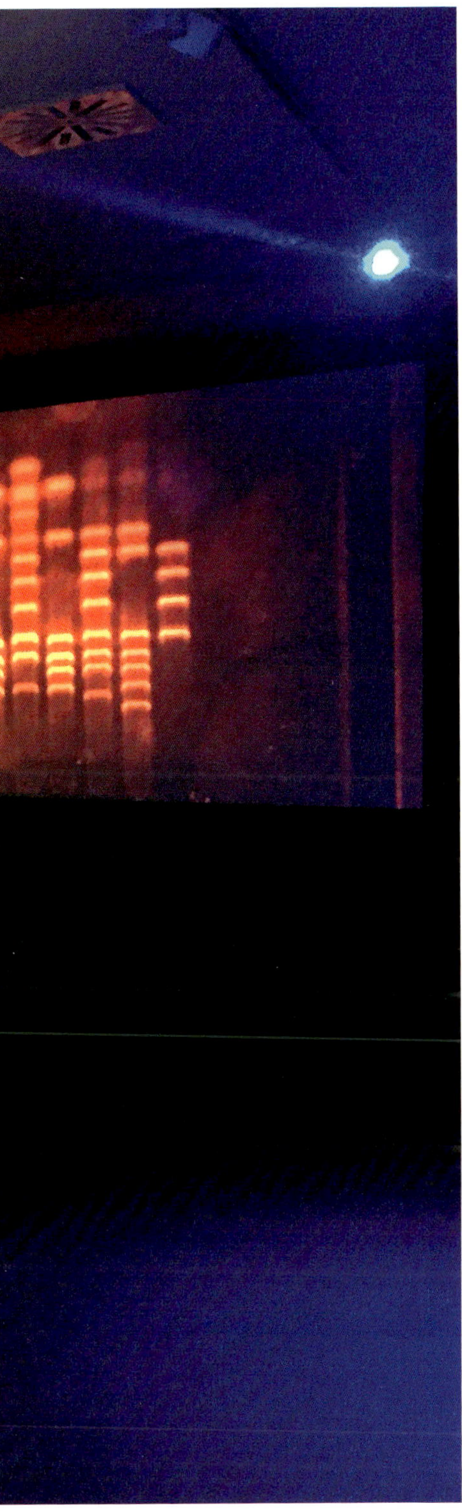

Paul Vanouse (American),
America Project, 2016,
spittoon and video projec-
tion. Courtesy of the artist.
Scientific collaborator:
Solon Morse.

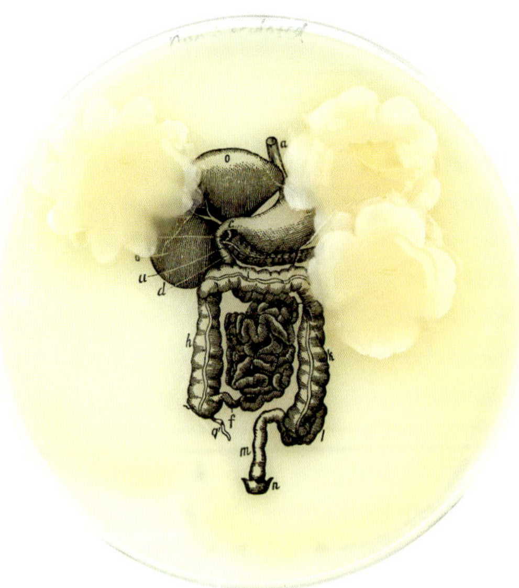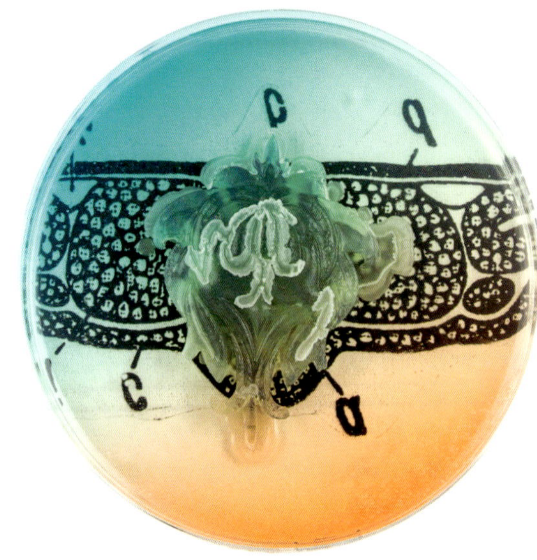

Baroque Biology (Paper Theatre)

Jennifer Willet (Canadian), *Baroque Biology (Paper Theatre)*, 2019, petri dishes, agar, GMO bacteria, collage materials, dimensions variable. Courtesy of the artist. Additional collaborators: Philip Habashy, Gillian Hughes, Lisha Laing, Aleeza Tariq, Jude Abu Zaineh. Mixed-media collages photographed by Justin Elliott.

Jennifer Willet's *Baroque Biology (Paper Theatre)* is a series of large LB agar petri dishes containing imaginary biological vignettes. In these visual narratives, non-human organisms teach humans complex biotechnological processes within the context of a paper theater show. The work is part of the series *Baroque Biology*, which includes quirky pieces of modified lab equipment/sculptures designed for installation and bio-art performances. The objects in this series are counterintuitive and imagine ecological and biotechnology research integrated into everyday life. They emphasize the role of play in our multiple understandings of biology—studying it and living it. These works are gaudy and fantastical with darker undertones that contrast with the aesthetics typically ascribed to a laboratory setting. The artist describes the work as engaging in unconventional daydreams, toppling hierarchies, and welcoming new actions and participants into the lab.

Willet's dishes are reminiscent of William Hogarth's serial engravings or fairy tales from a biotech future. Each allegory focuses on an organism (a fox or a microbe, a plant or fungus) that tries to communicate with humans in a helpful manner about the biological processes they employ for survival, reproduction, and/or aesthetic pleasure. Sometimes the human characters in these vignettes are open to receiving the communicated information, and sometimes they are hostile or ignorant to the messages they are receiving across species. Each petri dish contains paper cutouts, gold leaf, temporary tattoos, and 3D sculptural agar forms seeded with genetically modified rainbow-colored bacteria. This is a durational artwork, sealed in time by the camera, where the petri dishes slowly become confluent with microbes interacting with the collage elements in the dish.

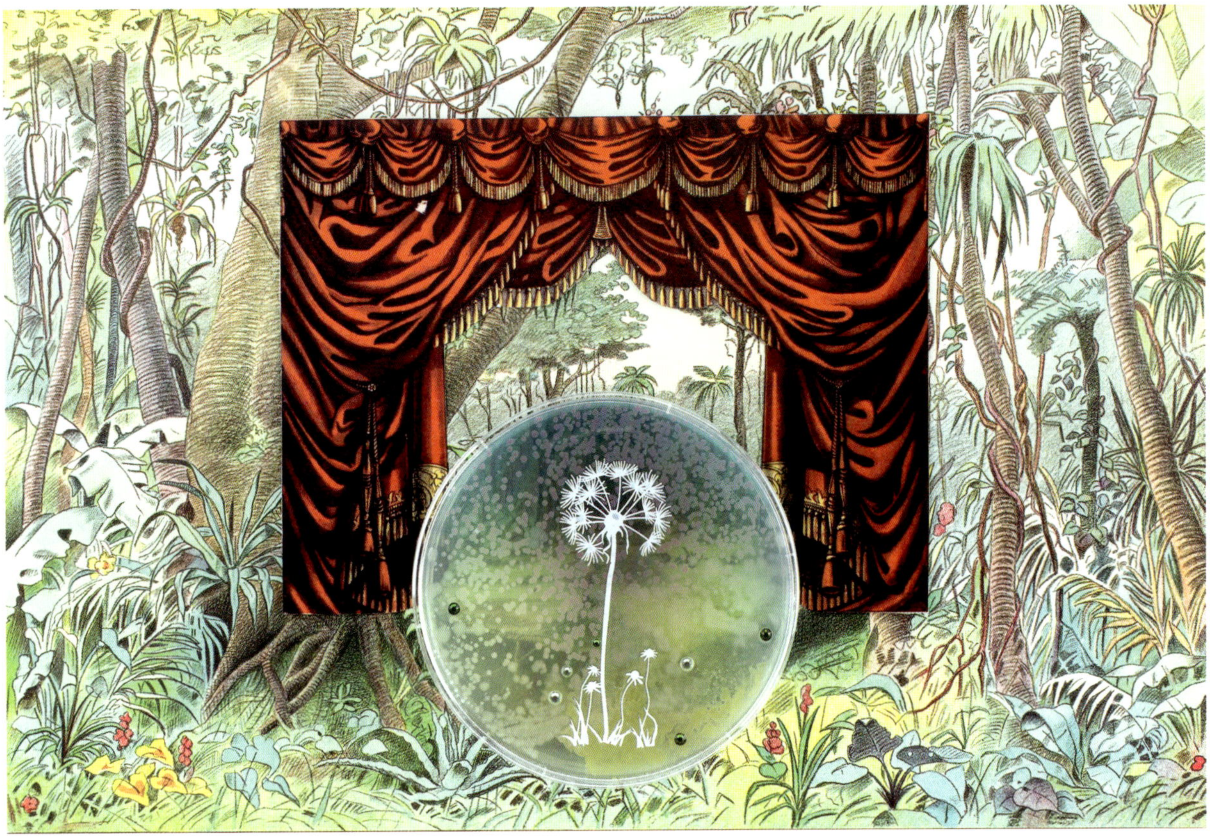

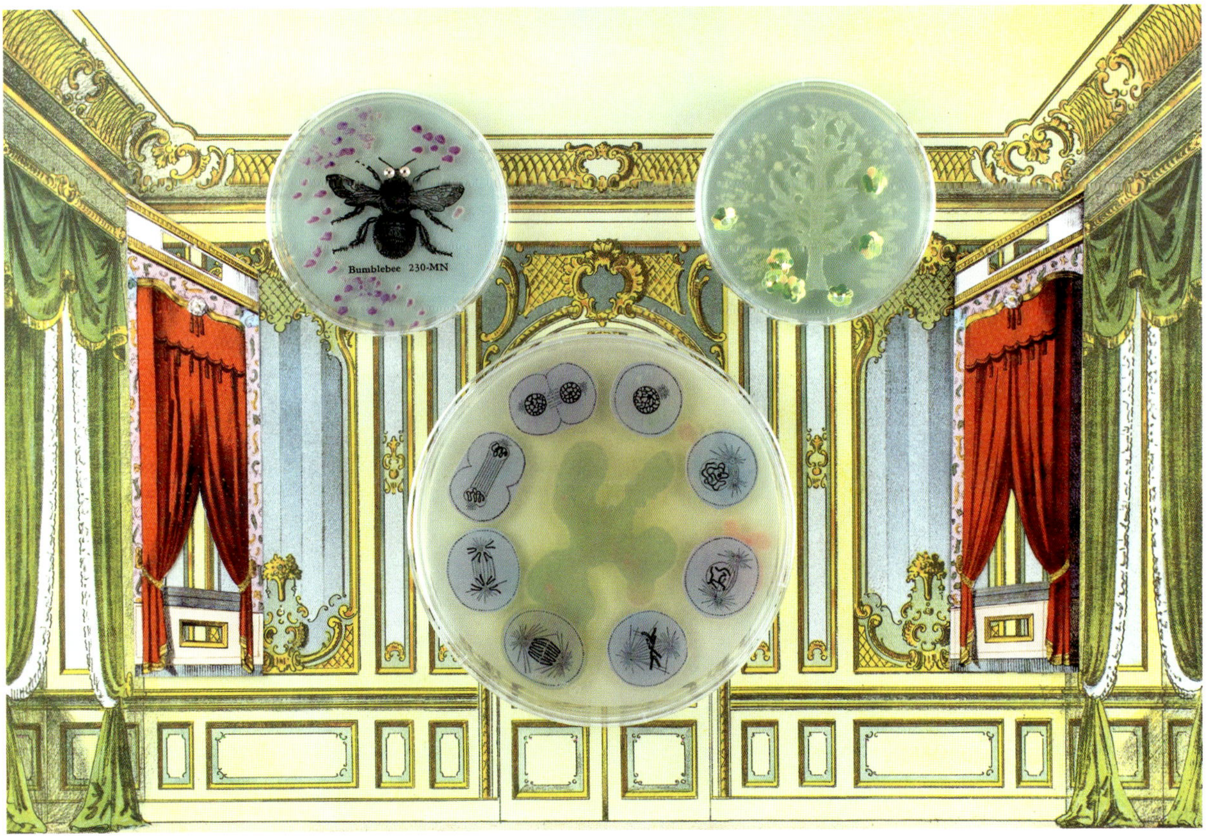

Bumblebee 230-MN

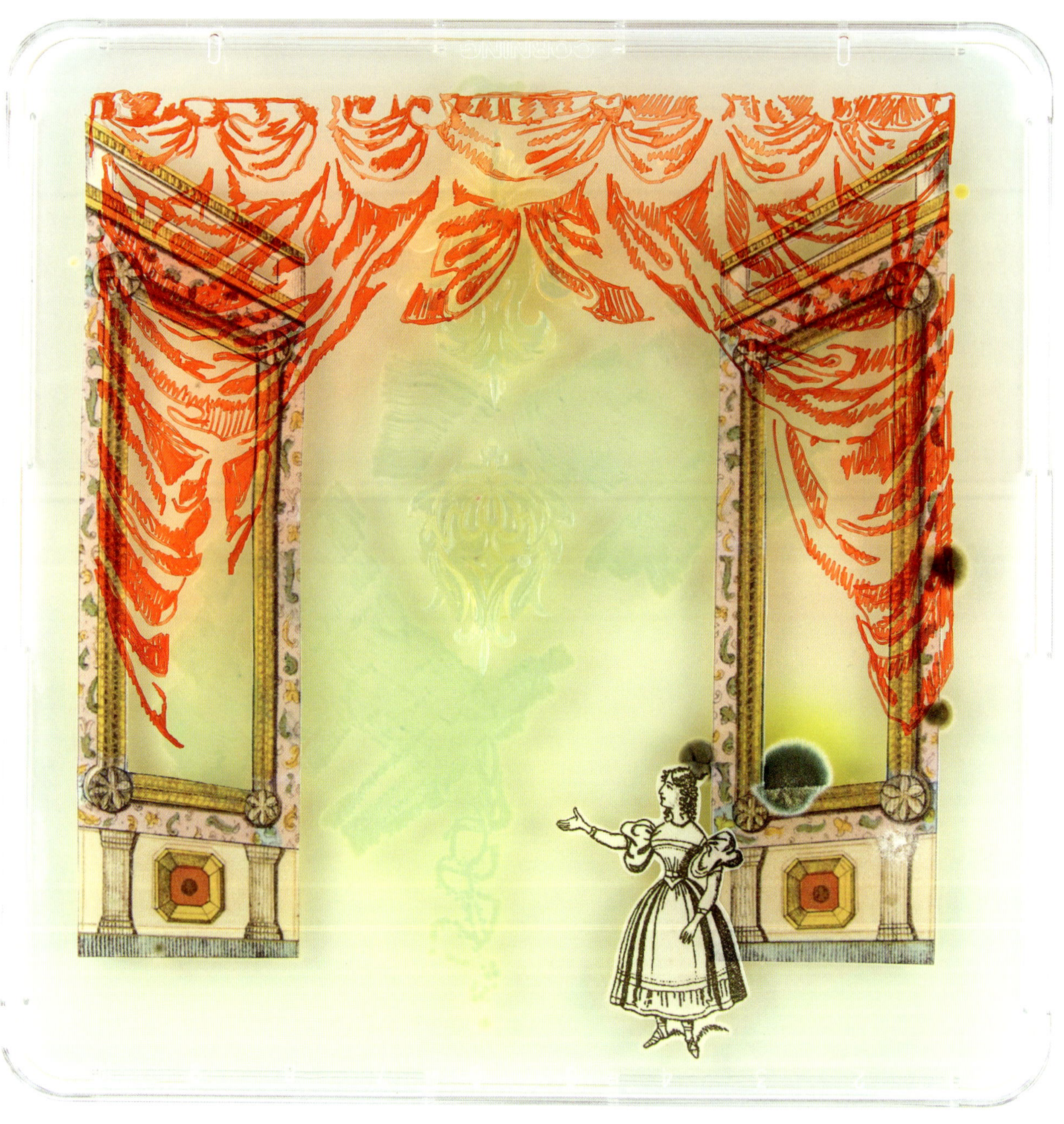

Jennifer Willet (Canadian), *Baroque Biology (Paper Theatre)*, 2019, petri dishes, agar, GMO bacteria, collage materials, dimensions variable. Courtesy of the artist. Additional collaborators: Philip Habashy, Gillian Hughes, Lisha Laing, Aleeza Tariq, Jude Abu Zaineh. Mixed-media collages photographed by Justin Elliott.

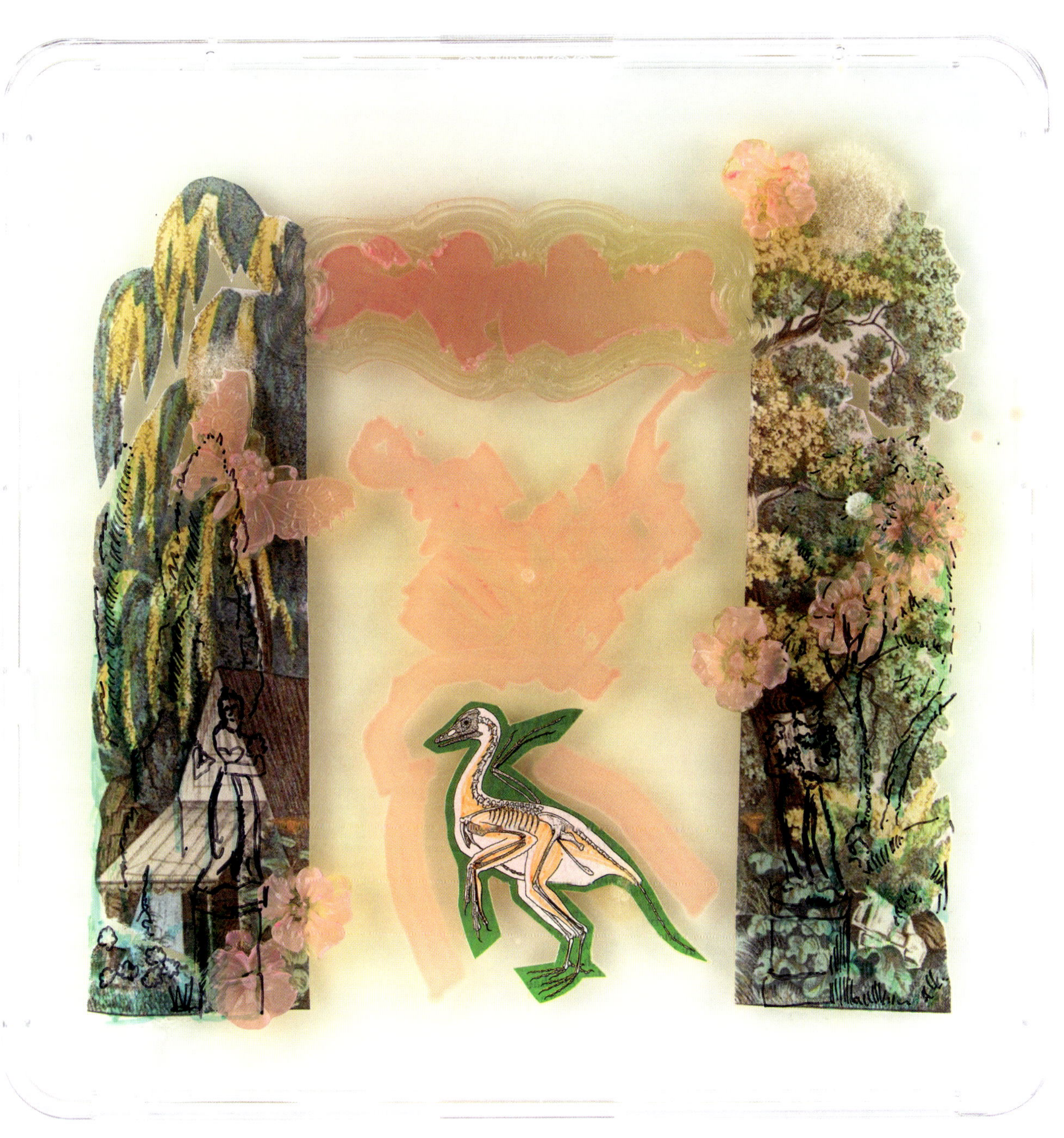

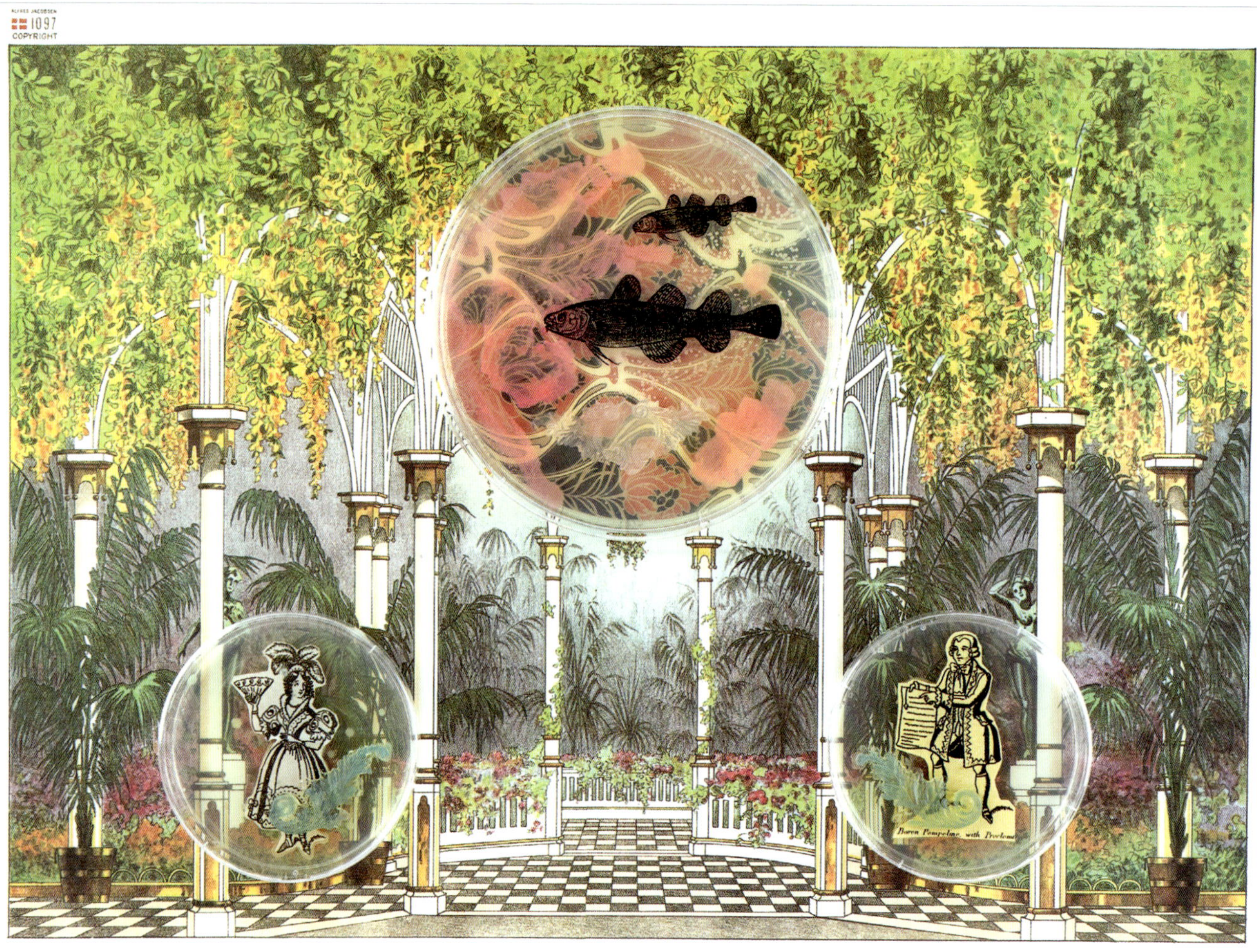

Jennifer Willet (Canadian),
*Baroque Biology (Paper
Theatre)*, 2019, petri dishes,
agar, GMO bacteria, collage
materials, dimensions
variable. Courtesy of the
artist. Additional collaborators: Philip Habashy, Gillian
Hughes, Lisha Laing, Aleeza
Tariq, Jude Abu Zaineh.
Mixed-media collages photographed by Justin Elliott.

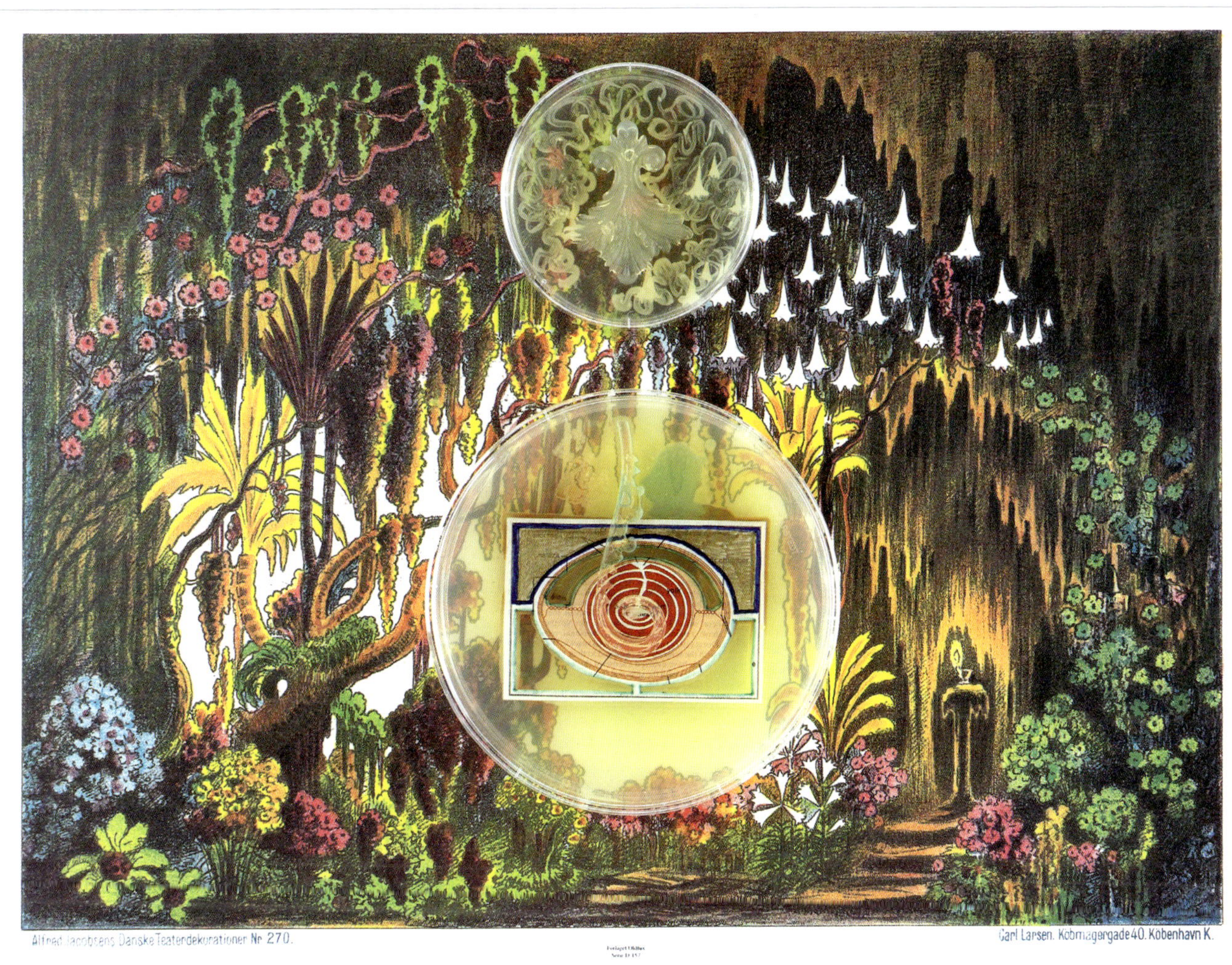

Alfred Jacobsens Danske Teaterdekorationer Nr 270.
Carl Larsen. Kobmagergade 40. Kobenhavn K.

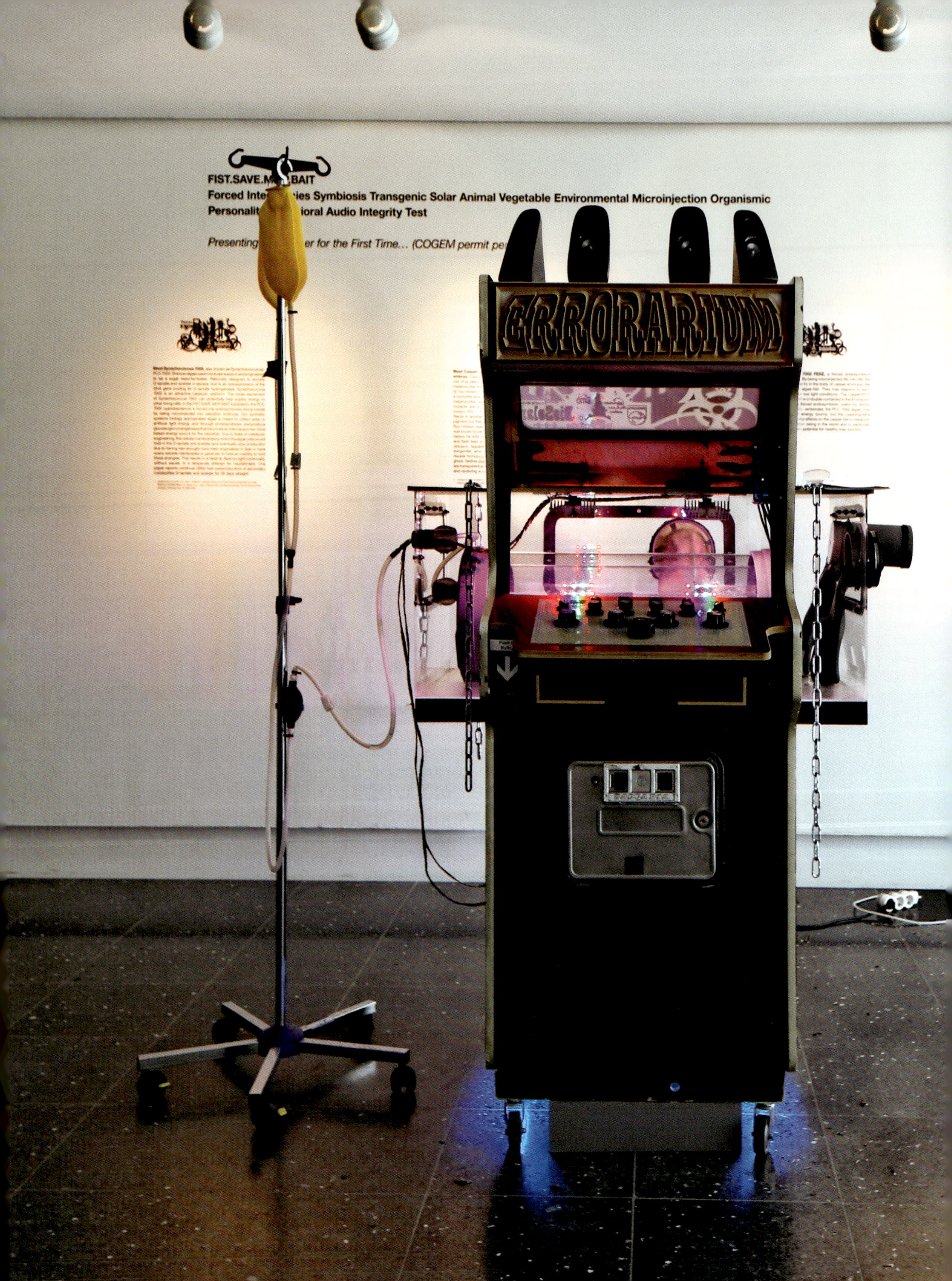

FIST.SAVE.MAKE.BAIT
Forced Interspecies Symbiosis Transgenic Solar Animal Vegetable Environmental Microinjection Organismic
Personality Behavioral Audio Integrity Test
Presenting Her for the First Time... (COGEM permit pe
ERRORARIUM

Errorarias: Bipolar Flower Enrichment

Artist Adam Zaretsky asks you to meet his "Bipolar Flowers" that are growing in the Errorarium. The artist describes the plants as "Bipolar (manic-depressive), Double Dipped, Zinc Fingered (ZF), GMO *Arabidopsis thaliana* plants." The Errorarium is a device for exploring the gamification of the forced genetic errors that may predictably or unpredictably appear in chamber-grown, zinc-fingered botanica.

The interactive installation is an enrichment terrarium that houses plants and subjects them to tests for photosynthetic and sonic engagement. Using the lights and sounds in the Errorarium, visitors can alter the environment of the growing organisms. The Bipolar Flowers must be contained, so they are grown, displayed, and publically entertained in the Errorarium. These plants have been "whole genome fracked" in a bipolar duet of two artificial transcription factors (activating and repressing) competing for the 524 GTA GAG GAG binding places on the *Arabidopsis* genome. These genes are regulated up and down according to the chance play of falling activation and repression domain inserts, claiming limited space in the plant's resultant bipolar disorder: mood (behavior), energy (physiology), and ability to function (development).

By changing the variables on the Errorarium, those interacting with the artwork are making the experiment non-repeatable and hard to utilize. Do you think you are enriching or stressing the plants with by manipulating the sounds and lights? What is the difference between enrichment and stress? These plants were created in the lab of Bert van der Zaal (in collaboration with David Lourier and Neils van Tol).

Adam Zaretsky (American), *Bipolar Flowers*, from the series *Errorarias: Bipolar Flower Enrichment*, 2012–ongoing, audio-photonic, environmental organismic personality, behavioral enrichment and integrity testing terrarium; bipolar double-dipped zinc-fingered *Arabidopsis thaliana* meant to house mutant organisms and subject them to tests for photosynthetic and sonic engagement, 39.5 x 69.25 x 35 in. (100.3 x 175.9 x 88.9 cm). Courtesy of the artist.

Bipolar Flower Plants designed and Inserted and bred in the lab of Bert van der Zaal (in collaboration with David Lourier and Neils van Tol).

Errorarium design: a Zaretsky/Juday/Edwards collaboration.

Frrorarium architecture and fabrication: Mason Juday.

Errorarium experimental light synthesizer engineer: Pete Edwards of Casper Electronics.

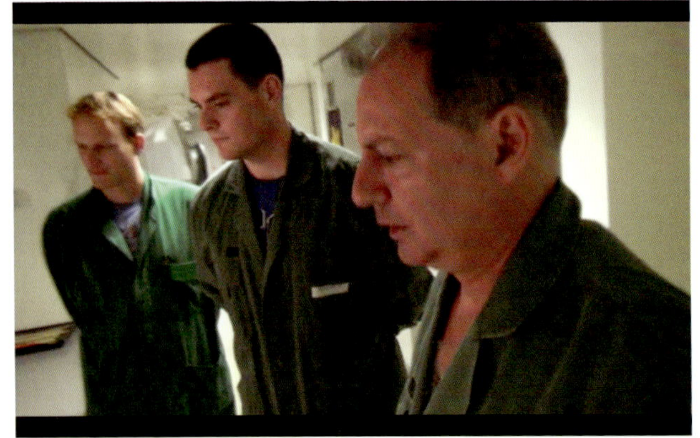
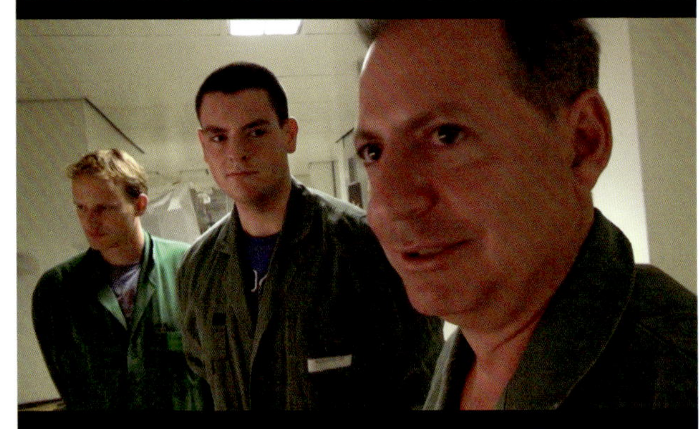

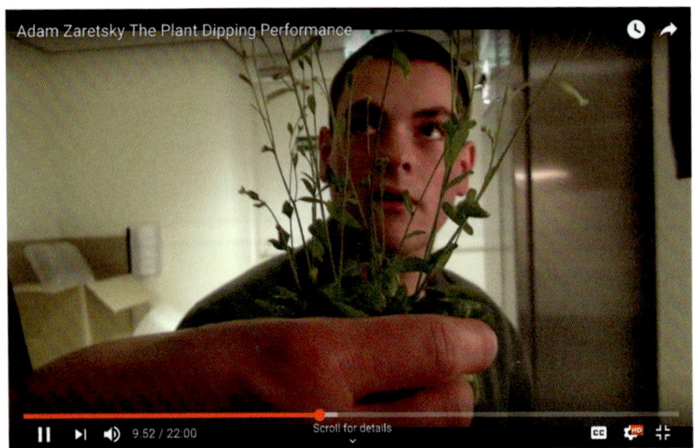
Adam Zaretsky The Plant Dipping Performance
9:52 / 22:00
Scroll for details

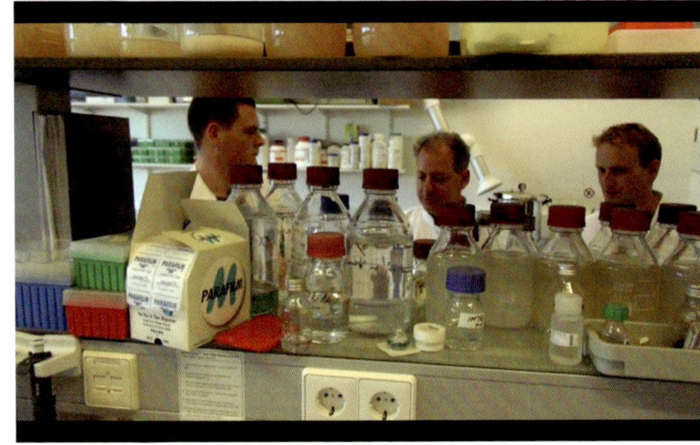

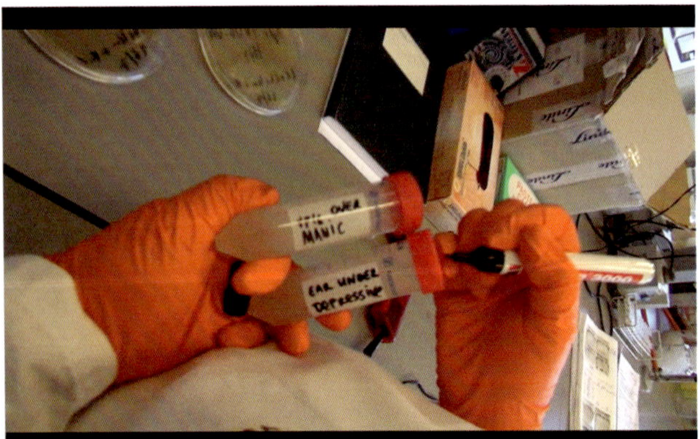
OVER
MANIC
EAR UNDER
DEPRESSIVE

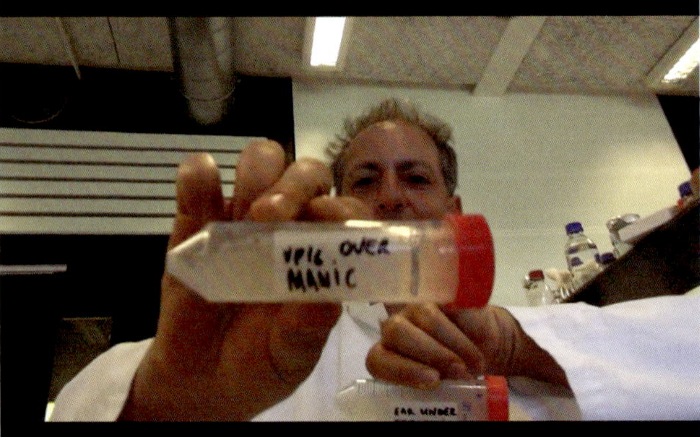
VP16 OVER
MANIC
EAR UNDER

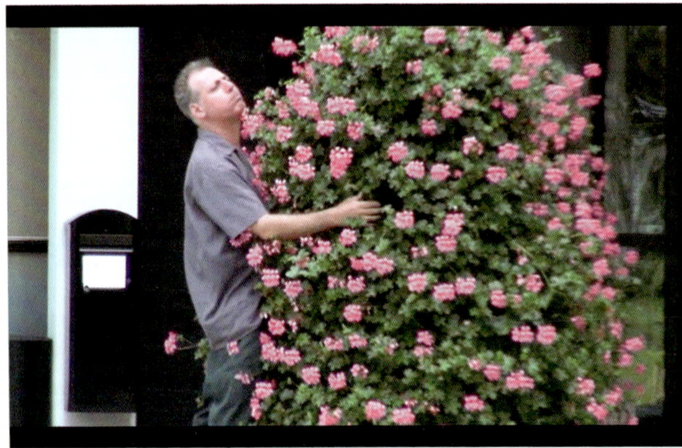
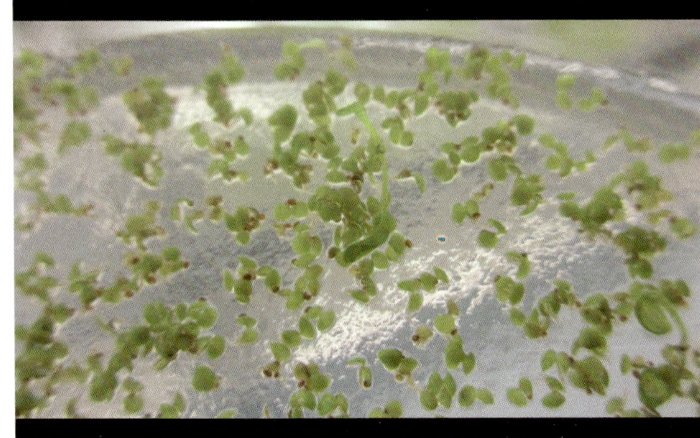

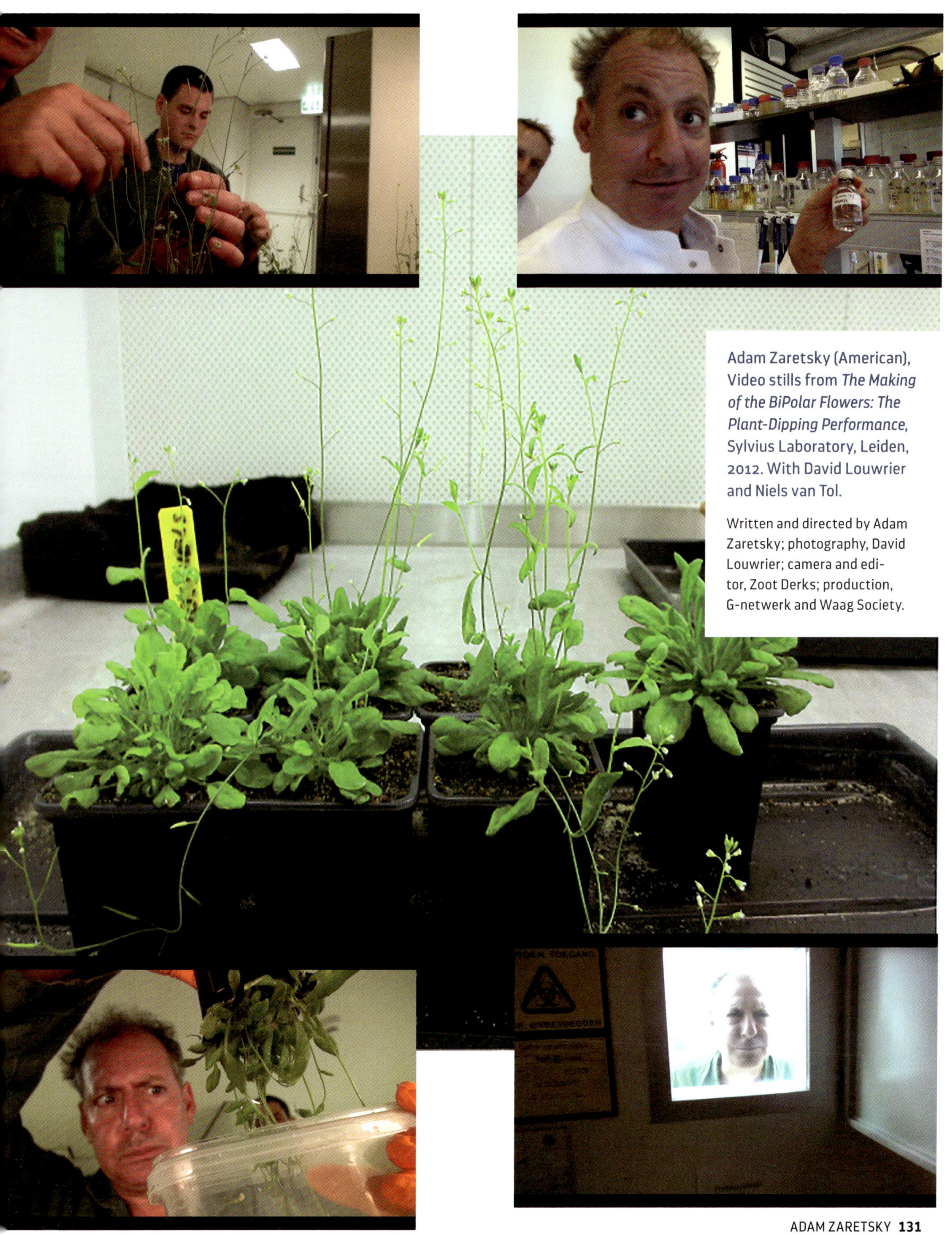

Adam Zaretsky (American), Video stills from *The Making of the BiPolar Flowers: The Plant-Dipping Performance*, Sylvius Laboratory, Leiden, 2012. With David Louwrier and Niels van Tol.

Written and directed by Adam Zaretsky; photography, David Louwrier; camera and editor, Zoot Derks; production, G-netwerk and Waag Society.

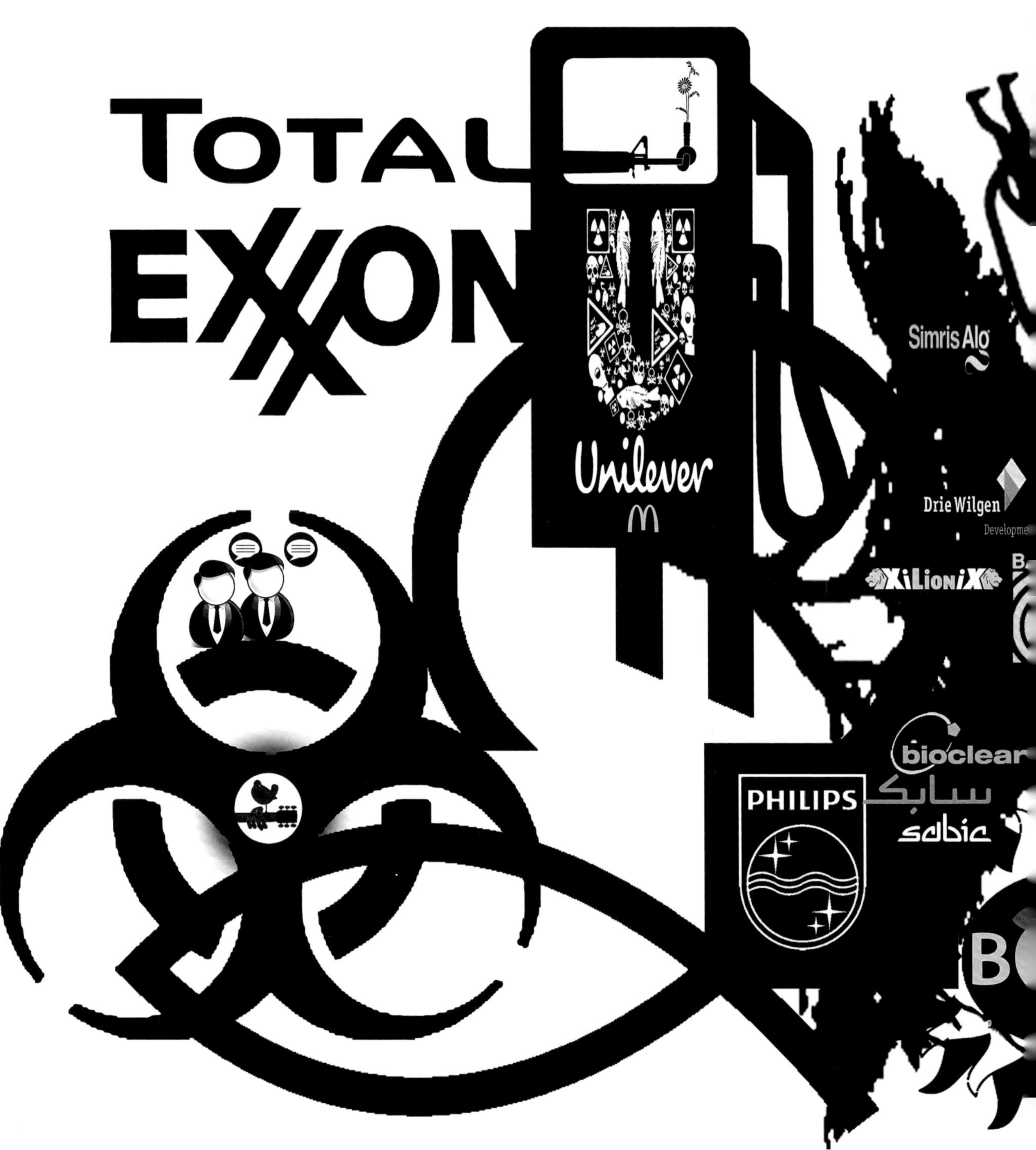

TOTAL
EXXON
Unilever
Simris Alg
Drie Wilgen
Developme
XiLioniX
B.
bioclear
PHILIPS
سابك
sabic
B

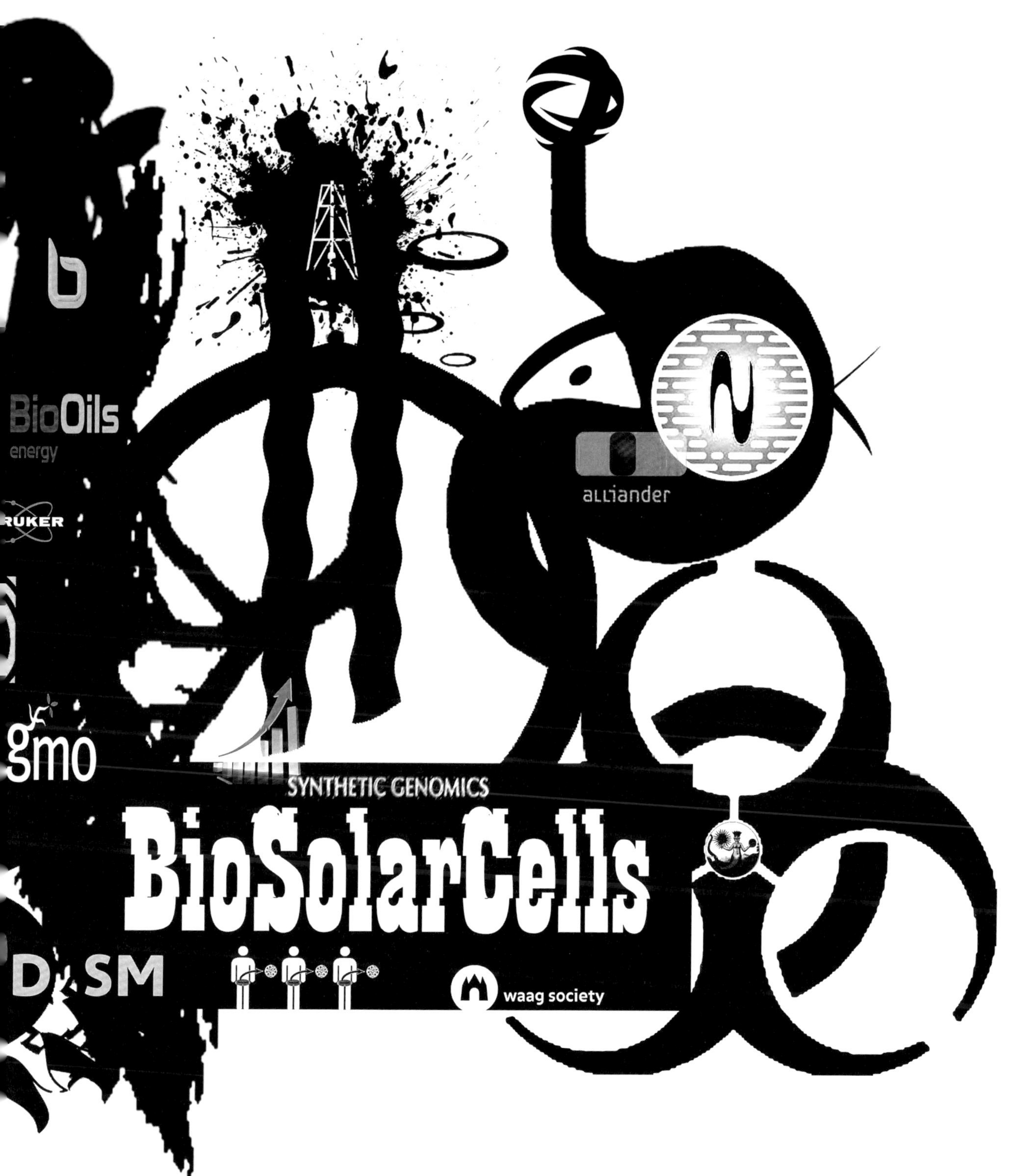
BioOils
energy
RUKER
gmo
D SM
SYNTHETIC GENOMICS
BioSolarCells
alliander
waag society

What is it that we as humans need from de-extincting a species? To showcase what we have lost and provide a sensory experience to hopefully change our destructive ways? Or to offer us an opportunity to pay homage to lost species? What if we had respected the natural world more to prevent these species from going extinct? And, if given the opportunity to resurrect these species, would we act any differently, knowing what our failures had caused before or relying on technology to fix our mistakes?

What Can Biotech Art Teach Us about Nature and Ourselves?

TODD KUIKEN

1. IUCN. 2019. *Genetic Frontiers for Conservation: As Assessment of Synthetic Biology and Biodiversity Conservation.* https://www.iucn.org/synbio.

2. United Nations Convention on Biological Diversity. 2010. *Strategic Plan for Biodiversity 2011–2020, including Aichi Biodiversity Targets.* https://www.cbd.int/sp/.

3. Tittensor, Derek P., Matt Walpole, Samantha L. L. Hill, Daniel G. Boyce, Gregory L. Britten, Neil D. Burgess, Stuart H. M. Butchart, Paul W. Leadley, Eugenie C. Regan, and Rob Alkemade. 2014. "A Mid-Term Analysis of Progress toward International Biodiversity Targets." *Science* 346 (6206): 241–44.

No corner of the earth, no matter how remote, is free from human influence—whether in the form of the altered atmosphere, expanding cities, ubiquitous pollution, invasive species, conversion of wildlands, loss of once-fertile farmland, or expanding exploitation and trade of wild species.[1] Governments have set ambitious targets for addressing biodiversity loss worldwide, such as the *Strategic Plan for Biodiversity 2011–2020, including Aichi Biodiversity Targets*.[2] To date, however, both the targets and the institutional arrangements that support them are failing.[3] Or put more simply, we as humans have failed to alter our habits, which has caused vast environmental destruction. So, are we forced to look towards technology to save nature (and us) from ourselves?

I've considered myself an environmentalist ever since I was a young kid in the 1980s on the Jersey shore. The beaches were closed because garbage and medical waste was washing onshore. "We" had decided to dump our garbage and medical waste into the vastness of the open oceans, only to realize later that the ocean would return our waste to us. I remember feeling saddened and I just couldn't comprehend how "we" would treat the oceans as our garbage cans. That experience led me to eventually become an environmental scientist focusing on the impacts of emerging technologies on the environment and trying, in whatever small ways I can, to prevent and undo the damage "we" have caused to the environment.

Art provides me a door into alternative realities. The exhibition *Art's Work in the Age of Biotechnology: Shaping Our Genetic Futures* provides me a glimpse into those realities—which I may or may not want to see—and forces me to contemplate both humanity's destruction of the natural world, as well as humanity's ability to use bio-technologies to reconstruct that natural world. The artwork in this exhibition challenges my desired magical world of mermaids portrayed in Disney's *The Little Mermaid* with the cruel realities of what science could achieve as Richard Pell has shown us in *The Mermaid De-Extinction Project*. Aaron Ellison and David Buckley Borden's triangular vortex, *Novel Ecosystem Generator*, forces me to imagine a switch I can flip to create new ecosystems or fix the ones we have destroyed. This work recalls Project Genesis from *Star Trek*, a theoretical process to terraform dead planets by means of a genetic explosion that would reduce the surface of a planet to its elementary particles. Fantastical imagery, yes. And yet, it's not far off when one considers the power that

4. Taylor, Bron. 2010. *Dark Green Religion: Nature Spirituality and the Planetary Future.* Berkeley: University of California Press.

5. Cramer, Phillip F. 1998. *Deep Environmental Politics: The Role of Radical Environmentalism in Crafting American Environmental Policy.* Westport, CT: Praeger.

6. Lewis, Martin W. 1994. *Green Delusions: An Environmentalist Critique of Radical Environmentalism.* Durham: Duke University Press.

7. http://www.symbiotica.uwa.edu.au/

gene drives hold and the kinds of uses of them that some have contemplated.

I am conflicted about the use of biotechnologies for conservation and environmental protection. This conflict is rooted in my training as an environmental scientist and in the environmental worldviews I hold, which often stand in conflict with one another. These views were formed in particular when I worked at the Oak Ridge National Laboratory studying the impacts of mercury on the environment and later at the National Wildlife Federation and the Woodrow Wilson Center. While these internal conflicts are my own, I believe they reflect the complicated and evolving relationship between biotechnology and its use in conservation and environmental protection. Much of the conflict around environmental protection stems from the philosophies, ethics, and religious belief systems of both individual people and entire societies.

While technology has always challenged these belief systems, the latest developments in biotechnologies are challenging those systems in more complex and extreme ways. Gene drives are being contemplated to introduce traits into a species that will be subsequently passed on from generation to generation, permanently altering its genome. Do we, as humans, have the right to alter a species or ecosystem in this way? Even if it's for the purpose of conservation or environmental protection?

Environmental worldviews vary in the degrees of care or responsibility that are placed on an individual or on whole societies. For instance, in Western society, "green religion" describes an individual's environmental behavior based on their perceived obligation; whereas a "dark green religion" perceives nature as having intrinsic, even sacred value, and therefore as being due reverent care.[4] Dark green religion emerges from deep ecology, first defined by Arne Næss in 1973. This worldview sees humans as just one species among many, having no special right to dominate or destroy the environment.[5] Its core belief is that "everything in the biosphere is interdependent, intrinsically valuable, and sacred."[4] It's concisely laid out in these four postulates:[6]

1. Decentralization of institutional power and control, leading to local autarky, is necessary for ecological and social health.
2. Technological advancements, if not scientific progress itself, are inherently harmful and dehumanizing.
3. Primal or primitive people exemplify how to live in harmony with nature (and with each other).
4. The capitalist market system is inescapably destructive and wasteful.

The argument against these postulates is more practical than philosophical: that after several decades of preaching these philosophies, the public remains, as before, "wedded to consumer culture and creative comforts".[6] So, despite "our" best intentions to protect the environment, our inability to change our actual behaviors leads us towards technology as a solution/scapegoat. This is reflected in Oron Catts' *The Autotroph* (2010), recently displayed at SymbioticA, "an overly technological and playful exploration of the immense complexity of dealing with ecological issues."[7]

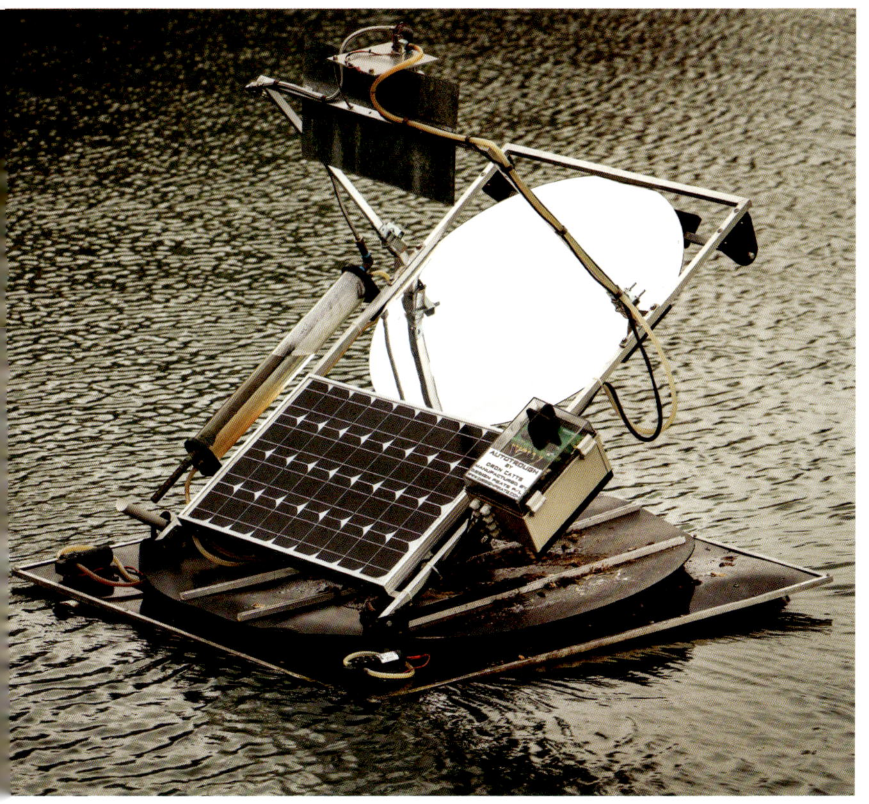

Oron Catts, *The Autotroph*, 2010. Photograph by Bewley Shaylor.

8. Gruen, Lori, Dale Jamieson, and Christopher Schlottmann. 2013. *Reflecting on Nature: Readings in Environmental Ethics and Philosophy.* New York: Oxford University Press.

As technology advances, its proponents challenge these ethics, as they are based on a premise of the division of humans from nature. For instance, Gruen, Jamieson, and Schlottmann ask: "If we are part of nature, then everything we do is part of nature, and is natural in that primary sense. When we domesticate organisms and bring them into a state of dependence on us, this is simply an example of one species exerting a selection pressure on another."[8] Yet Jeremy Rifkin describes biotechnology this way in 1983: "As bioengineering technology winds its way through the many passageways of life, stripping one living thing after another of its identity, replacing the original creations with technologically designed replicas, the world gradually becomes a lonelier place. From a world teeming with life . . . we descend to a world stocked with living gadgets and devices."[6] I view "biotech

art" as artists using or commenting on the technologies that make up "biotechnology," which is a slight variation from "bioart," where artists and designers are using biology to create pieces of art. This, of course, is my interpretation and is as subjective as trying to define what biotechnology is or art is in the first place.

This question of humans manipulating nature, either by direct means (biotechnologies) or through the co-evolution of species, reflects upon the broader concepts of "wildness" and "wilderness." Gruen, Jamieson, and Schlottmann suggest that a place is wild when its order is created according to its own principles of organization, and that what counts as wilderness is determined not by the absence of people but by the relationship between people and place. They cite Jack Turner's view of wildness: "To construct a new conservation ethic, we need first to understand why we impose a human order on non-human orders. We do so for gain, the gain being prediction, efficiency, and hence, control. Faced with the accelerating destruction of ecosystems and the extinction of species, we believe our only option lies in increased prediction, efficiency, and control. So, we fight to preserve ecosystems and species, and we accept their diminished wildness. This wins the fight but loses the war, and in the process, we simply stop talking about wildness."

So, is an ecosystem created or altered through Ellison and Borden's *Novel Ecosystem Generator* still considered wilderness or wild? And do other works not on display, like *Resurrecting the*

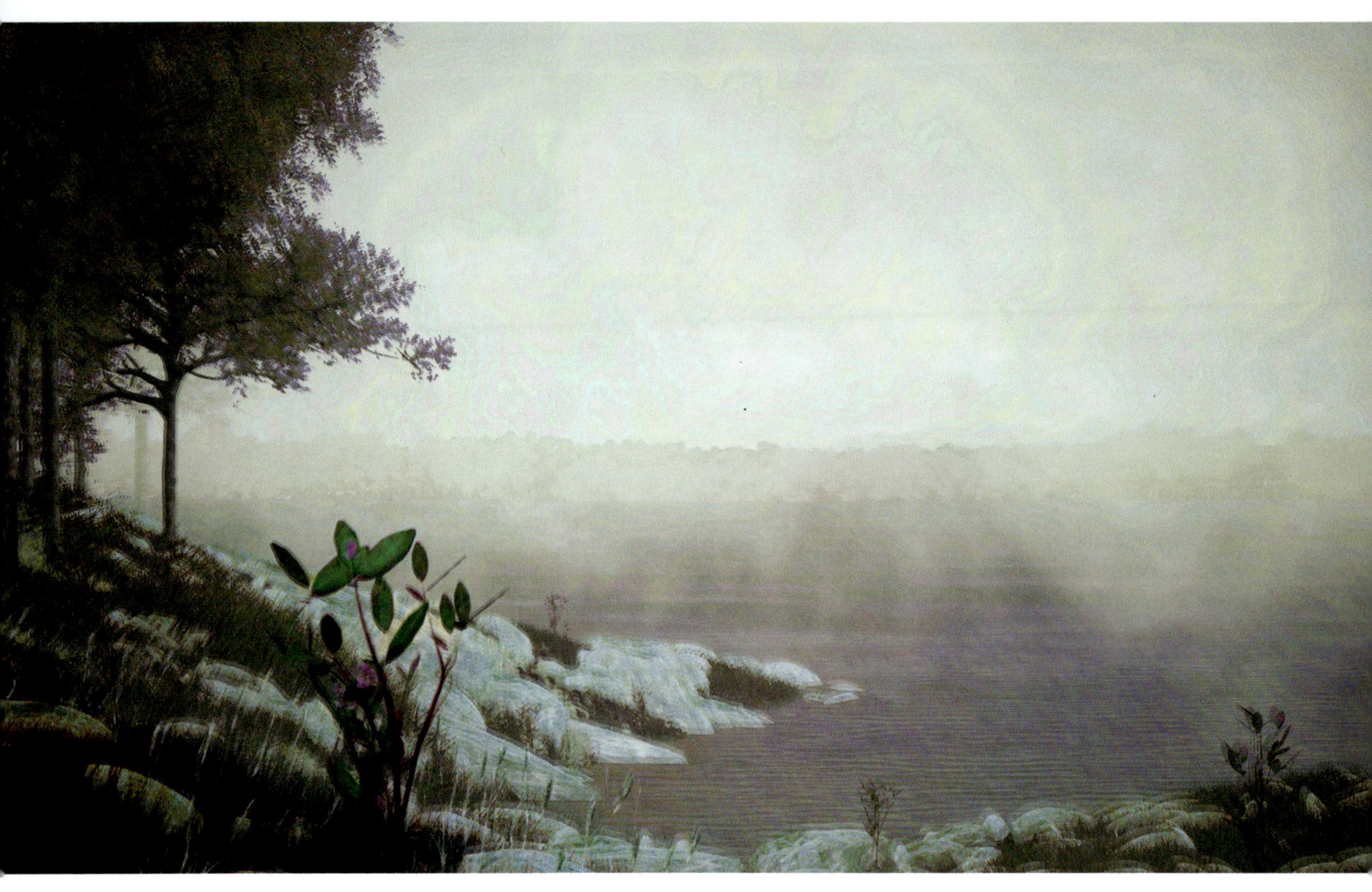

9. Ginsberg, Daisy, Sissel Tolaas, and Christine Agapakis. 2019. *Resurrecting the Sublime.* A sensory experience created by Alexandra Daisy Ginsberg, Sissel Tolaas, and a team of synthetic biologists at Ginkgo Bioworks led by Christina Agapakis. https://www.resurrectingthesublime.com/

10. Redford, Kent H., William Adams, Rob Carlson, Georgina M. Mace, and Bertina Ceccarelli. 2014. "Synthetic Biology and the Conservation of Biodiversity." *Oryx* 48 (3): 330–36.

Sublime,[9] remove the wildness of a flower once untouched by human hands? These strict interpretations of what is wild and what constitutes wildness deny a middle ground where responsible use and management of biotechnologies might create a balanced, sustainable relationship with nature. In 2013, at the first meeting of conservationists and synthetic biologists, Kent Redford made two notable observations. First, conservation practice tends to be reactive to change driven by other fields of human endeavor. The techniques and approaches used have been honed by decades of experience, through trials and tribulations, and are now well-defined with established practices and procedures. The second observation was that attitudes toward innovation are closely linked to attitudes towards risk.

Conservationists tend to be risk-averse in their practice of conservation. The stakes are high, and the fear of failure constantly reinforced, so the priority is generally to minimize risks of irreversible consequences of their interventions, especially given many practitioners' experiences of the outcomes from experiments in conservation.[10]

In *Resurrecting the Sublime*, artists, designers, and synthetic biologists give us the opportunity to experience the scent of an extinct species. (An earlier iteration of this piece was exhibited at our 2017 *Art's Work/Genetic Futures* field trial as *Extinct Perfumes*.) Scientifically this is an amazing accomplishment. Experientially this is surreal. One can imagine stopping on a hike to admire a flower's beauty while inhaling its scent.

But maybe we don't have the right to resurrect its scent or presence, like our loved ones given their final farewells as we bury them beneath the ground. Maybe that's where extinct species should remain, in their proper resting place removed from humans' interference once and for all? What is it that we as humans need from de-extincting a species? To showcase what we have lost and provide a sensory experience to hopefully change our destructive ways? Or to offer us an opportunity to pay homage to lost species?

I can't say for certain as I struggle to contemplate the power of biotechnology to enable this while reconciling our own destruction of the environment that caused these very extinctions. Yet, is this any different from the wonders I experience when I walk the halls of the Smithsonian and look upon the dodo bird glaring back at me in its skeletal form? Extinct less than eighty years after its discovery by Dutch soldiers around 1600 because of deforestation, hunting, and destruction of their nests by animals brought to the island by those same discoverers: should we have left those bones in the ground? Or has the reconstruction of these magnificent creatures provided me a better understanding of the natural world? *Resurrecting the Sublime* provides an opportunity in a new, immersive way to experience what is lost by extinction. It allows me to wonder "what if?" What if we had respected the natural world more to prevent these species from going extinct? And, if given the opportunity to resurrect these species, would we act any differently, knowing what our failures had caused before or relying on technology to fix our mistakes?

The artworks in this exhibition and others provide a unique space and opportunity to reflect upon our own personal philosophies and to share those experiences with others in order for us to collectively decide how we both value and coexist with nature. The relationship between technology and conservation is complicated. Does technology's use resign us to the notion that we have failed, and that consumerism, environmental exploitation, and unsustainable population growth are forgone conclusions? Or should technology be viewed as part of the collective evolution of humankind and nature? Could *Resurrecting the Sublime*'s sensory experience provide visitors with a path towards a better understanding of extinction in order to prevent further ones? Or does it allow one to rely on technology to simply remedy our failure to prevent those extinctions? Does the *Novel Ecosystem Generator* show us that the management or creation of new ecosystems is only limited by our imaginations? Or does it show the insanity of humans thinking they can create or control ecosystems? And does *The Mermaid De-Extinction Project* display the power of human scientific discovery? Or the cruelty of humanity's hubris?

Art is subjective, and this exhibition can't answer all of our questions on the role of biotechnology in our collective futures. It has, however, allowed me to escape the reality of our environmental failures while facing my own hopes and fears of using technology to make it right. It provides me a glimmer of hope for the environment's resurrection despite our inability to prevent its destruction.

Artist Biographies

SUZANNE ANKER is a visual artist and theorist working at the intersection of art and the biological sciences. Her practice investigates the ways in which nature is being altered in the twenty-first century through genetics, climate change, species extinction, and toxic degradation. Anker frequently works with "pre-defined and found materials," including botanical specimens, medical museum artifacts, laboratory apparatus, microscopic images, and geological specimens. Her work has been shown both nationally and internationally in museums and galleries including the Smithsonian Institute, the Phillips Collection, MoMA P.S.1, and the J. Paul Getty Museum. Her work has been the subject of reviews and articles in *The New York Times*, *Artforum*, *Art in America*, *Flash Art*, and *Nature*. As the chair of the School of Visual Arts (SVA) Fine Arts Department in New York since 2005, Anker continues to interweave traditional and experimental media in her department's new digital initiative and the SVA Bio Art Lab.

JOE DAVIS is one of the most influential artists working directly with scientists. He pioneered laser carving methods at Bell Telephone Labs and the University of Cincinnati Medical Center in the 1970s. In 1981 he joined the MIT Center for Advanced Visual Studies as a research fellow and lecturer. His *Microvenus* (1986) was the first genetically engineered artwork. Davis joined the laboratory of Alexander Rich at MIT in 1989 and the Harvard laboratory of George Church in 2010 as Artist Scientist. Davis is also affiliated with the Schwartz Lab at MIT and the Seifert Laboratory at the University of Kentucky.

JONATHAN DAVIS is a Research Triangle-based graphic designer and animator. He was a researcher for over ten years in the fields of plant biology and protein structure at the graduate and postdoctoral levels before leaving the laboratory to focus on exploring science through art, merging his experience as a scientist with a lifelong interest in computer graphics to create data-based CG works. Davis uses computer graphics and physics modeling as media to examine, explain, and explore science through art. Through his company, Scientific Studios, Davis collaborates with scientists and educators to visualize data and communicate scientific advancements.

HEATHER DEWEY-HAGBORG is a transdisciplinary artist and educator who is interested in art as research and critical practice. Dewey-Hagborg's work is held in the public collections of the Centre Pompidou, the Victoria and Albert Museum, and the New York Historical Society and has been widely discussed in the media, from *The New York Times* and the BBC to *Artforum* and *Wired*. She has a PhD in electronic arts from Rensselaer Polytechnic Institute. Dewey-Hagborg is an artist fellow at the AI Now Institute, an artist-in-residence at both the Exploratorium and the Science Center, and is an affiliate of the Data & Society Research Institute. She is also a co-founder and co-curator of REFRESH, an inclusive and politically engaged collaborative platform at the intersection of art, science, and technology.

AARON ELLISON and DAVID BUCKLEY BORDEN are a Cambridge-based creative team that unites art, design, and environmental science in place-based projects. Their art installations illustrate novel ecological systems ("ecosystems") that people create by changing the environment. In their creative practice, they engage with local communities to learn about their lives, practices, cultures, and customs, and create visual art that often uses vernacular tropes to envision our changing world. Their research-driven creations communicate abstract, often technical ecological concepts. Their installations provide spaces for thoughtful consideration and provocative discussions about how humans are altering the environment and the opportunities available to collectively rethink all our actions, for better or worse.

EMEKA IKEBUDE is based in Dallas, where he is a doctoral candidate in arts and technology at the University of Texas at Dallas. Ikebude holds master's degrees in art history (Ohio University) and arts and technology (UT Dallas). His artwork interrogates themes of dislocation and fragmentation from a biopolitical perspective located at the liminal intersections of tradition and modernity, and art and technology/biotechnology. His techniques include transforming everyday materials like wood, fabric, and metal into a distinctly characterized aesthetic. In much of his work, Ikebude employs the techniques of contouring, layering, mapping, digital visualization, welding, cutting, fraying, dyeing, gluing, and stitching. He uses these techniques to synthesize diverse, and often minute, forms into massive, variegated compositions because he is allured by the beauty and balance inherent in unity, and the force that forms when people unite.

CHARLOTTE JARVIS is an artist and lecturer working at the intersection of art and science. She approaches bodies as liminal spaces—sites for transformation, hybridization, and magic. Jarvis has been exhibited in ten international solo shows and over one hundred group exhibitions at venues including the Wellcome Collection, the Victoria and Albert Museum, the Kapelica Gallery, the Guangzhou Triennial, and the Venice Biennale. Jarvis is a past resident artist at the European Bioinformatics Institute, the Netherlands Proteomics Centre, and the Hubrecht Institute. She lectures at the Royal College of Art, Goldsmiths University, the Central Academy of Fine Arts in Beijing, and Imperial College.

KERASYNTH

DIANA EUSEBIO is an Afro-Latina fashion photographer, stylist, and activist based in Miami. Currently a rising senior at the Maryland Institute College of Art, Eusebio blends fashion and fantasy in her photography to engulf the viewer in a surreal and colorful world. Eusebio designs garments and accessories, styles sets and models, and curates them into meaningful photographs inspired by her Afro-Latina identity. From over eleven thousand applicants Eusebio was recognized as a National YoungArts Finalist, and has been a US Presidential Scholar in the Arts.

ERIN KIRCHNER earned their BFA cum laude in fiber from the Maryland Institute College of Art in 2018. Kirchner was a 2018 Nike Air Max Material Design Intern and a member of the 2019 Fueling the Future of Footwear X Asics Tiger class hosted by Pensole Footwear Academy. Kirchner's textiles-based practice concerns itself with the ethics of developing technologies, sustainability, and facilitating empathy for bodies considered "other" in Western society. By approaching these topics through the lens of "fibers," Kirchner hopes to change how bodies and systems in power occupy and operate in the physical/digital world and to create space for marginalized bodies and experiences.

GRACE KWON is an interdisciplinary artist interested in fiber, interactive arts, digital fabrication, and bio-fabrication. She has a deep investment in arts education and its intersection with technology. Her website is graceyoungkwon.com and her instagram is @glasskwon.

RACHEL RUSK was born in Ohio, and received a BFA from the Maryland Institute College of Art majoring in fiber arts. Embracing a wide array of tactics, Rusk employs digital, biological, and traditional artistic media to explore environments and their history, critically reflecting upon the manner in which they structure our society and shape us as individuals. Rusk's work is motivated by an interest in healing and repair, and in our relationships to each other and to the natural world. Rusk uses observation, process, and accumulated research to dictate her work. Rusk was a finalist in the MoMA Biodesign Summit two years running in *Kerasynth* and *Algae-Matron* collaborations. Her collaborative work has been featured in *Forbes*, *Smithsonian* online magazine, *Neo.Life*, and *Velocity*.

SYDNEY SIEH-TAKATAN is a New York–based fiber artist and aspiring medical illustrator focused on developing new ways of visualizing data and scientific information through weaving, embroidery, garment making, and storytelling. Her work explores the intersection between art and science, drawing inspiration from the natural world and digital technology. She values the meditative process of working with her hands in order to create sympathetic objects. Sieh-Takata received her BFA in fiber from the Maryland Institute College of Art in 2018. She has been a recipient of the Barbara Kuhlman Scholarship and the Betty Cooke '46 Scholarship, and she was part of the team that represented MICA at the 2017 and 2018 Biodesign Challenges at MoMA.

MARIA MCKINNEY is an Irish visual artist and a member of Temple Bar Studios in Dublin. She works across a range of media and has made a number of solo exhibitions, including at the Wellcome Collection (2018), the RHA Gallery (2016), Lokaal 01 (2016), and the MAC Belfast (2012). Her work was shortlisted for the MAC International Prize in 2014, selected by Hugh Mulholland, Judith Nesbitt, and Francesco Bonami. She has taken part in artist residencies including Skowhegan in 2017. In 2019 she will realize a project about the Jersey cattle breed on the island of their origin and namesake.

JOEL ONG is a media artist whose work explores emergent ways of interfacing with the natural elements through the lens of digital and moist-media technologies. He is an alumnus of SymbioticA and is also an artist with the UCLA Art|Sci Collective. Ong's individual and collaborative research in spatial sound, data aesthetics, bioart, and interactive media have been presented in festivals and conferences across Canada, USA, UK, Australia, Mexico, and Singapore. He is currently an assistant professor at the Department of Computational Arts at York University and is the interim director of Sensorium: Centre for Digital Arts and Technology. For this artwork, he has collaborated with Natalie Plociennik, a creative entrepreneur who produces illustrations, fine art, and artisanal tech products in Toronto. Plociennik's fascination with patterns found in nature led her to study earth and environmental sciences at McMaster University. She practiced fine arts at Centennial College where she developed her style in biomorphic art that is reminiscent of organic patterns, shapes, and structures.

RICHARD PELL is the founder and director of the Center for PostNatural History (CPNH), an organization dedicated to the collection and exposition of life-forms that have been intentionally and heritably altered through domestication, selective breeding, tissue culture, or genetic engineering. The CPNH operates a permanent museum in Pittsburgh, and produces traveling exhibitions that have appeared in science and art museums throughout Europe and the United States, including the Victoria and Albert Museum, the Wellcome Collection, the Museum für Naturkunde, the CCCB, the ZKM, the 2008 Taipei Biennial, the Carnegie Museum of Natural History, and the LA County Natural History Museum, as well as being featured in *National Geographic*, *Nature*, *American Scientist*, *Popular Science*, and *New Scientist*. The CPNH has been awarded a Rockefeller New Media fellowship, a Creative Capital fellowship, and a Smithsonian Artist Research Fellowship, and has received generous support from the Waag Society and the Kindle Project. Pell was awarded the 2016 Pittsburgh Artist of the Year. He is currently an associate professor of Art at Carnegie Mellon University.

CIARA REDMOND is an emerging contemporary artist working in mixed media, installation, and bioart. Redmond's work explores themes of identity, genetic destiny, gender, and the relationship between science and culture. She trained in materials conservation and works with artists and galleries to find innovative solutions for displaying unusual works and materials. Redmond is from Melbourne, and currently based in Tokyo. *We Make Our Own Luck Here* was developed with support from Waseda University.

KIRSTEN STOLLE is a visual artist examining the impact of biotechnology and agribusiness on our food supply. She is a Pollock-Krasner Foundation Grant recipient and her work is included in the collections of the San Jose Museum of Art, the Crocker Art Museum, and the Minneapolis Institute of Arts. Solo exhibitions include NOME, the Southeastern Center for Contemporary Art, the Turchin Center for Visual Arts, the Winthrop University Art Galleries, the Tracey Morgan Gallery, and the Jack Fischer Gallery. Group exhibitions include Balzer Projects, the Fridman Gallery, the Mint Museum, and The Billboard Creative. Her work has been published in *Poetry*, *Burnaway*, *Topic*, *Creators Project*, and *New American Paintings*.

EMILIA TIKKA is a Finnish artist working at the intersection of speculative storytelling and synthetic biology. Her interdisciplinary practice explores the philosophical dimensions and cultural implications of novel biotechnologies such as the genome-editing technology CRISPR. Her methods of research vary from designing objects, constellations, and fictions to hands-on experiments in a laboratory. She has been recently selected as Artist-in-Residence at Max Delbrück Centre for Molecular Medicine and the State Festival, the first European artistic residency on CRISPR. Her artwork has been exhibited at Ars Electronica, the Arts Center at NYU Abu Dhabi, and the EMMA—Espoo Museum of Modern Art, among others. Her work has recently been featured in publications such as *Nature* and *Süddeutsche Zeitung*.

PAUL VANOUSE is an artist and professor of art at the University at Buffalo, where he is the founding director of the Coalesce Center for Biological Art. His bio-media and interactive cinema projects have been exhibited in over twenty-five countries and widely across the US. Venues have included the Walker Art Center, the New Museum, the Museo Nacional de Bellas Artes, Haus der Kulturen der Welt, ZKM Karlsruhe, and the Albright-Knox Art Gallery. Vanouse's artworks have been funded by the Rockefeller Foundation, Creative Capital, the New York State Council on the Arts, the New York Foundation for the Arts, Sun Microsystems, and the National Science

Foundation. He has received numerous awards at festivals including a Golden Nica and two Awards of Distinction at Prix Ars Electronica. He has an MFA from Carnegie Mellon University.

JENNIFER WILLET is a Canada Research Chair in Art, Science, and Ecology and an associate professor in the School of Creative Arts at the University of Windsor. She is an internationally recognized artist and curator whose contributions influenced the development of the field of bioart. Her work explores notions of representation and body in relation to evolving biotechnologies with an emphasis on ecological metaphors. She has exhibited and presented her research extensively across Canada and internationally. Willett taught in the Studio Arts Department at Concordia University in Montreal from 2000–2007, and completed her PhD in the Interdisciplinary Humanities Program at the same institution. Willet also taught "Bioart: Contemporary Art and the Life Sciences" for the Arts and Genomics Centre at the University of Leiden in the Netherlands in 2008. In 2009 she opened INCUBATOR: Hybrid Laboratory at the Intersection of Art, Science, and Ecology, the first bioart lab in Canada.

ADAM ZARETSKY is a Wet-Lab BioArt Practitioner mixing ecology, biotechnology, non-human relations, body performance, and gastronomy. Zaretsky stages lively, hands-on bioart production labs based on topics such as foreign species invasion (pure/impure), radical food science (edible/inedible), jazz bioinformatics (code/flesh), tissue culture (undead/semi-alive), transgenic design issues (traits/desires), interactive ethology (person/machine/non-human), and physiology (performance/stress). Zaretsky runs the public life arts school VASTAL (Vivoarts School for Transgenic Aesthetics, Ltd.), teaching experimental bioart classes, messy labs, and hands-on biotech at art events, universities (including San Francisco State University, SymbioticA at the University of Western Australia, the Rensselaer Polytechnic Institute, the University of Leiden, Carnegie Mellon University, and New York University), and

in public venues. His art practice focuses on an array of legal, ethical, social, and libidinal implications of biotechnological materials and methods with a focus on transgenic humans.

Contributor Biographies

JOHN GODWIN is a professor of biological sciences at North Carolina State University and a member of the Genetic Engineering and Society Center. He and his students study behavior and sex determination mechanisms in a range of organisms including sex-changing reef fishes, flatfishes that exhibit temperature-dependent sex determination, behavior and neurobiology in zebrafish and mice, and, most recently, work in the area of genetic pest management focused on rodents.

FRED GOULD was born in New York City and grew up in New York and Rhode Island. He graduated from Queens College in New York City in 1971 with a BS in biology. In 1977, he received his PhD in ecology and evolutionary biology from the State University of New York at Stony Brook, with his thesis examining rapid host range evolution in a crop pest. He was then awarded an NSF postdoctoral fellowship to examine the relationship between insect adaptation to natural plant defenses and insecticides.

He was hired as a soil insect ecologist at North Carolina State University in 1979, and is now a distinguished university professor at that institution, with appointments in the Entomology and Biology Departments. Gould assisted in the development and deployment of insecticidal transgenic crops in ways that suppress the evolution of pest resistance. He is now focused on the potential for engineering insect pests to suppress disease and crop loss, and to protect endangered species.

Gould is co-director of the Genetic Engineering and Society program at NCSU. He has served on National Research Council committees, addressing regulation of genetic technologies in agriculture. He received the Alexander von Humboldt Award for most significant agricultural research over a five-year period, the Sigma Xi George Bugliarello

Prize for written communication of science, and the O. Max Gardner Award in 2012 for being the UNC faculty member with the greatest contribution to human welfare. He was elected to the US National Academy of Sciences in 2011 and serves on the National Research Council Board on Agriculture and Natural Resources.

TODD KUIKEN is Senior Research Scholar with the Genetic Engineering and Society Center at NC State University, where he explores the scientific and technological frontier, stimulating discovery and bringing new tools to bear on public policy challenges that emerge as science advances. He has numerous projects evaluating and designing new research and governance strategies to proactively address the biosafety, biosecurity, and environmental opportunities/risks associated with emerging genetic technologies. After completing his BS in Environmental Management and Technology at Rochester Institute of Technology, he worked on the biogeochemical cycling of mercury at the Oak Ridge National Laboratory. He earned an MA in Environmental and Resource Policy from The George Washington University while working at various environmental non-profits including the National Wildlife Federation. Kuiken earned his PhD from Tennessee Tech University, where his research focused on the air/surface exchange of mercury associated with forest ecosystems.

ROGER MANLEY became the director of NC State University's Gregg Museum of Art & Design in 2010. Prior to that, he worked as a photographer, folklorist, filmmaker, curator, and writer. He has curated exhibitions for more than forty other institutions, and has authored a number of award-winning books, catalogues, videos, and films, along with exhibitions of his own photographs of Australian Aboriginals, Hispanic farmworkers, Palestinian villagers, Gullah Sea Islanders, Navajos, Arctic gold miners, prisoners, textile workers, and self-taught artists. His feature-length documentary *Mana—Beyond Belief* premiered at the International Documentary Film Festival in Amsterdam and NYC's Lincoln Center, and was an opening night

feature at Durham's Full Frame Festival. Its awards included Best Cinematography at Avignon and the Grand Jury Prize at Rhodes.

Manley has had many international artist residencies and was a recipient of both the NEA Artists Fellowship and the NEH Scholars Fellowship. In 1992, he founded the triennial META Conferences at Black Mountain, which have brought together hundreds of artists, scientists, entrepreneurs, and other creative individuals from all over the world for regular collaborative exchanges.

WILLIAM MYERS is a curator, writer, and teacher based in Amsterdam. His book *Biodesign* (2018), published by MoMA, identifies the emerging practice of designers and architects integrating biological processes in their work. *Bio Art: Altered Realities* (2015), published by Thames & Hudson and launched at the Tate Modern, profiles art that uses biology in new ways or responds to advances in the life sciences that alter our notions of identity, nature, and the definition of life. His writing and exhibitions have been profiled in the journal *Science*, *The New York Times*, *The Wall Street Journal, New York Magazine*, *Smithsonian Magazine*, *Volkskrant*, and *Folha de São Paulo*, among others. Myers has lectured at Harvard University, RMIT, Universitário Belas Artes de São Paulo, International University of Catalunya, Oxford University, Leiden University, and the Royal College of Art. He has worked for MoMA, the Guggenheim Museum, the Smithsonian Cooper-Hewitt National Design Museum, RISD, Science Galleries in Dublin and Rotterdam, Vitra, TU Delft, and Het Nieuwe Instituut.

ELIZABETH PITTS is a member of the *Art's Work/Genetic Futures* planning team. She is an assistant professor in the University of Pittsburgh's Composition, Literacy, Pedagogy, and Rhetoric program. Pitts received her PhD in Communication, Rhetoric, and Digital Media from NC State University with a minor in Genetic Engineering and Society, and she also holds a BA and MA in English from Georgetown University.

MOLLY RENDA has served as exhibit program librarian at the NC State University Libraries since 2011. She develops, designs, and produces exhibitions in the D. H. Hill Jr. Library gallery that leverage the Libraries' Special Collections Research Center resources, as well as showcase faculty and student research and university history. Her background in painting and printmaking has informed a thirty-year career in graphic design. Renda holds a BFA from the School of Visual Arts where she studied with Bob Blackburn and Dale Henry, and later worked at Blackburn's Printmaking Workshop. She served as executive editor for design and production for *DoubleTake* magazine (1994–99), published by the Center for Documentary Studies at Duke University. Her book and publication design has been recognized by *Communication Graphics*, *Graphis*, the AIGA *50 Books, 50 Covers* exhibition, and the Association of American University Presses.

HANNAH STAR ROGERS is a curator, scholar, and poet. She received her MFA in poetry from Columbia University and PhD at Cornell University on the intersection of art and science. She curated *Making Science Visible: The Photography of Berenice Abbott*, which received an exhibits prize from the British Society for the History of Science and resulted in an invited lecture at the Smithsonian Archives of American Art. She is the past director of research and collaboration for Emerge: Artists and Scientists Redesign the Future 2016 and served as Guest Bioart Curator for Emerge: Frankinstein 2017. She is currently Visiting Scholar at the University of Edinburgh and teaches creative writing at the University of Strathclyde.

MEGAN SERR recently completed her PhD in biology with a minor in Genetic Engineering and Society at NC State University. She considers herself an interdisciplinary scholar and enjoys working on the biological as well as social side to conservation. Her primary focus is on invasive species and society.

ACKNOWLEDGMENTS

Art's Work in the Age of Biotechnology: Shaping Our Genetic Futures has been a four-year effort by a core team and the contributions of dozens of others. The exhibition evolved over time with the help of NC State University staff, faculty and students, and colleagues that span the sciences, the arts, and the humanities, who offered invaluable advice about planning for an international group show with invited and open-call artists.

The evolution of the final exhibition began after our one-night, pop-up field trial at CAM Raleigh in 2017. The following day, more than thirty NC State faculty, staff, and students, along with the six artists who presented at CAM, brianstormed together at our first symposium about the final, large-scale exhibition. These events were realized with grants from the North Carolina Biotechnology Center and the North Carolina Science Festival.

Staff from all collaborating institutions were vital to this project. Many thanks to the Gregg Museum of Art & Design and to the leadership of director Roger Manley, registrar Mary Hauser, preparator Matthew Gay, education curator Zoe Starling, communications coordinator Evelyn McCawley, assistant registrar Jordan Cao, and operations manager Hillary Leggette. We would like to thank Sharon Stauffer and Patti Mulligan at the Genetic Engineering and Society Center for their indispensable behind-the-scenes planning and public-facing communications. The NC State University Libraries supported the project from its beginning through the creative vision of director Greg Raschke. The talented staff from across the Libraries afforded access to subject and technical expertise that ensured the exhibition's success. In particular we want to thank Debbie Curry, Colin Keenan, Cindy Levine, Peter Schreiner, Travis Tyo, Jamie Chapman,

Robert LaSane, Thomas Derosier, and Jordan Booth. Special thanks go to Director of Program Planning and Outreach Marian Fragola and the External Relations team lead by Chris Tonelli: Charles Samuels, Brent Bradford, and Chris Vitiello.

As with any major interdisciplinary project, contributions from a variety of fields are needed. We would like to thank biologists and geneticists Rob Dunn, Carole Saravitz and her staff at the Phytotron, Jennifer Baltzegar, Anna Stepanova, Reade Roberts, Jim Mahaffey, and Bob Franks and arts and humanities scholars Patsy Sibley, Mark Olson, Priscilla Wald, Helen Burgess, Jason Delbourne, Jennifer Kuzma, and Darrell Stover for their support.

Thanks to conservation biologist Kent Redford for giving us the idea to make a corn maze, an endeavor that couldn't have happened without the indefatigable involvement of Bob Patterson, the advice of his student Elizabeth Carrigan of Carrigan Farms, and the generosity of Major Goodman. Jim Holland, and Dominic Reisig provided the teosinte and field corn seed. Ron Heiniger, Ryan Heiniger, Curtis Powell, and Chad Carter, also from the College of Agriculture and Life Sciences, lent their expertise and labor to prepare the seedbed. Mark Weathington and Bradley Holland of the JC Raulston Arboretum were also generous supporters. William H. Dodge collaborated on the maze design, and a host of local volunteers took on the challenges of growing and maintaining the quarter-acre stand of field corn. The North Carolina Museum of Art's Dan Gottlieb offered the use of park land in keeping with a long collaborative relationship with NC State University, and the museum embraced the suggestion to open the maze to the public in collaboration with Student Action

with Farmworkers' (SAF) annual end of summer celebration. Libraries colleagues Jayme Lachapelle, Hannah Rainey, and Natalia Lopez helped make the afternoon a success.

Thanks to the College of Design's Derek Ham and Patrick FitzGerald for their early thoughts on creating a VR corn maze experience, and to Payod Panda and Alberto Carrillo for their collaboration.

Our guest curator Hannah Star Rogers has been dedicated to the project since the CAM exhibition and workshop. She has shaped the vision for the exhibition and worked tirelessly to bring together a diverse, engaging group of artists.

Thanks go to catalog essayists William Myers, Megan Serr, and John Godwin for their insights and provocations; to copy editors Julie Johnson and Chris Vitiello; and to Friesens Corporation, Canada for their craftsmanship in printing and binding.

Most of all, we thank the participating artists whose work invites viewers to consider what art's work really can be in the age of biotechnology. By reaching out to the public, we hope these artists will help society make wiser decisions in shaping the future development and deployment of biotechnologies.

Both the corn maze and this catalog were made possible through the generosity of the NC State University Libraries' Goodnight Educational Foundation Endowment for Special Collections.

Finally, we thank the exhibition's visitors for their attention, observation, and personal responses to the artists' work. It is your ideas about the future of biotechnology and your interpretations of the artwork that we value most. Enjoy the exhibition!